DEAR MRS. ROOSEVELT

DEAR MRS. ROOSEVELT

LETTERS TO ELEANOR ROOSEVELT
THROUGH DEPRESSION AND WAR

EDITED BY CATHY D. KNEPPER, PH.D.

CARROLL & GRAF PUBLISHERS
NEW YORK

DEAR MRS. ROOSEVELT
Letters to Eleanor Roosevelt through Depression and War

Carroll & Graf Publishers
An Imprint of Avalon Publishing Group Inc.
245 West 17th Street
11th Floor
New York, NY 10011

AVALON
publishing group incorporated

Copyright © 2004 by Cathy D. Knepper

First Carroll & Graf edition 2004

Library of Congress Cataloging-in-Publication Data is available.

ISBN: 0-7867-1397-6

Book design by Maria Elias
Printed in the United States of America
Distributed by Publishers Group West

*Dedicated to all who look to the life of Eleanor Roosevelt
for inspiration*

"No woman has ever so comforted the distressed or so
distressed the comfortable."

—*Clare Boothe Luce*

Contents

Acknowledgments

D uring the creation of this book I was privileged to meet a
number of people who had Eleanor Roosevelt stories to tell.
When I explained my research, their eyes would light up and they
would eagerly tell me of the time they met Mrs. Roosevelt and shook
her hand, or listened to her talk at a high school in their town, or
glimpsed her on a South Pacific island during World War II. She
clearly made a profound impression upon those she encountered, and
this helped me to see her as they did, for which I am grateful. The
staff of the Franklin D. Roosevelt Presidential Library in Hyde Park,
New York, were at all times friendly, helpful, and resourceful, making
research there a real pleasure. Thanks go to Ken Spring and Ross
Knepper for wading through lots of letters and providing feedback;
Ross also contributed research assistance. Special thanks go to my
agent, Farley Chase, who understood what I was trying to do and
patiently guided me through the difficult task of shaping letters into
a book. As always, I owe a debt of gratitude to my husband, Mark,
who supports my compulsion to tell stories—true stories—about our
nation's past.

"I do not ask of any man alive
That he know all the answers. I only ask
A great caring—an honest and humble caring
About what happens to human beings and their hopes,
And that I ask of myself as much as another."

*—from a poem by Bonaro Overstreet, quoted by Eleanor Roosevelt
in her "My Day" column of November 7, 1944*

Introduction

Sunday, December 7, 1941, began as a peaceful morning at the White House. The weather was cool and crisp, with a brilliant blue sky overhead. While Eleanor Roosevelt entertained luncheon guests, President Roosevelt had a restful lunch on a tray upstairs with his old friend Harry Hopkins. At a little before 2 P.M. a Honolulu radio operator relayed the following message to the naval communications center: "AIR RAID ON PEARL HARBOR THIS IS NOT A DRILL." Secretary of the Navy Frank Knox phoned the president to give him the shattering news.

After Mrs. Roosevelt bid good-bye to her guests, an usher quietly told her the unhappy tidings. She waited upstairs until her husband was alone, hoping for a chance to speak with him briefly, but saw that he was focused entirely on what needed to be done. So she continued work on her mail, interrupted by luncheon, listening to the reports her husband received as people came and people went, patiently going through her letters as the world changed around her. She surely realized that the advent of war would increase her already overwhelming correspondence.

When her husband took office in 1933 she described her mail

this way: "Letters, and letters and letters: Wire baskets on my desk, suit cases of mail going home even on Sundays with my secretary, Mrs. Scheider. A sense of being snowed under by mail. This is a picture of our first weeks in Washington." Perhaps she should not have been completely surprised by this as she confessed: "The time was a serious one, and the need of the people seemed great. I had a feeling that even to be able to tell some one near the seat of government about their troubles, would be a help, so in a broadcast which I made I said I would be glad to hear from those who felt that any government department could assist them in their needs. Then began the avalanche!"

The First Lady also instituted a monthly column in *Woman's Home Companion,* called "Mrs. Roosevelt's Page," beginning in August 1933. The title of her first offering was, "I Want You to Write to Me," in which she declared:

"The invitation which forms the title of this page comes from my heart, in the hope that we can establish here a clearing house, a discussion room, for the millions of men, women and young people who read the *Companion* every month. . . . Often it is easier to write to someone whom we do not expect ever to see . . . Please do not imagine that I am planning to give you advice that will eventually solve all your problems. We all know that no human being is infallible, and on this page I am not setting myself up as an oracle. But it may be that in the varied life I have had there have been certain experiences which other people will find useful, and it may be that out of the letters which come to me I shall learn of experiences which will prove helpful to others. And so I close my first page to and for you, as I opened it, with a cordial invitation—I want you to write to me."

Mrs. Roosevelt intended for this correspondence to be directed to the *Woman's Home Companion,* where she would answer questions in her column. The people of America took her invitation seriously, their voices, via their letters, reaching out directly to her. She characterized her mail as "a varied collection that fills the wire baskets which constantly reappear on my desk and perhaps our system is not the best system in the world, but these are questions dealing with human beings and our main desire is to remember that each individual is a human being who feels that his problem is the most important thing in the world and as far as possible the problem should be met with that same feeling on the part of those who deal with it."

These voices, crying for assistance, came from a remarkable variety of people and places, asking for all manner of aid. And Eleanor Roosevelt at her desk might have been the image Americans had of her as they struggled to put their problems on paper. They often began their letters like this one, from an Oklahoma mother worried about her family in the Depression: "I have been tempted to write you so many times during these long agonizing months but hated to be an extra occasion for you to write or read another letter. However, today I felt I could not hold back any longer. In the strangest way I feel that I know you and that you will fully forgive my bothering you." During the Depression, thousands of people, rich and poor alike, lost not only money but also their sense of security. The world became a dangerous, frightening place. Thousands faced hunger and homelessness on a scale difficult for us to even imagine today. In response, many took what they viewed as desperate measures, such as writing to the First Lady, which they would never have contemplated in better times. Mrs. Roosevelt reflected: "I think the fact that the people in the United States, especially at this time, feel they can write just what they think and feel to people at the head of their government is a very healthy thing. I also think it an excellent thing that people generally feel that the President, his wife, and the people in the government belong to them and that they have a real stake in what is being done."

President Roosevelt's New Deal programs, created to assist the poor, the unemployed, and the elderly, eased the suffering of many people. Billions of federal dollars poured into government agencies, which generated employment and provided at least minimal assistance to the elderly. However, the massive bureaucracies that administered these programs proved daunting to many in need. Mrs.

Roosevelt helped those trying to find their way through the procedural maze, such as this South Dakota farmer's wife: "I want you to know how much we appreciate your aid in speeding up our home loan; we haven't it yet, but it seems like things changed for us after I wrote you." Mrs. Roosevelt forwarded queries she received on specific programs to the proper government agency and invariably received prompt, helpful replies. As the country gradually shifted from depression to war, which ended Depression-era assistance programs, she received letters like this one, in Braille, from a blind woman employed by the New Deal Braille Project : "Knowing that you are interested in all humanity, I appeal to you for help. Is there something that you can do to help extend the Braille Project?" By the time this letter was sent, in the late 1930s, the focus of the president and the country had turned from domestic to foreign affairs.

As more and more countries came under Nazi dominion, Mrs. Roosevelt received more and more frantic pleas from those in the United States with loved ones in Europe, as in this telegram from a New York City woman regarding her parents who were waiting for a visa: "Madame, to help save two valuable lives for this world please consider this case. Israel Schenkel and wife Lotte, Austrian refugees, sick and starving in a refugee camp in Marseilles, France, ask me, their only daughter for intervention in Washington. . . . Please help with advice whom to see and what to do."

American women residing in the Philippines wrote in July 1940 warning of Japanese aggression, saying, "American women, of whatever political affiliation, have learned to look to you as an unofficial helper in high places."

After U.S. entry into World War II, Mrs. Roosevelt's mail changed again. Not only soldiers, but soldiers' mothers, wives, and sweethearts wrote, all unhappy with their situation. Mrs. Roosevelt heartily endorsed the new military units for women in the army and navy, using her influence to assist in their creation. She traveled throughout the war period, to England, the Pacific, and the Caribbean, witnessing conditions for herself and meeting thousands of soldiers and sailors. With her own four sons serving in the military, she personally experienced what she called the "small death" that anxious mothers across the country experienced daily. As the war years dragged on, she received heartbreaking letters such as this, from a soldier's mother living in Franklin, North Carolina: "You may never read this letter, but hope you will. My son Pvt. George H. Dalrymple was reported to me by War Dept Washington D.C. as Missing in Action, in North Atlantic on Feb 2 1943 due to the sinking of a ship by enemy. Could you help me find out more about it?"

Mrs. Roosevelt also played an important role in boosting the morale of those at home. While her husband and Winston Churchill gave blood-stirring speeches, she quietly contributed to the war effort in any way she thought would be useful. The government clearly realized what an asset she could be, enlisting her help in publicizing programs from the selling of war bonds to the introduction of "Victory Mail," a new method of communicating with soldiers overseas. Even though circumstances had changed drastically, with the country facing war rather than depression, Eleanor Roosevelt worked tirelessly to maintain gains made in civil and human rights through the New Deal programs. Thus she took special care in responding to letters such as this from an African-American man in Washington, D.C., who wrote regarding the Red Cross policy of separating blood given by blacks from that given by whites: "With the appointment of a new chairman of the American Red Cross, can it not be possible for that organization to reconsider the policy of labeling blood supplied by Negroes? It is probable that a person not a Negro can not fully understand the inward disturbance the present policy causes Negroes." Yet, he wrote to a white, wealthy, upper-class woman with confidence that she would understand.

Mrs. Roosevelt's father had carefully imparted to the young Eleanor that a life of privilege incurred the responsibility of aiding those less fortunate. As she explained it, "Very early I became conscious of the fact that there were men and women and children around me who suffered in one way or another. I think I was five or six when my father took me for the first time to help serve Thanksgiving day dinner in one of the newsboys' clubhouses, which my grandfather, Theodore Roosevelt, had started. I was tremendously interested in all these ragged little boys and in the fact, which my father explained, that many of them had no homes and lived in little wooden shanties in empty lots, or slept in vestibules of houses or public buildings or any place where they could be moderately warm."

She also learned, during her unhappy childhood, that reaching out and caring for others provided a remedy for feelings of loneliness and self-pity. A woman writing to Mrs. Roosevelt in 1938 made a very prescient comment: "I first want to tell you I admire you very much, for the kindness you show to the young girls and boys, well not only that but you are an all round good woman; you appear to me as though you wanted to see others happy even if you were unhappy." This was entirely true; thus, her background and personality perfectly suited the situation in which she found herself as First Lady, faced with so many in dire need.

Mrs. Roosevelt's compassion and sincerity of interest conveyed themselves to the American people via a continual flow of communication: in "My Day," her daily (except Sundays) nationally syndicated newspaper column, her monthly column in *Ladies Home Journal,* as well as in constant lectures, personal appearances, press conferences, and radio interviews. In addition to hearing from Eleanor Roosevelt directly, Americans read and heard about her activities in countless newspaper and magazine articles, as well as on the radio, a medium of communication that both the President and the First Lady used to good effect.

While Americans listened to what their First Lady had to say, their First Lady listened intently to them. From their letters and in question and answer sessions on radio and in magazines, she heard what America was saying. In fact, Mrs. Roosevelt used letters as source material for her speeches and columns, always maintaining the confidentiality of her sources. It was well known that she donated to charity the money she received for her speeches and articles, leading countless letter writers to inquire if they could borrow money from her. A surprisingly large number of people, in this age before television, saw her in person, as she traveled widely in order to assess conditions for herself and to report back to her husband.

In her autobiography she explained the necessity of her travels: "One curious thing is that I have always seen life personally; that is, my interest or sympathy or indignation is not aroused by an abstract cause, but by the plight of a single person whom I have seen with my own eyes. It was the sight of a child dying of hunger that made the tragedy of hunger become of such overriding importance to me. Out of my response to an individual develops an awareness of a problem to the community, then to the country and finally to the world." Her constant travel led to a letter early in her tenure as First Lady from a farmer who told her he had named a new clock "Eleanor" because it was constantly "on the go."

It was not only the amount of communication, but the manner in which Eleanor Roosevelt expressed herself to the public, that enabled Americans to consider her a friend. In her "My Day" column she described her daily activities in an informal, chatty manner. She spoke with clarity, simplicity, and sincerity, whether holding a press conference, giving a radio interview, or answering questions in the auditorium of a local high school. She was described as "not a brilliant talker, but a brilliant listener." In her columns and articles she reported vividly on conditions she observed firsthand, while occasionally writing feisty essays on topics she felt were being ignored by policymakers. Mrs. Roosevelt's constant conversation with the public, in which she clearly listened and acted as well as spoke, caused Americans to feel that they did, indeed, know her personally. This helped greatly when she began her long term as First Lady in the midst of the Depression, and the lack of food, heat, clothing, and money caused many people to experience overwhelming feelings of helplessness. Through it all Eleanor Roosevelt radiated confidence, strength, and, most important of all, hope, serving as a beacon of light in the darkness.

As would be expected, letters to the First Lady revealed cultural patterns typical of the period. Even though conditions were desperate, with a 25 percent unemployment rate, those who wrote to her frequently felt shame and embarrassment, considering their difficulties to be their own fault. Some letter writers went to great lengths to conceal the fact that they had written to her. Many were self-conscious, others fearful of ridicule that they had taken such a step; many did not want family or friends to know the truth of what they were facing and didn't want people to laugh at or make fun of them. As I sat in the research room of the Franklin D. Roosevelt Presidential Library in Hyde Park, New York, sifting through file upon file of letters to Mrs. Roosevelt, I could visualize a parade of thousands of Americans reaching out for help.

And reach out they did. It is difficult to comprehend the amount of mail Mrs. Roosevelt received. Her papers at the library amount to 1,095 linear feet and consist of approximately 2,900,000 pages. Letters from the public from the years 1934 to 1945 total 3,000 boxes. Thus, the letters included here cannot definitively represent them all. They were, however, particularly selected for the voice of the writer, the nature of their distress, or the impact their letter, and others like it, had on government policy. President Roosevelt realized early on the importance of communication from "the people," pointedly commenting in his address on laying the cornerstone for the Roosevelt Library on November 19, 1939: "Of the papers which will come to rest here I personally attach less importance to the documents of those who have occupied high public or private office, than I do to the spontaneous letters which have come to me and my family and my associates from men, from women, and from children in every part of the United States, telling me of their conditions and problems, and giving me their opinions."

Not all members of the public supported the President and his New Deal or his activist wife. Asked about critics in a radio interview, Mrs. Roosevelt responded "I get very critical and very unflattering cartoons and critical articles, but you get, in a way, a little indifferent, you make up your mind what you want to do and you forget the other things." Some persistent critics, such as conservative syndicated columnist Westbrook Pegler, eventually infuriated her. In a column appearing in the February 12, 1942, issue of *The Washington Post* Pegler began, "For all the gentle sweetness of my nature and my prose, I have been accused of rudeness to Mrs. Roosevelt when I only said she was impudent, presumptuous and conspiratorial, and that her withdrawal from public life at this time would be a fine public service." He summarized his thoughts: "Still scrupulously avoiding impoliteness, I insist that Mrs. Roosevelt's activities have been not helpful but, on the whole, very harmful, that she has been guilty of imposition and effrontery that, for all her pleadings against discrimination for creed and color, has herself actively encouraged cruel discrimination against Americans refusing to join unions wherefore she should retire." Pegler's columns finally caused her to write to the attorney general, "I do think this is grounds for a libel suit. You, of course, will know far better than I, but it is so outrageous I had to protest." His reply could not have been satisfactory to her: "I do not think it is libelous, legally speaking, irrespective of considering the wisdom of taking action." Notwithstanding such critics, the vast majority of the First Lady's mail came from admirers who sought her help.

Mrs. Roosevelt, hearing daily from large numbers of Americans, quickly perceived the need for a well-organized system of dealing with her mail. She worked on it in the early morning and late evening hours, writing instructions for her secretary to follow in the replies. Due to the volume of mail, she issued the following as a guideline for individuals writing to government officials, a guideline she clearly felt applied to her own mail: "My plea to the general public would be not to look before you leap, but to think before you write. Make sure that you have exhausted every means near at hand which might solve your problem. Make your letter as brief and to the point as possible, and if you use a typewriter or you can find some one who does, have your letter typed. The long hand letters are the ones which consume time and cause the final nervous break-down for any secretary!"

Mrs. Roosevelt frequently referred letters to government departments for their attention; she assumed federal personnel would be happy to help the American public. As the letters she forwarded received immediate attention, she did not realize until much later that she had been quite naive in her belief that government bureaucracy responded eagerly to the general public. In a *McCall's* article of April 1954, she responded to a question placed by a reader: "In several books written since your husband was president, you are referred to as 'meddling' in government activities. As someone who loves and admires you, I'd like to hear your side of this story." Mrs. Roosevelt responded: "I was never conscious of meddling in government activities. I realize I passed on inquiries, complaints and suggestions which were sent to me and since then I have learned that even high department heads felt that my interest meant an obligation on them to do things which they did not think they should do. I am shocked and grieved. I had always supposed they would do only what they thought right and not permit me to do anything which they considered wrong. However, I suppose I must accept the fact that without any intention on my part I did meddle in things which they considered I had no right to do. I regret this and I can only say it was done without intention."

After examining hundreds of letters, it became obvious that Mrs. Roosevelt developed personal guidelines to deal with her correspondence. During the Depression she received constant requests for money or for specific items such as food, clothes, housing, or a job. These she referred to appropriate government agencies or private charitable organizations for assistance, and when no sources seemed available, she sent regrets that she could not help. During World War II, she made it clear that she would not interfere in military matters, saying that her "help" might do more harm than good, but referred those requesting deferment, leave, or changes in their status to the Morale Branch of the War Department. Her tact and diplomacy were frequently called upon to bridge gaps in communication and understanding.

Mrs. Roosevelt's responses to letter writers revealed much about her own personality. While usually sympathetic in dealing with the misfortunes of others, she definitely did not deal as charitably with those individuals whom she considered the cause of their own problems, such as drinkers and gamblers. She disliked self-centered people and responded unfavorably to their letters of self-pity. She most admired those who were struggling to help themselves, but who because of their gender, race, or class were having difficulties; these people she would help in any way she could. Thus, her responses to her correspondents faithfully mirrored her approach to life: "The thing which counts is the striving of the human soul to achieve spiritually the best that it is capable of, and to care unselfishly, not only for personal good but for the good of all those who toil with them upon the earth."

Issues and problems existed that were far beyond the scope of what a First Lady could accomplish, as Mrs. Roosevelt realized: "The variety of the requests and the apparent confidence that I would be able to make almost anything possible always worried me," she wrote in her autobiography. A St. Louis, Missouri, mother pleaded with her to intercede with the state welfare organization for her children's return: "Please Mrs. Roosevelt help me to get them back will you. If you will do this for me I will never, never forget." But matters such as this remained solely under the jurisdiction of state authorities. A Glenelg, Maryland, woman wrote: "From what I have read in the papers and heard at differing places over the radio the good deeds you have done for poor people, . . . I am appealing to you for help. In 1925 . . . my husband [had] an unavoidable accident while on employment of the state road . . . and [is now a] cripple for life. . . . I feel sure you will let me hear from you in the near future as I am in need." This was, again, purely a state matter and even a sympathetic First Lady could not provide assistance.

When her husband became president, Eleanor Roosevelt was already well known as a champion of the downtrodden; people trusted her. If supporters viewed Franklin Roosevelt as the savior and father of the country, there could be no doubt that Eleanor Roosevelt was regarded as the mother. She served as First Lady at a pivotal time in American history, symbolizing the ideals of our country: hard work, respect for individuals, and equal justice for all. She passionately felt that "staying aloof is not a solution; it is a cowardly evasion," and immersed herself in everyday America. She was regarded in life as she is in history, as a source of hope and pride. And so it was that she attracted a phenomenal number of letters from a wide spectrum of the American population. People whose circumstances could not have been more different from her own felt free to unburden their hearts, to reveal secrets and troubles that weren't even shared within their families. The letters illustrate how different life in America was in the 1930s and 1940s, when sheer survival proved an exhausting task for many. The letters also show us that basic human nature does not change; men and women struggled then with their fear, financial loss, illness, and troubled family relationships as they do today.

Eleanor Roosevelt elicited from the people unvarnished and candid appeals that provide a unique history of the time. The immediacy of the letters transport the reader from Oklahoma families forced to abandon their farms, to mothers dealing with the blight of urban poverty in Washington, D.C., to the proud elderly all over the country quietly facing homelessness and hunger, to soldiers in Europe worried about their families at home, to servicemen in the Pacific, desperate for a break from long years of war. Because Eleanor Roosevelt drew forth all these voices, we can hear them still.

Notes on the Letters

The letters presented in this book are as near the original as possible, modified only when necessary for clarity, as the goal is to give the reader the flavor of the original. The letters may be found in Series 70, Correspondence with Government Departments; Series 75, Old Age Pensions; Series 100, Personal Letters; Series 100.1, Letters from Servicemen and Women; Series 102, Refugee Children; and Series 150.1, Material Assistance Requested. Mrs. Roosevelt's comments used throughout are found in the originals of her "My Day" columns and in the Speech and Articles Files; all materials are in the papers of Mrs. Eleanor Roosevelt, Franklin D. Roosevelt Presidential Library, Hyde Park, New York.

In addition to missives to government agencies, this correspondence includes letters to charitable organizations and other nongovernmental groups to whom Mrs. Roosevelt wrote for advice and aid. Often the entire series of letters between Mrs. Roosevelt and her correspondents no longer remains in the files, not surprising given the volume of mail dealt with on a daily basis. She received more letters from women than men; women felt comfortable in writing to her with their troubles, in a way they wouldn't have with a man. Due to the President's polio, people with handicaps of varying kinds implored her help, feeling that she would be particularly sympathetic to their plight. She also received occasional letters from con artists, those out to profit at the expense of others. Even though clearly sympathetic to the trials and tribulations of those who wrote, she did check into the facts.

Mrs. Roosevelt's correspondents usually assumed she would send their mail to others for aid if that proved necessary, so they did not expect confidentiality. However, if the writers made it clear that they did not wish their name revealed, she abided by their wishes. Using this as my guideline, I omitted the name from any letters in this work in which the sender requested anonymity. In addition, I would be delighted to hear from the descendants of families whose letters are included in this volume.

In selecting letters, I attempted to cover a range of issues, include writers from all over the country, encompass varying ages and races, and illustrate the prevailing themes of the time. Mrs. Roosevelt frequently received letters intended for her husband; evidently the correspondents felt that the likelihood of their letter receiving FDR's attention would be increased by sending it in this manner. Mrs. Roosevelt referred these to FDR's secretary, Grace Tully. Mrs. Roosevelt also referred a number of additional letters to her husband. These either contained information she thought he should know or regarded causes she wished to bring to his attention. Sometimes she merely sought his advice on a delicate issue. FDR had a basket by his bedside in which Mrs. Roosevelt placed these letters; they would be returned with his comments the next day. This "passing of baskets" illustrated the way in which the President and First Lady worked together on issues both large and small. He relied on her for information on what was happening in the larger world, since his polio made it difficult for him to move freely. She depended on him to push a social justice agenda whenever it was politically possible to do so.

The individual Mrs. Roosevelt relied on most to deal with the mail was her secretary, Miss Malvina Thompson, nicknamed

"Tommy." Tommy was born in the Bronx in 1892 and began work for Mrs. Roosevelt in 1928, serving as Mrs. Roosevelt's confidential secretary until her death in 1953. She thus worked for Mrs. Roosevelt throughout the White House years. Tommy married Frank Scheider in 1921 and divorced him in 1939, which is why some letters are addressed to Malvina Scheider. To Tommy fell the task of sorting the mail and dealing with the daily deluge at Mrs. Roosevelt's direction. Tommy accompanied Mrs. Roosevelt on her travels, which led to some interesting experiences. "There have been days when my typewriter was perched on a rock; sometimes on my lap in a fast moving automobile. We have used the bed in a hotel room when no table was available and my position was a little awkward; on a destroyer lurching from side to side and on trains with the typewriter sliding under my eyes when keeping my eyes on its movements was a bit disconcerting." In a 1939 interview, Mrs. Roosevelt referred to Tommy as "the person who makes life possible for me." Tommy herself stated that "everything I do is conditioned by her needs. I never do anything else." Mrs. Roosevelt was at her bedside when Tommy died on April 13, 1953, and felt her loss greatly.

Ralph Magee, head of the Correspondence Unit, supervised the handling of Mrs. Roosevelt's mail when she and Tommy were away. He oversaw a staff of two dozen people, some of whom dealt with the more traditional social correspondence every First Lady received. They would open, sort, and answer letters as they felt Mrs. Roosevelt would wish, until she returned. Mail did follow her to the presidential home in Hyde Park, New York, so she got little respite from the deluge. In spite of the aid Mrs. Roosevelt could provide to many, she must have felt an incredible burden, receiving a daily stream of problems from those who imagined she could accomplish virtually anything.

Part One

The Great Depression

As President Roosevelt famously pronounced: "I see one-third of a nation ill-housed, ill-clad, and ill-nourished. The test of our progress is not whether we add more to the abundance of those who have much; it is whether we provide enough for those who have too little." In his first inaugural address he spoke of his belief that the major stumbling block for the American people was fear: "So first of all let me assert my firm belief that the only thing we have to fear is fear itself—nameless, unreasoning, unjustified terror which paralyzes needed efforts to convert retreat into advance." First Lady Eleanor Roosevelt also realized the significance of the constant sense of dread felt by many Americans in 1933: "The worst thing that has come to us from the Depression is fear. Fear of an uncertain future, fear of not being able to meet our problems, fear of not being equipped to cope with life as we live it today." The letters to the First Lady at this time reveal massive fear of the future, of not having enough work, money, food, or clothing—all the basic necessities of life.

The Great Depression began in the United States with the crash of the stock market on October 28, 1929; in a few weeks, stocks lost 40 percent of their value. While affecting all levels of society, the

Depression especially wreaked havoc on those of the lowest strata, who had marginal resources. At its worst, unemployment levels reached 25 percent in 1933. President Herbert Hoover took steps to deal with Depression conditions, but they proved insufficient for the scope of the problem. The large-scale economic downturn, characterized by sharply reduced industrial production and widespread unemployment, lasted virtually until the United States entered World War II, when the demands of war production pulled the economy out of the doldrums.

Widespread poverty posed problems enough, but mother nature added even more. Farmers throughout the Great Plains could have been forgiven for thinking they were on the receiving end of the Biblical plagues of Egypt as they struggled with extreme drought, dust storms, and hordes of grasshoppers. At the same time, severe flooding wreaked havoc in the Midwestern states. Countless families reeled under a series of blows, such as lost farms or wages, combined with family illness, which reduced them to the breaking point. If the family breadwinner lost his job, became ill or incapacitated, left home, or died, the spouse and children frequently had no way to replace this income and suffered greatly. For many letter writers, their obvious mental anguish matched or exceeded the physical deprivation they suffered.

Depression conditions must have been extremely frustrating for Mrs. Roosevelt because she truly wished to help her correspondents, but all she could do in most cases was refer people to federal or state agencies, as appropriate, or private charities, whose funds were often exhausted. Plain and simply put, the majority of those seeking her aid needed cold, hard cash. The fertile imaginations of Americans conjured up numerous ways to improve their situations. Opening a tea shop or boarding house, taking in washing or sewing—all were good ideas but all required substantial financial resources to get started, money people did not have and hoped to get from Mrs. Roosevelt. However, the money she gave to charity generally went to an agency such as the Red Cross or the American Friends Service Committee for distribution, and not to individuals.

Because she could actually do little financially to help in the face of such massive need, Mrs. Roosevelt felt it extremely important to travel the country and assess conditions for herself, and then report to the President, feedback he used to help create the New Deal. She learned early on that a visit from her and positive comments in a newspaper could create an easier path for the unfolding government programs. In a radio address she described the conditions she found:

"I have talked to girls who work in department stores, to women whose boys are in C.C.C. Camps; I have seen the inside of share croppers homes in Arkansas; and cabins with mud floors in the Ozarks. There is little that I haven't seen in the course of the last few years which touches the third of the nation which is ill fed, ill housed, ill clothed and I think that estimate of a third is a low estimate.

"There is little I can do about it except to talk about it. The government alone can only make a few patterns which point the way to what might be done by people in their communities if they so desired. To know about these sore spots, is to be impelled to go out and tell other people in order that they can go and see for themselves but it is important that before they go they should be prepared and understand what they see. Therefore, those having this understanding have an obligation to interpret these sections of our country; this portion of our people to the rest of the nation which is more fortunate." Mrs. Roosevelt utilized her "My Day" column and other speeches and articles to this purpose.

Even in the face of what was obviously widespread suffering, individuals often felt they were somehow to blame for their problems; most felt shame and embarrassment in having to ask for assistance, with their pride suffering greatly. Perhaps the most heartbreaking aspect of the Depression was not the material privation but the effect it had on people's hopes and dreams, which had to be deferred or completely abandoned. The letters that follow illustrate the desperation as well as the courage in the face of despair revealed by Americans as they endured the years of the Great Depression.

—CDK

The Great Depression

May 16, 1933

Dear Mrs. Roosevelt,

Tired after all mornings ironing, I sat down by the radio to patch. Idly turning it on to the only station I could bring in with enough volume to hear, imagine my surprise and delight to hear you being introduced—and your fine talk.

It is inspiring to know we have as our "First Lady," one so really **great** and influential, who is so kindhearted—charmingly simple and wholly unselfish.

I love you with a reverence that amounts almost to worship for what you have done for our Bobby. He has been at Warm Springs[*] since October and (altho' I'm half sick with longing to see him) I pray God he may stay until he's well.

No one will ever know how my heart swells until it **hurts** when I think of you doing all that for us—I will probably never have a chance to favor you, but will do my best for someone else, and to be worthy, and raise my 5 children to be one hundred percent American!

---

* Under the influence of President Roosevelt, Warm Springs, Georgia, became a treatment center for polio victims.

You seem so interested and friendly I felt I must write and thank you **again**.

Yours sincerely,
Mrs. A. L. Holland.
Siloam Springs, Arkansas.

[One page handwritten]

In a radio program on April 19, 1935, regarding her mail, Mrs. Roosevelt quoted the sentence above: "I will probably never have a chance to favor you, but I will do my best to help some one else and to be worthy and raise my five children to be 100 percent American," so this letter of gratitude must have touched her greatly.

June 8, 1933

Dear Mrs. Holland:

Thank you so much for your very lovely letter. It has made me very happy indeed to be able to do what I could for Bobby. I have not heard from Dr. Hooke recently, but I feel sure that he is getting along very nicely, and I hope that he will be able to return to you at the end of the year very much improved.

With all good wishes, I am
Cordially yours,
Eleanor Roosevelt

Mrs. Roosevelt was probably telling the story of this family in an unpublished article she wrote about her mail for Vogue *magazine in 1940:*

"To give you some idea of the type of thing which comes to my desk and how it is handled, let me tell you a story of a letter written on six sheets of cheap pad paper. It was a mother's story of her family. She spoke well of her husband but he had been unfortunate. They lived in a poor part of the country; a part-time job which the father held had been lost; the land was poor

and produced little; their cow had died, and there were five
children to be fed and clothed and then one of them, a little
fellow of some five years old, had infantile paralysis. He lived,
but one leg was badly crippled. How was he going to meet life?
She had heard of Warm Springs, but she could not take the trip
and she could not pay for the care. What could she do?

The letter rang true, but I asked a friend to visit them
and find out if circumstances were as she described them.
They were, and then with the aid of some friends, a fund was
raised which paid for the small boy for the long months that
he had to stay in Warm Springs; for his trip and for one older
person to make the trip with him and settle him there. He
stayed until the doctors felt that they could do nothing more
for him. When he went home he was sufficiently improved
to go to school with the others. He learned to get about on
crutches, even to walk on them the half mile to and from
school every day."

• • •

January 8, 1934

My Dear Mrs. Roosevelt

From what I have read in the papers and heard at differing
places over the radio the good deeds you have done for
poor people, you are a wonderful woman and a good sensible one and now I am appealing to you for help in some
way and when I explain to you I know you will understand
my situation. My husband had a letter written to your
President but he never received any answer to so I don't
think he received it. In 1925 on July the 7th my husband
hapen to an unavoidable accident while on employment of
the state road as patrolman and he was in the Hospital
and had extra pictures taken and was pronounce cripple
for life and has bin on cruches ever since not able to do

anything not as much as pump me a buckett of water. I even have to put his shoes on and lace them up so the state paid him compensation of twelve dollars a week untill Oct 23th 1933 and since then we haven had a cent and hear I am with kidney trouble sick one day feel right good the next not a cent for doctor. and when he got hurt we was paying on a home so it caught us with nine hundred dollars mortgage while ever we got the compensation we could keep the intrust paid taxes and insurance up but now we cant do nothing we have nothing but poor humble home and about to loose it he is willing to do anything he can do siting down he hassen got learning enough for bookeeping or any thing like that now what am I to do.

I cant be turned out sick with a criple husband he got hurt giving the state a good honest day's work and has worked for the state for twelve years and they should care for him the balance of his life. I and my husband both worked hard to put you two in the White House and worked for that party 4-5 years and now I know if there is anything you can do to help me you will do it please given this your attention at once and I feel sure you will let me hear from you in the near future as I am in need.

Respectfuly
Mrs. Henry O. Ridgly
Glenelg, MD

[Four pages handwritten]

• • •

January 12, 1934

Dear Mrs. F. Roosevelt:

I do not expect you will remember me writing you, telling you about my husband having his application in at Navy

Yard. I just wanted to let you know he has been sent for and is working there now. When I wrote to you asking help rather than telling you about it, I never dreamed of you taking so much interest in my letter. I also had a letter from the captain telling me you had sent my letter down there. I know it is through your kindness that he has been called. I never will be able to thank you enough. It has meant so much to me. I wish I could thank you in person but I know that is impossible, so I thank you from the bottom of my heart. I would love to come to Washington but it seems like everything is so uncertain; I am afraid to seek work there so will look around here. Sometimes when I am sitting alone I wonder what you are doing. I am every once in a while going to drop you a card just to let you know I am thinking of you if I may take the pleasure to do so. I just had to write to thank you again. My best wishes for you and our President, hoping that God will give the strength and courage to go on which I hope he will because we all believe we have the right one to help us all the best that he can. If only the people will stand by him everything will be alright. I hope my letter reaches you, and many thanks again for your kindness and interest.

Remain

Mrs. Lillian Higgiston

In a 1936 speech, Mrs. Roosevelt addressed the issue of joblessness this way:

"Another task for us to undertake and a very important one, is to convince many unthinking people that the unemployed are not a strange race. They are like we would be if we had not had a fortunate chance at life. Some of us regard the unemployed remotely, as if they were thousands of miles away and had no personal call on anyone's sympathy. It isn't the intention to be cruel and indifferent. It's just that it is very hard for people who do not come face to face with suffering to realize how hard life can be. I have a feeling that in the next few years in addition to helping out the unemployed themselves, we in this group, must take on the task of educating the fortunate people into an understanding of the lives of the unfortunate."

. . .

February 26, 1934

Dear Madam,

I am writing you this letter to ask you if you could help get my children back. The children Board of Guardians took them away from me. They promised that if I would let them operate on me[*] they would give them back to me but they haven't. The only reason that they took them away from me for was because my husband was out of work and I went to the Provident Association for help. They were the ones who had them taken away from me. My husband is working now and I have a home and everything ready for the children if I could get them. I love them so much and sure miss them. I guess you know how I feel since you are a mother yourself. How do you think you would feel if your children were taken away from you. Please Mrs. Roosevelt help me to get them back will you. If you will do this for me I will never, never forget. I guess this is all. Please answer this and let me know if you will help me.

From a mother who loves her children and would like to have them back.

Mrs. G. Riddle
St. Louis, Missouri
(Please answer soon)

[Three pages handwritten]

---

[*] sterilization

March 6, 1943

My dear Mrs. Riddle:

Mrs. Roosevelt asks me to acknowledge for her your letter
of February 26, and to express to you her regret that she
can do nothing personally in the matter of which you
write, as it seems to be one which would come under the
jurisdiction of State authorities.

Very sincerely yours,
Malvina T. Scheider
Secretary to Mrs. Roosevelt

• • •

October 24, 1934

Dear Mrs. Roosevelt:

I am sending you a card of Thanks. I don't suppose you
remember the letter I sent you last year shortly before
Christmas telling you about my husband having his application in the Navy Yard in Washington and how he was
waiting to be called, and after receiving my letter you
sent it to the Captain in the Navy Yard and in return I
received a very nice note telling me you had forward my
letter there. It wasn't very long before my husband was
sent for. I knew it was through your interest and kindness that he was sent for. To you I suppose it meant such
a little thing to do, but you will now know the happiness
it has given us. I only hope that my husband will be able
to keep his position. We have a home, of course, we just
pay rent, but it is home after all. I think of you so much
and hope you and our President will have all the joys and
happiness of life. He is trying so hard to bring peace and
work and yet there are so many can't see it. I hope he
won't get discouraged and I don't believe he will. Please

don't think I want to bore you with my letter but just once in a while I like for you to know how thankful I am. Will close with all my best wishes for your success and happiness.

I remain:

Mrs. Lillian Higgiston

Brooklyn, Maryland

[Four pages handwritten]

• • •

March 29, 1934

Mrs. Franklin Roosevelt

Dear Madam:

I now drop a few lines to ask you a few questions as I can not find out any place else.

Now as my daughter die and left 3 little girls 4 years ago and as time have been so hard on us and as I have been told by folks we should have a pension for to help support the girls and as I have try to find out here and I can not. I have been told to write to you and ask you about it. Now I do not care to part with the little ones and as last year was a very hard year on us and we are a family of 9 and as my husband has been work on the PWA Project but it sure is very hard to keep 9 on $12. Others say for me to see if I could not get a pension to help care for the 3 girls for I am glad to keep them at home if I can only have a way. Now I have to school the little ones. They need clothes and things and as I can not get any help to take care of them they are in the 7th grade, 5th and 3rd grade and now is the time I like to be able to keep them going right along. Would like to hear from you to see if they are entitled to a pension.

I also have 2 boys in the 8th so I have quite a bit to care for. I will close hope this reach you all right and hope you can understand this all right.

From Mrs. Nellie Allen
Knoxville, Illinois

P.S. As we were try to buy us a small Place and as we were out of work and as the cinch bug and dry weather kill all of our crop now we have to move if we can find a place we do not know where we go so Please let me here right back as our time is out April 4, we try to get 5 or 10 acre so we can raise most of our living.

Answer soon.
And oblige me,
Mrs. Allen

[One and a half pages handwritten]

April 5, 1934

My dear Mrs. Allen:
Mrs. Roosevelt asks me to acknowledge for her your letter of March 29, and to express to you her regret that she can do nothing personally in the matter of which you write, as it seems to be one which would come under the jurisdiction of State authorities.

Very sincerely yours,
Malvina T. Scheider
Secretary to Mrs. Roosevelt

• • •

April 12, 1934

My Dear Mrs. Roosevelt—Mother of our country

I am writing you a letter to ask you to help my poor boy. They have taken his pension away. They cut him to $13.15 now he has got word he will not get that after April 1. He had an operation at the Bronx Hospital last October and has not had any work since. He is a drugist with the depression he lost all he had. Will you please try and place him in one of the Soldier's Hospitals any where. I am his poor old Mother 68 years old and not abel to work only at times. I have no money.

Mary Robinson Schrader
Troy, New York

My son's name is George Evans Robinson, 40 years old and Served from August 23, 1918 to March 18 1919. I will be most thankful to you if you will try and do something for my poor son. May God bless you and yours.

M.R.S.

[Three pages handwritten]

April 26, 1934

My dear Mrs. Schrader:

Mrs. Roosevelt asks me to send you the attached copy of letter she received from the Administrator of Veterans Affairs, to whom she referred your letter concerning your son.

Very sincerely yours,
Malvina T. Scheider
Secretary to Mrs. Roosevelt

My dear Mrs. Roosevelt:

Replying to your letter of April 18, 1934, you are advised that this veteran enlisted on May 16, 1918, and was honorably discharged on April 3, 1919. He, therefore, would be eligible for domiciliary or hospital care, if indicated, as far as his military service is concerned.

Application should be made to the Veterans Administration Facility, Bronx, New York. That station has been advised of the status of the case, and you may be assured his application will receive prompt attention.

Sincerely,

Frank T. Hines,

Administrator of Veteran's Affairs

• • •

May 4, 1934

Dear Mrs. Roosevelt,

I am a widow and have worked in the laundry of Miss Evans, East 125 St. N.Y. for seventeen years. My only child, a daughter, is very delicate. She is married, and has one child. Her husband is out of work and the man he worked for owes him for many months work.

My daughter and I were trying to pay for our little home in Floral Park Long Island. Now that my daughters husband is out of work I am the only one bringing in any money.

Miss Evans place has been taken by the city for the Triborough Bridge and is to be torn down this month. The city has not paid Miss Evans for the house and she does not know how she is going to set up another laundry till she is paid.

Will you please forgive the liberty I am taking in

asking you to do something to help us so that Miss Evans will be able to keep up her laundry and I will not lose the work I need so badly.

Yours respectfully,
Mrs. Emily Schwarz
Floral Park, Long Island

[One page handwritten]

• • •

December 29, 1934

Dear Mr. and Mrs. Roosevelt
Once more our blessed Christmas Day is over and with a sigh and tears to many, eyes so dim and road so rough. May power through God be given to man to lift this depression from over us, by doing so will give us new light up on our God Almighty.

Dear Mr and Mrs Roosevelt I am just a little woman of 64 yrs. I havent got the power but I have a heart of deepest sympathy and a real good knowledge of just and unjust and one of our most unjust situation of today is the machenery taking the place of all working class of people which is a dirty deal. South Gate is a city of 25,000 or more inhabitants five years ago most all owned their own homes or paying for one, prosperous little city and as a hole a good class of people. Today it is a bankrupt city lost their jobs, lost their homes, lost in banks, lost money loaned out, lost money through sharks, and elderly people who had a little means helped their married children, thinking the married children would soon get jobs but that day never come. Now the only escape from starvation is charity or suicide which is all around us, with in couple of blocks from my home a poor widow poisened herself and three little children, another case four blocks away a man shot his sweet 16 year old daughter then himself, this daughter was his favorite of his two daughters. He had become so weekened in body and mind looking and waiting for a job. O, yes let the men head of the machinery have the jobs they say the machinery must go on it can not be stoped the working class of people was put here on earth (**by God, long before machinery was ever made**) they come first and they are going to make serious trouble if they can not hold their just rights that God gave them.

God has never left a message no where that machinery has the right to take our working class who are among our **best people** and make **paupers** out of them. Give them dole, sneer at them, and in many cases treated with less respect than the lower animals. Most of our young people coming out of high school and colleges are at the end of the road don't know which way to go, so they cut corners and land on Bum St. There they fall in with company who will help create a job that job is made up of different acts. Kidnapping, robery and when cornered shoot to kill innocent people. Let it be one two three or more. Then comes that long drawn out court trial and we tax payers has to pay the cost of trials. When 2/3 of our city fails to pay their taxes and assessments we others haft to pay up thir delinquit bills. IT CANT BE DONE IT RUINS US ALL. How shameful that our hard working class people seeking their own homes and a good majority are AGED PEOPLE. From my early childhood days I always knew that my parents paid taxas twice a year and along life' journey up to 64 yr. And my husband 72 yr we have lost property, lost loaned out money and have a loan on our home we have not paid taxas this fall, some has not paid taxas for 2, 3, and 4 years back. **the torture of mind and body it has given us**

and no homes in our older days (THERE IS NO PLACE LIKE HOME) WHO HAS ROBED WE ELDERLY PEOPLE OF OUR HOMES???

I suppose some of these day we will see in our papers that the machinery has started to break ground to build more pore houses to put all the old people in. Do you wonder why I got out and worked for the Townsend pension plan* it was the only thing that we could see that would take care of the younger people as well as the aged people. Our young people must have work. Dear Mrs. Roosevelt we all see you have a very dificult problem to solve may you be blessed with higher power to help solve the problem.

A sincere true friend Mr. and Mrs. Van Wagoner
South Gate, California

[Six pages handwritten]

• • •

April 2, 1935

Dear Mrs. Roosevelt:

I'm writing you for some advice and a little help if you might count me worthy. I am a girl of 19 yrs. have been raised in a respectable home and have had a respective

---

* The Townsend plan, drafted by Dr. Francis E. Townsend, proposed giving $200 per month for every person over sixty years of age. In a U.P. story of Dec. 24, 1934, Mrs. Roosevelt condemned the Townsend plan as impossible to carry out. She commented, "I have worked for old-age pensions. I believe them vitally important to any society that plans for the future. But I do not believe in the Townsend plan. It is utterly impractical. It is unfortunate that the impression should be given that such a plan can be accomplished, for it cannot." It never had a realistic chance of passage, but the Social Security Act in 1935 created a modest pension program. See Part Two.

living by honest hard working parents. Have had 2 yrs. high school and helped with the support of my mother and 1 younger sister and brother until lately.

Last summer I kept company with a young man whom I trusted to marry and care for me as he promised to do. Now I find I am to become a mother soon, the young man is gone. I can no longer support myself or help mother and she is not able to carry on alone. What am I to do, Mother has no way to take care of the extra burden. We can't hardly have the things we really need. We have always made our way and never have had help or Relief. We have always thought everyone should be self-supporting. Relief here is taking care of all they can or say so. I have read and heard so many good things about you and your kindness to others. I decided I would pour out my heart to you **unknown to any body.** Hoping that you might help me thru this. Until I can get on my feet again. I promise to do as you advise and surely will be grateful for your help as I surely need a few dollars and advise. I feel so badly to set down unable to help mother carry on the expense and burden. Thanking you in advance and may God Bless you and help you in every task you undertake.

A Friend

Flora, Illinois

P.S. Will anxiously be waiting for your reply.

[Two pages handwritten]

April 8, 1935

My dear Miss A:

Mrs. Roosevelt asks me to acknowledge your letter and to tell you she is very sorry to hear of the difficult time you are having.

She regrets that she can do nothing personally to help you, but if you care to have her, she will be glad to ask some one to go to see you and assist in whatever way it is possible to do so.

Very sincerely yours,

Malvina T. Scheider

Secretary to Mrs. Roosevelt

The "some one to go see you" in the above letter probably refers to an informal system described in a 1940 article written for Vogue *magazine but never published. Mrs. Roosevelt described it as "an unofficial organization of some one in almost every state in the union, who could investigate a particularly interesting or appealing letter if it seemed necessary."*

• • •

April 23, 1935

Dear Mrs. Roosevelt

As I am in great trouble and can not get you off my mind you seem to allways be with me. I have never seen you but have seen your picture a good many times. I have no one but my husband and he is 54 and I am 48. We used to farm and have a plenty in 1931 we had a good crop of tobacco— and a hail storm tore it to pieces and 1932 the river got our corn crop or at least the best part of it and our tobacco did not bring anything. 1933 we went in debt and made another crop and it did not bring enough to pay what we owed so we had to give up farming. My husband worked at a sawmill last year and he is only getting one dollar a day. I pray every day and night that something will start up so he can make more. We live near the gap of Smiths Mountain and there is nothing he can get to do and he can not go off whear he can not come home at night as I am in such a bad condition. I thought I would write and ask you to make up a good will offering for me at the White House. We are good honest hardworking Christian people and love to go to church but we do not go as we have nothing deacent to wear. I had rather have a cow than most any thing on earth as we are not able to buy seed to have a garden and it is so hard to just have meat and bread. You get so tired of it. I shall not tell no one I have written to you as the people around hear would only laugh at me. But I do not feel like you will so that is why I am writing to you if you send me any money please do not send check if you can help it just put the money in a letter and send it.

Mrs. B.
Sandy Level, Virginia

[Five pages handwritten]

April 26, 1935

My dear Mrs. B:

Mrs. Roosevelt asks me to acknowledge your letter and to express her regret that because of the great number of similar requests she receives, she has found it impossible to attempt to comply with them, much as she would like to assist all those who appeal to her.

Assuring you of Mrs. Roosevelt's sympathy, I am

Very sincerely yours,
Malvina T. Scheider
Secretary to Mrs. Roosevelt

In a radio program of July 25, 1940, in which Mrs. Roosevelt had been asked to characterize her mail, she described the hundreds of letters she got similar to the above:

"Other people ask for money outright. Some threaten or

insinuate that dire things may happen if the check is not forthcoming by return mail. My heart goes out, as would yours, to people in need. I can not often give money directly to those who write for it. First, it is difficult to investigate each case. Second, charitable organizations have been formed for just that purpose and it seems more sensible to work through them."

• • •

May 8, 1935

Dear Mrs. Roosevelt:

Over a year ago I discovered an ingredient of vegetable extraction, which removes dandruff.

I have demonstrated my mixture before several eminent persons, who are interested in hair and scalp research, but who seem to resent the fact that I, not a medical student possess that marvelous formula.

Doctors tell me that eight out of ten people have dandruff, it is an unsanitary condition of the scalp that nothing as yet has been able to combat.

Realizing how badly in need of this remedy thousands of people are, I find it difficult to make the proper contact.

Knowing of your great interest in the betterment of all things, I have taken this privilege of writing you for whatever advise or guidance you can give me. Am willing to demonstrate my claim and prove this wonderful achievement, the elimination of an unhealthy and unsanitary condition which exists among all people.

I'm fully aware of the fact that your time is valuable, but I'll be grateful for a word of advice you give or any suggestion you may have.

Thanking you in advance, wishing you and yours the best health, I am always very gratefully and sincerely,

Mrs. H. Goldfarb

Brooklyn, New York

[One and a half pages handwritten]

May 17, 1935

My dear Mrs. Goldfarb:

In reply to your letter of May 8, Mrs. Roosevelt suggests you get in touch with the Patent Office, Department of Commerce, Washington, D.C., for information on the value of your medicine.

Very sincerely yours,

Malvina T. Scheider

Secretary to Mrs. Roosevelt

• • •

October 17, 1935

Mrs. Franklin Roosevelt:

Dear First Lady,

I am the wife of a Georgia farmer, which is very much interested in our President and his family and the good he has done, and is doing now.

I am very much in trouble now, and feel like I must have a little help. I have a family of six children which have all finished high school, two daughters married, and are in Washington. One having an apartment on Erie Ave. Takoma Park, Md and Mrs. Meacham the daughter in which I am writing you is staying with her at the present time, working at Heckt Co. Dept Store. She had 20 cents in her purse when she landed there. She started working the second day she landed but gets a very little. At first, she didn't have a thing for winter, not even a coat or suit. She says its getting cold and she wants to go to night school and take typing so as to get a better position, but cant stand to go out in cold without sufficient warmth. What can you do to help her and me. Can you make some arrangements for a coat, have you one you could give her. One of your daughters would fit her I think. Could you see her sometime at Heckts or have your secretary to see her. She is a sweet deserving girl just 23 years of age. And so ambitious. I am so sorry to have to ask this favor but, it seems my only chance. As you know farmers are pretty hard up at the present time.

If you should call her up or see any reason for seeing her, Mrs. W. W. Meacham at Heckts Dept. store and I shall some day, I hope be able to repay you if you will only help her to get some warm cloths or a coat. Just what ever you can do for her would be such a help to both of us. For you know how close a mothers daughter is to her. Wish you could know her.

Sincerely
Mrs. Victor A. Purvis
Culverton, Georgia

[Two pages handwritten]

• • •

January 6, 1936

Dear Mrs. Roosevelt
I am writing you on behalf of my son, George Menear, who

is sixteen years of age and whose right side is paralyzed due to a serious illness two years ago. I have had him to several doctors, but they say the only thing that can help him is the treatments given at the institutions for paralyzed children. Our county health doctor advised me to write to you, as you had helped another child in this vicinity to their treatments. A welfare nurse filled out an application several months ago and sent it to Charleston, but has not received a reply.

George is in Junior High School and greatly interested in his studies, but is greatly handicapped by not being able to write, since losing the use of his right hand. It is impossible for him to go to school when the streets are slippery, as he has very little use of his right leg, which makes walking very difficult and dangerous.

My husband has been out of work almost a year and a few weeks ago we were forced to seek help from the relief. My son's only hope is that you will heed his plea for your help. Your kindness will never be forgotten I am sure. May I hear from you soon, please?

Very truly yours,
Mrs. Victor Menear
Flemington, West Virginia

[One and a half pages handwritten]

January 18, 1936

My dear Mrs. Menear:

Mrs. Roosevelt has asked me to acknowledge your letter. She is indeed sorry to know of your boy's illness but hopes that with time he will completely recover.

It is suggested that you communicate with Mr. Paul H. King, President, International Society for Crippled Children, 542 Buhl

Building, Detroit, Michigan, who may be able to give you some helpful information.

Very sincerely yours,
Malvina T. Scheider
Secretary to Mrs. Roosevelt

Because she had a husband with polio, Mrs. Roosevelt received many letters from family members of those suffering from a wide variety of physical handicaps. In 1945 she wrote an article addressing the situation, as the number of disabled had greatly increased due to war injuries. She concluded this way:

"Some of the most useful people I know are people with physical handicaps. They are useful because they remind other people of the real values of life without ever having to say anything. If they can get an education, earn a living and in addition contribute good cheer in their social relations, they will send out rays of hope and courage throughout the world which none of us could possibly equal no matter how much enthusiasm we put into leading our normal lives."

• • •

[undated]

Dear Mrs. Roosevelt

I presume you will think this a strange request I am asking you. We have no radio and now it seems everything is radio. I have a daughter who has been ill for several years. She doesn't have any enjoyment and never goes any where. She is longing for a small radio to enjoy the programs. No one in our family is working. My husband spent the past 2 years in hospital a victim of a hit and run driver. Do you have a discarded one she can have? Thanking you

Mrs. B. Meade

P.S. I have tried every way to get a radio but so far have had no success, and don't know how we can get one, so I decided to write to you.

Sincerely,
Mrs. B. Meade
Chicago, Illinois

[One page handwritten]

· · ·

March 6, 1936

To your Highness
Mrs. F. D. Rosevelt
Dear madam
I don't know just how to begain this letter and yet this is the only way I can get in tuch with you because you see I am Colored and I would not be permitted to see you. Your Highness please don't take ofence at what I am going to say. You see my wife and I are trying to get to New York to try out on the Major Edward Bowen amateur hour and if you can help us we will be very gratefull to you. I know this letter sound foolish for me to write it to you but I have to do something for I only have one arm and I can not work like other men and all I can do is dance for a living and with three little children to looke out for besides a mother and a sister it is pretty hard. Your Highness please don't think rude of me for I would not ask you if we could work around here. But this means so much to me and my

family and I am not trying to get something for nothing. I have always work for what I have gained and I want work now the kind of work I can do, so if you wish to look in to my case I live at George st. here in Grand Rapids. The paper said you help people who need help and I and my wife need a little now. I hope I have explained the best I can do. Thank you

Mr. Coppins Carew
Grand Rapids, Michigan

[Four pages handwritten]

• • •

March 6, 1936

Dear Madam.

Please read this before burning.

I am a poor Mother with 10 children 9 are boys and I have no way of making a living. Now I have an **old clock** 35 yrs old in good running order. I was wondering if you knew some rich old Genelman who would buy it to help me out.

You know all these old Millionairs surley some one could help a Mother with 9 boys to feed. I feel a Mother that has 9 boys living ought to be able to at least get one meal a day. This clock is an old wooden clock that strikes 1/2 hours and hours. That is the only thing I have in this world to sell. Hope you can help me and thanks.

Mrs. G.
Bruce, South Dakota

[Two pages handwritten]

March 11, 1936

My dear Mrs. G:

Mrs. Roosevelt asks me to acknowledge your letter and to express her regret that because of the great number of similar requests she receives, she has found it impossible to attempt to comply with them, much as she would like to assist all those who appeal to her.

Assuring you of Mrs. Roosevelt's sympathy, I am

Very sincerely yours,
Malvina T. Scheider
Secretary to Mrs. Roosevelt.

• • •

April 7, 1936

My dear Mrs. Roosevelt:—

You no doubt receive so many letters that this one may find your waste basket and if so I would not blame you. I have been debating with myself now for three weeks as to whether I should do this, and I have finally decided to take my chance as it really seems the only course left.

My husband was out of work for nearly two years except for odd jobs but, last May he received one with this village. He was so glad to get it and the whole world changed but the comptroller of the village is making the men pay up their old bills and my husband only receives four dollars per day for five days unless extra work given them on Saturday. With four children to feed and clothe besides your current bills it is mighty hard. The utility company shut our lights and gas off seven weeks ago for an old bill and it has made my work so hard. I wanted to give them four dollars per month on it but they will not accept it. They do not understand how hard it is to wash by hand being men, but I don't hold that against them as they have a duty to perform. However I must keep my children clean because I feel that sort of thing must be bred in them as they grow and my oldest son 13 yrs old has been making progress in cartooning. The art teachers are interested in his work so I would like them to continue so.

Mr. Campbell has tried to borrow money here to get straightened around but every one seems to think his wages are too small to keep it up. I don't understand why when a fellow is down everyone seems to delight in his misery. He has a chance for a better job in a month or so but with these bills it will be difficult to get one as they'll probably come there. I know very well you are busy as anything and I should know enough not to bother you but Mrs. Roosevelt you seem so broadminded, I had to come to you to see if you don't know some one who is willing to trust a poor man with one hundred dollars and allow him to pay it back at four dollars per month so I can pay my utility bill and straighten out with these others then the cheque might be enough to get my children some clothes, a little something each pay day. Do you know any one who will do this for me? I don't ask for a gift I want a loan and I know I'll have a little interest to pay. Im honest and I do so want to kind of relax again as this worry is very hard on our nerves. Altho you have never had the experience I believe you do understand. If you can help me Mrs. Roosevelt Ill pray for you the rest of my life. Thanking you anyway and wishing you and President Roosevelt a Happy Easter, I am yours truly

Mrs. Fred Campbell
Maywood, Illinois

[Four pages handwritten]

April 10, 1936

My dear Mrs. Campbell:

Mrs. Roosevelt is very sorry that she cannot grant the loan you desire. So many people appeal to her as you have done that she has found it impossible to help individuals in a financial way. She is sure you will understand that she cannot do for one what she is unable to do for all, and sincerely hopes you will be able to find some way out of your difficulties.

Very sincerely yours,
Malvina T. Scheider
Secretary to Mrs. Roosevelt.

• • •

April 15, 1936

Dear Mrs. Roosevelt,

Will you please consider this request before you consign it to the wastepaper basket. You must receive a lot of annoying letters and I know you are very busy because I follow you in magazines and on the radio, but will you consider this just a little different as I have tried hard to earn my request by the little poem. You may smile at the poor thing as you can clearly see I am no poet. I have always admired your husband as a president as millions of others do and you as such a fitting helper for him.

Now I will tell you my trouble. I want to see my mother and father, I have not seen my mother and younger brothers for 10 years and my father for six years. My father had a cerebral hemorrhage in the winter. He has recovered but with a very high blood pressure and bad heart the doctor said that he will not live more than 6 months or a year and may go at any time.

My mother has had diabetes for nine years and is very poorly.

They are Mr. and Mrs. M. F. Cornish at Jacobson Minnesota that is the post office so you can confirm this if you like my father was in the University Hospital at Minneapolis when he was so sick this winter. I want to go home to visit them this summer as soon as school is out which will be the last of May. We have a car and I drive although I have had only one arm since I was two years old. My husband promised us (I have four children) that I could drive home when school was out if we could manage the money for gasoline and oil, but since the daughter had her tonsils out, my husband broke his arm and several other unlooked for expenses arose until now he tell me it will be impossible for us to go. I am heartbroken but I haven't given up hope I am trying in every way I can think to get the money for that gasoline. Could you use this little poem in the presidential campaign? It expresses what so many people feel and although it isn't very poetic if it were used on a poster or where people could see it I'm sure it would help a lot.

If you could not send the money, could you arrange with some gasoline company for a pass for gasoline during the months between the middle of June until the middle of August?

The **Youngstown Telegram** just came and I picked it up to read your daily page of "My Day," of your trip, your husbands speech, etc., so you feel very close to me.

I am praying for your help and every day I shall look for an answer. Our minister is Rev. Wm. Roberts, Mineral Ridge, Ohio if you wish to look me up. Thank you very much for taking time enough to read this.

Sincerely,

Mrs. A.W. Carlisle

Mineral Ridge, Ohio

Mineral Ridge is a small town near Youngstown. We imagine it will take two hundred gallons of gasoline for the trip.

The following poem accompanied the letter:

Roosevelt

This is one man, who did not rise from lowly station
To become the leader of our mighty nation
Like one of royal line
He came from one of America's best families.
This did not protect him from the dread disease that beset his youth,
His great courage was put to the test until at last his young body stood strong as the best.
From one position of trust to another did he advance
Until lo! He stood at the great White House entrance
He had no more than the oath of office taken
Until he began to gather the reigns of governing into his hands.
From chaos and despair the sun began to shine,
Hope and faith to the people came back once more.
And the wheels of industry began to roar.
He came at this time of great depression
The kindness of his big heart to give expression.
The hungry were fed and the shivering were clothed;
Millions of men put back to work;
The nation rebuilt and new forest began;
As a great Father he cared for the victims of flood and of storm;
Yes and "Thank God," kept our country safe from war.
I say to the people of this nation,
"Could you ask for more!"

[Six pages handwritten]

. . .

May 20, 1936

My dear Mrs. Roosevelt:

May I ask an appointment with you to talk about a Susan B. Anthony stamp? I do not recall a more graceful gesture toward women past and present than the issuance of this would be. I hope so much you can give me the time. Mrs. Robert Andaman of New York and New Jersey has interested herself greatly in trying to get this long overdue stamp. If you will receive me, may I bring Mrs. Andaman with me?

Sincerely yours,
Abby Scott Baker
(Mrs. Robert Baker)
Washington, D.C.

[Two pages handwritten]

May 25, 1936

Hon. James A. Farley
Postmaster General
Washington, D.C.
My dear Mr. Farley:

Mrs. Roosevelt asks me to send you the enclosed letter from Mrs. Robert Baker, Washington, D.C., who writes concerning a Susan B. Anthony stamp. Will you let Mrs. Roosevelt know about this?

Very sincerely yours,
Malvina Thompson Scheider
Secretary to Mrs. Roosevelt

June 1, 1936

My dear Mrs. Roosevelt:
The receipt is acknowledged of your letter of May 25,

through your secretary, Mrs. Scheider, concerning the letter of Mrs. Robert Baker to you asking for an appointment relative to the proposed issuance of a Susan B. Anthony postage stamp.

We have had many requests for the issuance of such a stamp, but our program has been such that it could not be given favorable consideration. The postage stamps already committed for this year, namely, the Arkansas, the Oregon Territory, and the Army and Navy group of ten, will tax the facilities of both the Department and the Bureau of Engraving and Printing.

However, I suggest that it would be very proper to give careful consideration to the issuance of a postage stamp for Susan B. Anthony sometime next year.

Sincerely yours,
James Farley
Postmaster General
Washington, D.C.

Later in 1936 the government issued a three-cent Susan B. Anthony postage stamp, based on Adelaide Johnson's 1921 sculpture of Lucretia Mott, Elizabeth Stanton, and Susan B. Anthony. The stamp commemorated the sixteenth anniversary of women's suffrage.

• • •

September 21, 1936

Mrs. Franklyn D. Roosevelt.
Washington, D.C.

I am writing you pleading for **help**. My husband is an invalid for 6 years and I have worked untill I have given out physically. I have been keeping house for my widowded daughter with 4 in family and my husband and I six in all doing all laundry and everything, I have once had a beautiful home of 12 rooms and I kept boarders, but I lost this home on account of the depression they closed us out of it for a small mortgage, so I am homeless and penniless, and if I could get you to finance me a house for 1 month I could be self supporting again. I am still able to look after a house and have been called a splendid maniger of a house so I and my husband are entirely thrust upon our one daughter, who has all she can do for her children, to live.

I can furnish affidavits from several doctors as to our condition. I have never been on relief and never expect to be. I am writing for help and when I can make it if you can help me I will return it. I know of a large house in a college town if I can get the money to start that I want, but it will take three hundred to handle it, it would soon pay it back. Please do not make this public, if you do not care to believe I am a worthy person, just thrust it in the waste basket, but I believe you will respond in some way.

Very Truly,
Mrs. T.
Plant City, Florida

[Two pages handwritten]

· · ·

January 11, 1937

Dear Friend:-

My last hope is to raise $100 to buy a Acousticon Hearing Aid. I've gone to two specialists and both tell me there is no other help.

We are just getting started in married life—have been married a year and my deafness is quite a shock to both of us. And where can I get $100 elsewhere. You have plenty and will have for the next 4 years. But us, why we think we are doing good to get enough to eat and wear. First it's a flood and then drought. Now please Mrs. Roosevelt give this your personal consideration and try and help someone who is really in need. No one knows just what a terrible handicap it is to loose your hearing. I am just a young woman 24 years old. Can't you send me enough to buy the Aid that will help me. Hoping to hear from you at once.

Yours truly

Mrs. Russell Ballentine

Belvue, Kansas

If you don't believe me write to
Dr. E. A. Dranke   Or Dr. H. L. Kirkpatrick
Manhattan, Kansas   Topeka, Kansas
Both tell me there is no help for me.

[One page handwritten]

January 21, 1937

My dear Mrs. Ballentine:

I am sorry to tell you that, owing to the great number of requests for assistance, Mrs. Roosevelt is never able to give money nor to help anyone personally. She has much sympathy for you in your difficulties, and asks me to give you the name and address of an organization which may be able to advise you:

The American Society for the Hard of Hearing
1537 35th Street N.W.
Washington, D.C.

Very sincerely yours,

Malvina T. Scheider

Secretary to Mrs. Roosevelt

• • •

March 6, 1937

Dear Mrs. Roosevelt,

I am bringing my problem to you, as I have tried for 18 years to solve.

My daughter, who is now 18 years old, was a forcep delivery in a small Texas town where abdominal delivery was unheard of, I suppose, for her head was so badly mashed and has several large scars still very plain, but it all shaped up nicely except her nose was so badly injured it didn't develop and of course ruins her looks.

This has over shadowed her personality all these years she has been so unhappy and prefers to be alone to avoid stares and remarks from thoughtless people, of course she has no social life, she is far above the average in intelligence is a very sweet girl and would be beautiful if I could only have a plastic operation on her nose.

Mrs. Roosevelt I haven't any money to have this done, you are a mother and such a broad minded woman I am coming to you as my last hope that you can help me solve it. Do you know of a fund anywhere for facial deformities? Anyone can get loans to finance farms, houses, business, why not a human life it seems much more important to me.

I am enclosing a letter from Dr. V. P. Blair of St. Louis, Mo. he will do the operation free but there is hospitalization operating room and other expenses besides I would have to go with her I have two little girls I couldn't leave alone.

Please Mrs. Roosevelt can't you help me to help my little daughter.

Sincerely

Mrs. V.

Bowling Green, Kentucky

My husband was in the Worlds War at the time of my daughters birth. Please keep this letter confidential.

Thank you.

[Three and a half pages handwritten]

April 16, 1937

My dear Mrs. V:

Mrs. Roosevelt read your letter with understanding of the problem which is giving you so much anxiety and she wishes that she could help your daughter personally, but, unfortunately, the demands upon her are too many and all of the money which she is able to give is pledged.

Mrs. Roosevelt knows of no fund such as you mention, but suggests that the Children's Bureau, Department of Labor, Washington, D.C., might be able to advise you. You might also inquire of the welfare agencies in your own state as to any facilities near at hand for the treatment of cases such as your daughter's. Could you not get the interest of some of the women's organizations in your community? Very often they are able to give helpful advice or to assist in raising funds for deserving people.

I am returning the letter which you enclosed and deeply regret that Mrs. Roosevelt cannot be more helpful.

Very sincerely yours,
Malvina T. Scheider
Secretary to Mrs. Roosevelt

• • •

March 26, 1937

Mrs. Franklin D. Roosevelt

Worthy Mrs. Roosevelt

Being somewhat timid to write to our "First Lady," I am confident that you would not turn down a petition of a poor mother who has tubercolosis. Every week I see in the paper where you give various lectures in order to raise money for some unfortunate people, which is praiseworthy and certainly will linger long in the memories of our people.

Although I never read much in former years, I am sure there was never a President whose wife was so interested in the welfare of the people. May God bless your effort. Every day I pray fervently that, "he," might send money some way to help us through this siege of tubercolosis. Surely you will have a means to raise money for me, by giving a lecture on this disease which would be appreciated by the public. The people in the city seem to get help in so many ways such as city hospital and sanitation. We live on a farm and had a total crop failure. The county court has been very kind and allowed us $7.50 a month but this does not go far. Also by reference they tried to get me to the state sanitarium at Mt. Vernon but had no room besides the doctor did not urge me to go as I could be cured at home. It is over 400 miles and would not help me any to go so far away from the family. My husband had to go to P.N.G. Mark to buy feed with the money he earned. But must quit to plant and sow. Carpenters volunteered to make a sun porch for me but have no money to buy lumber. We need ice to keep my eats fresh and were not able to pay last years ice. Have to have the children examined as the State Board of Health insists on it. Besides the wholesome eats that the children need to keep their vitality. I must close as I cant write anymore. Trusting that you will be able to send me several hundred dollars as I am so worried. Thanking you in advance I am cordialy

Mrs. H.

Hermann, Missouri

P.S. Please do not publish name as we have growing children who would hear this all their life. Do not mention name any-time.

[Four pages handwritten]

April 2, 1937

My dear Mrs. H:

Mrs. Roosevelt asks me to acknowedge your letter which she read with sympathetic interest. She is very sorry she can not comply with your request, as the money earned from her lectures has already been pledged and allocated. If you will communicate with Mr. F. D. Hopkins, National Tuberculosis Association, 50 West 50th Street, New York, New York you may receive helpful information.

Very sincerely yours,

Malvina T. Scheider

Secretary to Mrs. Roosevelt.

• • •

June 9, 1937

My dear Mrs. Roosevelt—

Please pardon me for writing this letter. I have heard so much about you helping the poor. Will you please help me.

I am 73 years old and sick. I haven't one soul who can help me. I haven't really any place to lay my head. I am proud, do not want to call on the town for help, and I do not want anyone to know my circumstances, as I am a lady who has seen better days. I am really ashamed to be so poor. When my husband passed away I had some money invested in stocks but eight or ten years ago I lost every cent I had, so here I am proud and poor. We can't get a pension in Maine, they do not have the money. They may be able to get it by this fall.

What I am worrying about is what will I do untill then. Cant you help me along untill Fall. Please do if you can. Just enough to bridge me over. If they can not raise the money by Fall perhaps you could help me get into the Home for aged people. We have to have $1,000 to get in the Home. We have a lovely Home in Farmington for old people.

I have got to leave this place June 20th as they are selling the place. Will you please write me any way. I am so down hearted and discouraged I worry and cry half my time. To think what little I had is **gone**. I do hope you will be able to read this letter and do please help me.

I have heard how good you are to the poor and needy. May God bless you all the days of your life.

I think our President is one of the most noble men in the world I am proud to say I voted for him.

I wish you could come to Farmington again and come talk with me. I am as honest as the days are long.

You cant imagine how pleased I would be to get a check from you. I would cry with joy.

If you do think enough of me to answer this letter. Please do so before the 20th of this month.

Mrs. Roosevelt—you do not know what it means to be old with no home and every one that belongs to me have passed away. I never had any children. Hoping to hear from you soon. Good bye with best wishes for every thing that is good.

Mrs. G.
Farmington, Maine

[Six pages handwritten]

June 11, 1937

My dear Mrs. G:

Mrs. Roosevelt has asked me to acknowledge your letter for her. She is very sorry indeed to hear of your difficulties and regrets that she cannot comply with your wishes. She receives so many requests for financial aid that it is impossible for her to do as you ask.

Assuring you of her regret that she cannot help you, I am

Very sincerely yours,

Malvina T. Scheider

Secretary to Mrs. Roosevelt

• • •

July 2, 1937

Dear Mrs. Roosevelt,

I am an ex newspaper woman, proofreader, reporter and typesetter, editor of a weekly newspaper and an all around business woman, but NOW I find my strength giving out, I am 56 years old and cannot even walk more than a block at a time, and when I dress to go out the trip to the store or to New York tires me in an hour, and I NEED a little old USED car to deliver my sewing to customers, but I CANNOT make the FIRST down payment, WILL YOU HELP ME? I can carry on if I can get the required down payment on a good used Pontiac 1934 coupe which will answer my purpose as well as a new car. I have a nice sewing machine and I make beautiful dresses for children and dolls, and also ladies evening dresses, but I MUST have a means of transportation, on account of my feet being almost useless when it comes to walking.

I know how you help others and I have hesitated to

ask you to do anything for me, but tonight as I sat here ALONE wondering how I could get that little old used car I thought of you and decided to ask you, I can easily pay you back $25 a month if you request it and also finish payments on the car because I have no other debts. WILL YOU PLEASE GIVE this request your PERSONAL attention? If there is any way in which you can arrange for me to get this help I will be FOREVER grateful to you. This is the FIRST and only request I will ever make, and it will SURELY make me happy to get the car so that I can deliver my garments and also take orders from others enroute, which is the way I make my living now. Enclosed is my photo so that you will know to whom you are confering this favor, if you really do see fit to help me. Forgive me if I have bothered you too much.

> Please write me as follows
> Yours Very Truly
> Mrs. Bertha M. Alden
> Teaneck, New Jersey

P.S. I sent you one of my little organdy aprons 2 years ago and was so glad to get your letter of thanks.

[One page typed]

July 8, 1937

My dear Mrs. Alden:

Mrs. Roosevelt asks me to write and tell you she is very sorry she cannot lend you money for a down payment on the car you wish to purchase. Unfortunately, so many people ask this of her that she has found it impossible to comply with such requests, and, in any case, all the money she has to give has been pledged. She hopes you will find some way out of your difficulty and sincerely regrets that she cannot be of assistance.

Very sincerely yours,
Malvina T. Scheider
Secretary to Mrs. Roosevelt

• • •

March 12, 1938

Mrs. Roosevelt
First Lady of the House
Kind Lady
I was 69 years old the 5 day of this month and I am in a
Serious condition. I got Run over with a car and Got my leg
Broken in three Difernt Places and Knocked out of Joint at
the hip and I aint Got no money to Go to the Hospital on and
Cant Get it as I am a Verry Poor man and I am asking you
to send me $50 that I can have something done for myself
at once if you will send me the $50 I sure will appreciate it
as mutch as anybody in this world. Mrs. Roosevelt, I would
not ask you for this money if it had not ben nessary but it
is nessary as I am in a Condition that I have Got to have
something done and done at once. So Pleas send the money
to me and I know that it will be another Star in your Crown.
I would not ask you for this money if I dident haft to and I
feel like you will Send me the money as I Know you have a
feeling for a Poor man in my shape.

So Please let me hear from you at once.
Yours Truly
George W. Watters
Allardt, Tennessee

[Two pages handwritten]

March 14, 1938

My dear Mr. Watters:

Mrs. Roosevelt and her secretary are away, and in their absence I have been asked to acknowledge their mail.

Owing to the great number of appeals for financial assistance which Mrs. Roosevelt receives, she finds it impossible to help every worthy case brought to her attention, much as she would like to do so. The money she has at her disposal for philanthropic purposes has already been pledged and allocated.

Very sincerely yours,
Administrative Officer
Social Correspondence

In a radio broadcast of July 25, 1940, in which Mrs. Roosevelt discussed her mail, she remarked:

"The letters which distress me perhaps the most are those from people who are ill or who have members of their family who need and can not get medical attention. When these writers come from certain states or from small towns and rural districts of many states where I know there are no available clinics, I am often at a loss to know how to reply."

• • •

March 1938

Dear Mrs. Roosevelt:—

As I am almost desperate I am writing you this letter hoping and praying that in some way as you read it God will help you to see my need and understand the truthfulness of these statements and from the depth of your generous Christian heart you will help in this case.

My husband up until the depression was a successful lumber man; while we were not people of wealth had a comfortable living and shared it with many who were not as fortunate as we.

After loosing our home and all money we had, today we are in destitute circumstances and cant meet the great need that is facing us. And I assure you Mrs. Roosevelt it is very difficult for me to bring my self to asking this favor of you, and if it was not under these critical circumstances a dear life at stake I could not do so.

Five years ago my son of 19 had a good job at Guntersville Dam; core drillers making $30 per week. he had a very serious attack of influenza which he has never fully recovered from, as it left him with an infection in his spleen causing muscular rheumatism. he has not been able these past two years to even stoop to tie his shoes and most of time had to be lifted out of a chair.

This past Dec. 3rd he collapsed and had to be carried to hospital in a serious unconscious condition temperature 105, 106 and 107 off and on for nearly four weeks.

We tried to get him there as a charity patient but the hospital being a small one can only accomodate a certain number and his heart being so involved we could not delay in getting the medical attention he had to have.

My husband operates a gas boat here but for the past year has not been able to get enough work for us to hardly exist on, so we were completely out of funds.

We borrowed $25 to get him in, had to give notes for the rest $200 which falls due April 10th which I see no hopes of his even paying the interest on and renewing them. And my son still in a critical condition and unless we can pay this cant get further treatment for him and unless he can get it cant possibly live.

He is a fine good Christian and so deserving of attention and help and it is tearing my very heart out of me to see my only boy suffer and die for the need of medical aid where there is so much that could be done to save him.

We are both 53 years of age and need him so much and his father has almost gotten down on his knees begging work to support him. But it seems now we are utterly helpless to do any thing else and in my despair some how I have thought of appealing to you. Feels like with the fine handsome boys you have you will understand more than any one else what it would mean to give even one of them up. If you feel like in your heart you would like to help this boy get well I will appreciate any thing you can do and will say if he ever gets able to work he will gladly repay in the very best way that he is able.

Best wishes to you and our beloved President and your entire family and to hear from you soon.

Respectfully

Mrs. E. H. Duffy

Decatur, Alabama

[Three pages handwritten]

March 31, 1938

My dear Mrs. Duffy:

Mrs. Roosevelt and her secretary are away, and in their absence I have been asked to acknowledge their mail.

I know Mrs. Roosevelt would be very sorry to hear of your son's illness and would like to help you. Unfortunately, she receives so many appeals for financial assistance that she finds it impossible to help every worthy case brought to her attention. The money she has at her disposal for philanthropic purposes has already been pledged and allocated.

If you will write to the United States Public Health Service, Washington, D.C., perhaps that agency may be able to suggest something that will be helpful to you.

Very sincerely yours,
Administrative Officer
Social Correspondence

• • •

September 2, 1938

Dear mother of the Nation:

Dear Mrs. Roosevelt, before I start this letter, I beg you to please excuse my writing and mistakes. I'm all nervous and confused, asking myself how I dare to write and bother you, but only my great misery and nessisity obliged me to do it. Mrs. Roosevelt, I'm a young mother 21 years old and I have 2 babies and a good and devoted husband. He is a candy peddler, doesn't make much, but we live struggling. Dear lady you might wonder why I'm writing you and perhaps taking your time, but please read all my letter. You see I was born in Texas and raised there and never went out until I came to California 3 years ago. I hardly know people here and I don't see a way out in my situation but you, you was my first thought. I have heard so much about your kindness to the poor and your big charities and I'm sure you'll feel sorry for me. You see, I been having a heart disease since I was a child, and now I'm expecting another baby in December and the Doctor suggests a Ceasarian operation for I can't give a normal birth on account of my heart its too weak and just imagine my dispair I don't have a single penny the operation costs $80. Mrs. Roosevelt I'm not asking you to give me that money but I'm only asking you to please lend me $80 for my operation and I promise that we'll pay you back next year. I went to a clinic for some glasses for I can't see well and believe me I haven't got them yet they cost $10 so I have to get ten dollars out of those $80 for my glasses that I need them so badly. Some times I think I'm losing my mind. The creditors knock at my door all day and warn us to pay, but how? I'm very gratefull to our dear President, who has done so much for us. Remember that I love you and respect you deeply and I beg you forgivness of my daring to write you for I'm so humble and you are so great. I hope to hear from you soon. Please don't publich this letter its very private. Receive all my love and affection and love from my dear children. Your dear citizen friend.

Yours sincerely,

Mrs. L.

Los Angeles, California

[Four pages handwritten]

September 13, 1938

My dear Mrs. L:

Mrs. Roosevelt and her secretary are away, and in their absence I have been asked to acknowledge their mail.

So many appeals for financial assistance come to Mrs. Roosevelt that she finds it impossible to help each worthy case brought to her attention, much as she would like to do so. The money she has at her disposal for philanthropic purposes has already been pledged and allocated.

Very sincerely yours,

Administrative Officer

Social Correspondence

• • •

September 26, 1938

Dear Mrs. Roosevelt:

Permit us, the patients of the National Leprosarium, Carville, Louisiana, to humbly submit our petition, enthusiastically approved by our Medical Officer in Charge, Dr. H.E. Hasseltine, Medical Director, for the transferring of our Colony to Fort Stanton, New Mexico, or some other suitable location.

Be assured this is no momentary result of restlessness but a long-desired-for event which we hope and pray will become for us a reality and a blessing—a blessing in many ways, and perhaps, another advancement in the cure of leprosy. For, gathering together statistics and data, as well as is in our power to do so, we have compiled a "summa" of reasons for the presentation of our petition which is as follows:

First, the Hansen Bacillus, as we understand it, is very similar to the Tubercle Bacillus in its structure, its growth, and its attack upon the human body, save that the Tubercle Bacillus is confined principally to the lungs, bones, and throat, the lesions of which are internal; while the Hansen Bacillus attacks principally the nerves, bones, skin, eye, ear, nose, and throat, producing external lesions and disfigurement. Both are maliciously destructive. If this is true, should not the treatment also be somewhat similar? Thanks to the Government, we do receive good, wholesome food, fresh country air, and unlimited rest, but—what about the climate?

The growth of the Tubercle Bacillus is retarded by high altitude and dry climate but becomes prolific in low, humid areas, moisture and warmth being most conducive to rapid incubation. Hypothetically speaking, can we not then place the Hansen Bacillus in the same category? Who would ever suggest this swampy, semi-tropical country as beneficial to a tuberculous patient? This climate is universally known as "bad" for well people not to speak of those infirm, regardless of the nature of their illness; yet year after year, we see some of our fellow patients succumbing to the ravages of tuberculosis and the fury of pneumonia. As dreaded winter approaches, we often ask each other as well as ourselves, "Who's next?" Is not leprosy in itself enough—and more than enough? Review the records of the past nine months and you will find that death's toll was indeed heavy, pneumonia carrying by far the heaviest rate. Throat conditions are on the increase to such an extent that the number of tracheotomy tubes has become discouragingly great.

Second, after studying graphic charts from various sources and tracing the shaded areas where leprosy is found, all of the recent issues show these locations to be in the tropical and semi-tropical countries with very few exceptions, three or four at the most. Does this not point to the theory that the heat and moisture or some climatic or elemental condition of the tropics are conducive to the growth of leprosy? True, history does give at certain times instances when leprosy was almost pandemic. Yet when these various epidemics subsided, it left leprosy practically confined to the tropics. To further substantiate this theory, the statistics as taken among ourselves show that practically 95% of the patients here at Carville are of themselves from the tropical or semi-tropical countries or have lived there over a period of time sufficient to have contracted the disease. Our patients are mainly from along the Gulf Coast, in and about the borders of Mexico, the Hawaiian Islands, the Philippines, China, Southern France, Spain, Italy, Central, and South America. Of these a large number comprise our native born Louisianians.

Third, aside from climatic conditions, there exists the danger we are in, year after year, from the threatening torrents of the Mississippi River. Should that levee beside us break, we and the whole colony would be swept from the face of the earth. Recall the danger of 1927—how we passed anxious days and nights, ever alert and ready for the signal to board the barges, if we could get to them! The levee was moved back and reenforced, yet the same danger threatened us again in 1937! Should you spend the money appropriated for the renovation of this place, and should, in a few years to come, the levee break—or, again have to be moved back, to what purpose will your money have been spent? For, another strip taken from our colony would leave us indeed only a miserable strip in which to live. Why invest money in such a perilous site? Why invest lives in such a perilous site? True, we are afflicted with leprosy, but do we not still remain human beings? Are not our lives as dear to us as those in Washington, New York, or elsewhere? Aye—perhaps more so, for "health and wealth are appreciated when **lost,** knowledge and virtue when found." And in our case, the loss of health has not only cost us physical suffering, but has cost us, and dearly too, the deprivation of our homes, our families, our loved ones. Yet, we are still human beings with human hearts, human sufferings, and human hopes. Our hopes—the hope of at least some alleviation from pain, if not a restoration to health—we place in your hands. Will you—can you blight our hopes?

As to the Government of the United States of America, we trust her implicitly. We trust that our beloved President will make this last resort for the cure of leprosy the crowning act of his administration. We trust, hope, and pray that this movement will mark a new epoch in the treatment of leprosy, made possible by that Nation who has proven to the world her Democracy of a "Government of the people, by the people, and **for** the people" even to the very least, as the public at large considers those stricken with leprosy.

This, dear Madam, is our "summa" which we humbly present to you for the transferring of our Colony to Fort Stanton, New Mexico, or some like climate.

Trusting that our plea will sow its seed on fertile ground and bear early fruit, we remain

Humbly indebted to a beloved Government,

Ever gratefully,

Joseph L. Trahant

U.S. Marine Hospital

Carville, Louisiana

[Four and a half pages typed, edited for length]

[marked "Copy"]

October 6, 1938

Dr. Thomas Parran
The Surgeon General of the United States
Washington, D.C.
My dear Dr. Parran:
This seems to be quite an appeal and it probably has been brought to your attention before this. However, Mrs. Roosevelt asks me to send you the letter and to ask for your opinion in the matter.

Very sincerely yours,

Malvina C. Thompson

Secretary to Mrs. Roosevelt

October 14, 1938

My dear Miss Thompson:

In the absence of Doctor Parran, your note of October 6, 1938 transmitting a letter addressed to Mrs. Roosevelt by Mr. Joseph L. Trahant and requesting his opinion in the matter of the suggested relocation of the National Leprosarium at Carville, Louisiana, has been referred to me for answer.

Mr. Trahant wrote an identical letter to Doctor Parran. We have also received several letters on the same subject from Mr. E. D. Lewison, Chairman of the Executive Committee of The Patients' Federation at Carville, copies of which are inclosed, and I believe I can best give you the consensus of opinion of the Surgeon General and his associates by forwarding herewith copies of the replies from this office.

I am also sending you copies of correspondence between Doctor Parran and Mr. Wm. Jay Schieffelin, President of the American Mission to Lepers.

If you wish further advice in the matter, please call upon me.

Very sincerely yours,
Robert Olesen
Acting Surgeon General.
U.S. Public Health Service
Washington, D.C.

October 18, 1938

My dear Mr. Trahant:

Mrs. Roosevelt has received a report from the Public Health Service concerning the matter of the National Leprosarium at

Carville. It seems that the Surgeon General has taken up this matter with you in detail by letter of September 9 and that it has been given careful consideration. Mrs. Roosevelt is afraid that there is nothing further she can do inasmuch as the matter has had the attention of the proper authorities.

Very sincerely yours,
Malvina T. Scheider
Secretary to Mrs. Roosevelt

In 1894 the state of Louisiana transported seven leprosy patients from New Orleans to what was then the deserted Indian Camp Plantation. The state purchased the property and provided custodial care for the patients. On February 3, 1917, an act of Congress established a National Leprosarium on the site, headed by William M. Danner of the American Leprosy Missions. In 1921 the United States Public Health Service took control and the "home" became the United States Marine Hospital Number 66. In the 1940s Guy Henry Faget, M.D., director of the hospital, pioneered sulfone drug therapy, and in the 1950s patients began to receive rehabilitation training and education. In 1981 the United States Public Health Service established Regional Hansen's Disease (leprosy) Clinics to provide outpatient care around the country. In 1992 the National Park Service placed the Carville Historic District, which now includes a museum, on the National Register of Historic Places. In 1998 the Hansen's Disease Center relocated to Baton Rouge, Louisiana, and in 1999 the state of Louisiana received the title to Indian Camp Plantation back from the federal government. The state started a program on the site for at-risk youths, supervised by the Louisiana National Guard. Approximately sixty Hansen's patients still live at Carville, where they may remain as long as they wish.

· · ·

[Date-stamped June 15, 1939]

My dear Mrs. Roosevelt,

I am going to ask you something that I do not think I could speak of to anyone else—my husband died six years ago. His illness continued for many, many months, so that after his death I had nothing left, and I lost my home and am sixty four. However I have managed to earn a small living.

Two weeks before my husband's death I had no money with which to pay his nurses, $3 per week. And so because I had already sold everything I had to obtain money for my husband's care, I borrowed enough money on my engagement ring to see me through.

I have never been able to get it back, six years—

But I have paid interest and the reduction payment the President-Savings Assn. requires annually. So it is still mine—

But this year, because I have been severely ill I could not save the money for this purpose. I must pay $25.40 in ten days from this date, or my beloved ring is gone. I could not bear it. I have kept my chin up and fought a good fight for sixty years, but this would be the last straw. Would you make me a loan of $25? I would repay it. I have tried in every way to get this sum but it is impossible. Please understand, that if I had not been ill for so long, I would have saved the money.

I apologize for writing you and can only say that this letter is a prayer. I believe you will understand my acute fear of losing this ring.

Very sincerely,
Mrs. E. P. Hazel Kelley Hatch
Old Greenwich, Connecticut

[Three pages handwritten]

June 19, 1939

My dear Mrs. Hatch:

Mrs. Roosevelt asks me to acknowledge your letter and to tell
you she is so sorry she cannot do as you wish. A great many
appeals for financial assistance come to her each day, but,
unfortunately, the demands on her resources are so heavy that
she has found it impossible to respond to these appeals.

Very sincerely yours,
Malvina Thompson
Secretary to Mrs. Roosevelt

• • •

July 25, 1939

Mr. and Mrs. Franklin D. Roosevelt
The White House
Washington, D.C.
Dear Sir and Madam:—

Hardly expect this to reach you personally but I simply
have to write to some one about the hopelessness of our
trying to earn an honest living.

We are a family of four, one boy to enter high school
this fall, the other boy in junior-high. We've been married
sixteen years, happily, in spite of the terrific struggle
trying to make both ends meet.

Our problem is the same as hundreds, more likely thousands of others. We started out with doctor and hospital
bills the first few years of our married life and are still
trying to pay them off. We make a fair living wage but can't
live even comfortably on it as most of it goes to pay these
old bills, all drawing interest now. We have tried to get on

a cash basis but then the creditors press us. No matter how we try the future hasn't a sign of a rose tint. Is there a solution?

The whole family needs dental and eye care but how can it be managed? Husband's insurance even had to be dropped and his work is far from safe but what else to do?

We don't ask for charity or relief, but just help to get on our feet and free of debt.

Isn't there aid of some sort for the honest people, trying to get along? How can people be happy, contented and good Americans when every cent is needed for old accounts? I personally know dozens of families, struggling just as we are. What is to become of us? We can't save for a rainy day because every cent is needed for bills.

We want to educate our boys but we can't even be sure we can manage high school. We've tried to get a loan at the bank, enough for all bills, not more than $500, then we'd only have to pay interest on one account and could easily pay interest on one account and could easily make monthly payments on one account. The banker advised bankruptcy, said we didn't have a chance other wise. They are justly owed bills and we want to pay them if possible.

Please tell us if anything can be done. After each pay day when there is only a dollar or so left after creditors have been pacified I wonder if it's worth the struggle. Can you, yourselves realize the fight we're making to live decently and honestly?

In this glorious land of plenty of ours how can a common person get a start when he's burdened with old doctor bills and other small accounts??

With all the really big problems you have to ponder hope you can give a few minutes to this one, really big to the people concerned.

You are both doing a wonderful job but I'm hoping you can give us a bit of advice too.

Very sincerely
Mrs. Ivan G. Martin
Foster, Oregon

[Four and a half pages handwritten]

August 8, 1939

My dear Mrs. Martin:
I am writing to acknowledge your letter, which I will be glad to give to Mrs. Roosevelt as soon as possible.

Very sincerely yours,
Malvina Thompson
Secretary to Mrs. Roosevelt

• • •

December 23, 1939

My Dear Mrs. Roosevelt
To the many such letters as this you receive, am very reluctantly and as a last resort, adding another, which I would not do were I not driven to it by dire need and dread of the poor house.

Will be 80 years old on the 4th day of January; have been lame since infancy, in 1918 fell and fractured the weak knee and since then have been obliged to use a cane, sometimes two of them when walking. Was until failing sight and hearing compelled me to give up, was a rural school teacher. Most of my teaching days were before the days of good wages or good roads but I did manage to get a little home on which there now is a mortgage of eight-hundred dollars, while it is not yet due, am now unable to keep the interest paid and am dreading foreclosure. Hearing that you give in charity the proceeds from your lecturing tours, am humbly and earnestly asking you to add to your many charitable deeds another to an old woman who needs very badly that amount to free her home from its encumbrance.

May God who has dowered you with so much of this world's good incline your kind woman's heart to heed the request of old woman so much in need of it.

Wishing you and all dear to you a joyous Christmas and many of them am

Respectfully yours
Mary Mahan
Iowa City Iowa

[Two pages handwritten]

December 28, 1939

My dear Miss Mahan:

Mrs. Roosevelt asks me to acknowledge your letter and to express her regret that she can not do as you ask. Owing to the great number of appeals for financial assistance which come to her, she finds it impossible to help every worthy case brought to her attention, much as she would like to do so. The money she has at her disposal is pledged and allocated.

Very sincerely yours,
Malvina Thompson
Secretary to Mrs. Roosevelt

• • •

September 17, 1940

Mrs. Elinor Roosefelt

Washington, D.C.

Beloved First Lady, I write this because I love you so, also Our President, yet loving you as I do, I envy you your lovely new cloths, and it makes something dirty in my heart to know I am in such desperate need (Through no fault of ours) and havent had a new dress or underlings in ten years. We are all workers never asked for one cent of relief, I washed outside, hung wall paper and painted for 10 years, and nursed in T.B. hospitals several years. Now I'm broke down at 55. We have had four hospital bills in 5 months. It started when my only child a son, was nearly burned to death in an explosion on Pennsylvania Railroad. They paid his hospital bill and care only. He's worked all his life since 16 for this and his young wife is ill with cancer and now he has contracted T.B. from emery dust. No, the railroad hasn't even given him a cent of relief, the aid ignores our request for aid although we pay regular in the Pensylvania aid. We have morgaged even the bed we sleep in, now the last hospital bill is to be paid on monthly $12 per month. Some days we hardly can have food sometimes just popcorn. I can't see how I can go on, and yet hearing of thousands of dollars going overseas, and lovely clothes by wealthy, no wonder we feel envy. I don't, God knows, envy one cent going to Europe. I am simply distraught with having folks say "they pity us so in our misfortunes but must have their money" which is true. I go hungry to pay, yet I can't get out, I can't see my way through.

I understand, of course, you must have nice cloths to meet the public and you do so much good, maby a prayer for me and mine, by you and God will help me. **I have even**

thot of destruction of my self, but that is such a cowardly way out. But new fall cloths, and money for Europes destitute. My dear it makes me have an ugly heart which I pray God to erase. A small town can be a cruel town. I would be so sneered at if they knew I had dared write the "first Lady." I wish I had a mother, old as I am. I am just a little weary girl needing a word of encouragement. So please forgive my presumption Lady Roosefelt, and enjoy your deeds of kindness and lovely cloths, but I only ask of you a prayer that somehow I can pay all and enjoy one free breath from debt before I have to march on.

Sincerely your good friend

Mrs. F.

Bradford, Ohio

[Four pages handwritten]

• • •

November 8, 1940

Dear Mrs. Roosevelt:

While reading about you in today's **Chronicle,** I wondered, perhaps as many others, if you would help an individual.

I'll be frank about it, Mrs. Roosevelt, I'm a Republican, never the less I enjoy your broadcasts and especially your writings. I started a correspondence course in Journalism but have had to give it up, hoping some day to be able to finish.

We were on a farm but because of ill health Mr. Kern was forced to quit. We could not afford to hire anyone to help.

We rented a small tourist camp and gas station, which gave us a fair living through the summer but not enough to carry us through the winter. We are located on Route 5 but out in the country where there is not much in local trade, although we have acquired quite a bit of local trade, which makes us feel good as we were strangers here.

We both are looking for work this winter but honestly it's just impossible to get it. Everything calls for experienced help and at the age of 50 it throws you out. It makes a poor outlook for the future.

The banks require so much credit and we just can't give it.

I'm not asking for charity, Mrs. Roosevelt but I am asking if you would lend me $200 with the understanding that if we get work, which I earnestly pray we do, we would pay back in monthly payments this winter, and if not, pay it next summer when the tourist season opens.

Mrs. Roosevelt, can you and will you help me? If not this amount, will you let me take $100? I will repay every cent and with interest.

If I can get the $200 it would help me fix a lunch room so I could have home cooked meals and get the truckers to stop, for there are a lot of trucks. If I could only get started but it takes money and I haven't it.

You've no idea Mrs. Roosevelt how some of us try to get along. I haven't had a new dress in 3 years, not even a house dress. I keep them washed and mended so I can at least look clean. Life gets pretty drab sometimes, with so much sickness and no work. If it were not for my trust and faith in my God, I sometimes don't know what I would do. I am only one of many I suppose. It does seem as though there must be a break soon.

Now, Mrs. Roosevelt, I told you that I am a Republican but I'm not a narrow minded one. Thank God I can count myself out of being that.

We have four long hard years ahead of us and I sincerely hope and pray that each and everyone of us will do our utmost to make it a happy and prosperous four years with you and Mr. Roosevelt. May we work in unity and peace.

Very sincerely yours,

Mrs. Leonora Kern

LeRoy, New York

[Three and a half pages handwritten]

November 25, 1940

My dear Mrs. Kern:

Mrs. Roosevelt and her secretary are away and in their absence I have been asked to acknowledge their mail.

I am sure Mrs. Roosevelt would be very sorry to hear of your difficulties, but know she could not lend you the money you need. Unfortunately, the number of demands on her resources make it impossible for her to respond to requests for loans, much as she would like to do so.

It is suggested that you write to the Reconstruction Finance Corporation, Washington, D.C., as this agency may be able to give you some helpful advice.

Very sincerely yours,

Administrative Office

Social Correspondence

• • •

November 23, 1940

Mrs. Roosevelt:

Dear Friend:

As one friend to another I write you this letter to-day. With all the trouble and uproar that is raging in the foreign countries, I doubt if you or the President either can pay any attention to what I have to say. I know you and the President both have a lot to think about and do more for the good of our country than any other two people living in it could do. I always read our local papers about how you help different organizations. Mine is a very small family organization. My two daughters and my self. My husband was killed nearly three years ago by an automobile.

Now I will begin what I wanted to say to you. I am working in a clothing factory here in Richmond, and I make less than $20 a week. Last year I made $840. I have rent, electric bill, coal and every thing to pay for out of my small earnings. My oldest daughter who will be 16 years old July 24, is in second year high school at John Marshall. I cant give her clothes like the other girls have, she cant go to none of the parties the school gives because she doesn't have clothes decent enough to go. My youngest daughter is in the 6th grade. I have been laid off from work for nearly three weeks. I will go back the 27th of this month. I am so far back in **all** my bills. My rent is due the first of December. My grocery bill is way overdue. I don't see my way where I can get the children any thing for Christmas.

Mrs Roosevelt I thought if I wrote to you, you might be able to help me. I feel like if some one would help me to get straight I might some day in the near future be able to help some one just like my self, which I know there are thousands, all over the world. Mrs. Roosevelt I am sending you pictures of my daughters.

Edna May is 15 and Virginia Arlene is 11, will be 12 Jan. 12th. If you will help me some day I might be able to help you, the good Lord only knows,

Very sincerely
Mrs. Ruby Ogden
Richmond, Virginia

[Three pages handwritten]

December 4, 1940

My dear Mrs. Ogden:

Mrs. Roosevelt and her Secretary are away and in their absence I have been asked to acknowledge their mail.

Mrs. Roosevelt receives a great many appeals from those who are in need of financial assistance, but, unfortunately, it is not possible for her to respond to these appeals. All the money she has at her disposal for philanthropic purposes has been pledged and allocated for some time to come. I am sure she would regret being unable to help you.

> Very sincerely yours,
> Administrative Officer
> Social Correspondence

• • •

September 26, 1941

Dear Mrs. Roosevelt

I'm coming to you with our problem because I must. Three weeks ago tonite I desperately prayed for a solution to our problem and this is what happened.

It seemed as if Someone was standing just back of me and spoke and this is what was said "Write and ask Mrs. Eleanor Roosevelt for a loan of $500, tell her you'll pay her back at the rate of $10 per month with yearly interest and dividend, to all be handled thru a Waukesha bank and explain why you need this amount."

I've prayed each nite since then and as soon as I ask for guidance it seems as tho some one says "You know what to do. Now do it." So that is why I must write you and ask help.

Mr. Simpson and I are married 8 years now since the 14th of this month. We have 5 children and the catch is 2 doctors told me I probably never would have any children, before I was married.

We married on $20 a month on a farm job. By the time we got to $30 we had Bud and Mr. Simpsons Dad to support. Before we knew what to think hardly, Gail and Michael were both born, then to top it off Gail had to have an operation and our house burned down. We boarded with a farm family all that winter and Doris was born in July. The next Spring I injured my back and ran up another Doctor bill. Doris is now 4 years old and Bud 7.

Last Feb. Sally was born. When she was 3 weeks old we moved 90 miles to come down here. We got a job at $70 and house rent, light, fuel and milk, garden etc. with a bonus of $100 at the end of the year. We had figured that I'd have to spend 4–4 1/2 hours each day in the barn and milk house on this dairy farm but found it is closer to 8. We decided we'd try to keep it tho as Bud and Gail are both very good at helping and did take good care of Sally.

Only we hadn't figured on Sally getting a severe case of whooping cough when she was only two months old.

You see our old job only paid $40 per month and extras and we figured we would get all our bills except $100 paid this year. It would take a lot of planning but we thot we could do it. So promised so much each month to our creditors. We lost that job in July. The one we have now pays only $60 and we must buy 2 quarts of milk extra each day, pay for our fuel. So now with our creditors wanting their money and winter almost here, we just don't know which way to turn. Our creditors say with business being diferent now they must have their money and we can't pay. We have no furniture to sell or anything else. I sold my washer 2 years ago when we needed money badly. So can't even help that little now.

If you could arrange this loan Mrs. Roosevelt you'll never know how much we'd appreciate a real start not to be weighted down with more than we can handle. To be able to plan meals that cost more than 60-75 cents per day for this whole crew would be so grand. I'm thanking you for taking time to read this.

Sincerely

Mrs. Leroy H. Simpson

Waukesha, Wisconsin

P.S. You could have the Waukesha State Bank investigate us if you wished.

[Seven pages handwritten]

September 29, 1941

My dear Mrs. Simpson:

Mrs. Roosevelt regrets that it is impossible for her to respond to your appeal, as all the money she has at her disposal for philanthropic purposes has been pledged and allocated for some time to come.

Very sincerely yours,

Malvina Thompson

Secretary to Mrs. Roosevelt

• • •

Part Two

The New Deal

On July 2, 1932, after his selection as the nominee for president, Franklin Roosevelt addressed the Democratic Convention, boldly asserting: "I pledge you, I pledge myself to a new deal for the American people . . . " The actions of Eleanor Roosevelt served as an important facet of the New Deal, as she traveled everywhere, popping up in unlikely places ranging from coal mines in Appalachia to migrant work camps in California, relaying to her husband the problems she saw, thus bringing the White House directly to the American people. She said of these ventures: "My trips around the country gave me a wonderful opportunity to visit all kinds of places and to see and get to know a good cross section of people. Always during my free time I visited as many government projects as possible, often managing to arrive without advance notice so that they could not be polished up for my inspection. I began to see for myself some of the results of my husband's actions during the first hundred days of his administration, and in meeting and talking with people all over the country I got the full impact of what the new programs had meant to them. It was evident that the home and farm loans, for example, had saved many a family from outright disaster." Thus, both the President and his wife firmly believed that the federal government could serve as a force for good.

Actions by the administration of President Roosevelt eased the suffering of many. His creation of the "alphabet agencies," numerous government bureaus and programs to help the poor, did much to restore confidence as well as employ thousands of people without work. The largest such employment program, the Works Progress Administration, later called the Work Projects Administration, presided over by Harry Hopkins, received an initial allocation of $1.5 billion to create work for the unemployed. Using unskilled labor, and with a lack of advanced planning, the WPA quickly hired as many as possible, while at the same time contriving useful activities. The WPA furnished jobs for 8.5 million workers on 1.4 million individual projects. The newly employed built highways, roads, and streets, erected 125,110 public buildings, and created 8,192 public parks. The WPA constructed roads, trails, and buildings in national parks, built dams in the West, compiled indexes of census rolls at the National Archives, and hired white-collar workers for the Federal Theater, Federal Writers, and Federal Arts projects.

The Public Works Administration, headed by Harold Ickes and working at a slower pace, hired the unemployed to construct roads, highways, sewage and water systems, gas and electric power plants, schools, courthouses, hospitals and jails, dams and canals, levees and bridges, viaducts, docks, and tunnels. The Civilian Conservation Corps hired young men who lived in camps with military discipline to make improvements to forest and recreational resources. The National Youth Administration found appropriate work for urban young adults.

The New Deal by no means solved the country's problems, as even with all of the programs in operation many of the unemployed could not find work. And most of those who did have government-created jobs remained poor, as the pay provided was meager. As the Depression lingered, workers on the public payroll discovered they had to deal with the stigma associated with being *on relief,* which followed them when they sought employment in the private sector. Many others went to extreme lengths to avoid relief, knowing in advance the slur that would attach to their reputations. Other problems inherent in any large government project arose: both political influence-peddling and graft meant that the neediest did not always receive what was intended for them. However, considering the speed with which the programs were initiated, and their size, they remained largely honest and nonpolitical. A substantial improvement in economic conditions did not occur until well into World War II, when defense production provided an almost unlimited supply of jobs.

The Great Depression dealt a particularly devastating blow to the elderly. Letters to Mrs. Roosevelt revealed the desperation felt by many of them, as writers begged her to use her influence toward the creation of an old-age pension program. The Townsend plan, drafted by Dr. Francis E. Townsend, proposed giving $200 per month for every person over sixty years of age, but it never had a realistic chance of passage. Another simplistic plan put forward would have allotted $1 a day to older people. The Social Security Act, when finally passed on August 14, 1935, broke new ground conceptually, for the first time creating federal responsibility for the welfare of the American citizen, but it remained modest in the actual help it provided. Composed of three major parts, the first and most important one involved retirement insurance. A new compulsory tax, assessed in equal parts on employers and employees, would fund this program. However, it excluded farmers, domestic workers, and the elderly, who together made up half the population. The second provision created unemployment insurance, setting up a mandatory system of payments to those who lost jobs; it was managed by the states, thus creating a system of wide variation in what were always limited payments. The third provision in the Social Security Act funded federal money to match what had been traditional state pensions for the aged, dependent mothers and their children, the blind and crippled. All of these programs are taken for granted today, but in 1935 they gave great encouragement to those in need who were desperately seeking help.

As might be expected, many of Mrs. Roosevelt's correspondents wrote of their difficulties in dealing with the numerous federal government bureaucracies; Mrs. Roosevelt forwarded these to the proper departments for action. As the 1930s advanced, the tenor of the letters Mrs. Roosevelt received changed. In 1938 and 1939 many wrote protesting the elimination of New Deal programs, as government interest and money refocused on events outside of the United States. Mrs. Roosevelt did what she could to assist both programs and individuals, because the New Deal as a whole reflected her central beliefs as expressed in her book *Tomorrow is Now*: "One of the basic elements in our whole way of life, one of the elements that, for two hundred years, has attracted the peoples of the world to our shores, is our belief that each individual has a right to a better life and to better working conditions and a larger share of the prosperity of his country because, by having them, he can develop his maximum potentialities as a human being."

—CDK

The New Deal

January 4, 1934

Our dear Mrs. Roosevelt:—

Your kindness and thoughtfulness for others who are in need of a friend—and—counselor, has encouraged me to come to you for advice. I'm a widow, 65 years of age. In 1927 my husband and I contracted for this little home place. We put over $1,400 in it, besides the upkeep, taxes and insurance, which has mounted up in to the hundreds of dollars. **We wanted a home** (never had had one of **our own**). Yes we wanted a little home where we could spend our last days knowing we didn't have to move. My husband was killed on the streets of Kirkland Jan. 29 1933. I kept up the payments as long as I could and last Feb. I got my application in for a Home Loan. Property has decreased in value, since 1927. We have paid as much as the place would sell for now. But a contract is a contract, and you know what that means. The Home Loan Co. offered the holders of the contract $760, they turned the offer down, asking for

$1,000 loan. I was willing to resume that much (although with my regular income of less than $15.00 a month and what little a woman of my age can bring in besides) I was willing to resume that much, rather than lose the first and only home we ever tried to have, even if I'd have to live on less, if it were possible. Last month, the Home Loan Co. wrote me the funds would be exhausted before my application could be cared for.

Now, Mrs. Roosevelt, what shall I do? I have the taxes paid, the buildings insured up until this coming March. The people are urging me to pay or get off. The only way I see out now is if we can get an Old Age Pension. I, with thousands of others can buy us a home, and live in peace and comfort the few remaining years we are here. May I ask your advice and that **you use your influence** to help us get an Old Age Pension. Remember there are thousands of us standing back of you and the President with our prayers and hopes and love.

We believe you have, as Esther of old, "come to the kingdom, for such a time as this" (quoting from the Bible). God bless you and yours, with wisdom and courage, and all you need to help you in your trying position. And may He help us all to be true to you.

Sincerely yours.
Mrs. Georgia H. DeWeese
Kirkland, Washington

[Three pages handwritten]

. . .

[undated]

My Dear Mrs. Roosevelt

I cut from our daily paper—*Boston Post*—a little bit concerning your interest in old people and the establishment of assured pension for them. It touched me in a vulnerable spot. I am seventy four, in receipt of five dollars weekly, and the town of Braintree is in such financial straits that I never feel quite sure how long I may receive the allowance. If a measure could be enacted whereby all old people could be mortally set at rest as to tenure of home, food and fuel, it seems to me it would be an act not only of great philanthropy but almost of necessity.

I truly and fervently pray to Almighty God to further your effort in this time. I, for one cordially appreciate your spirit and good will towards us.

Very sincerely yours,
Cora Allen
East Braintree, Massachusetts

[One and half pages handwritten]

January 12, 1934

My dear Miss Allen:

Mrs. Roosevelt has asked me to acknowledge your letter and to thank you for writing her.

She has always felt that some provision should be made to take care of those who have worked hard during their lives, and through circumstances over which they have no control find themselves in need in their old age. She has endeavored to do what she could toward attaining this goal, and hopes that the day is not far distant when the problem will be satisfactorily solved.

At the present time, many of the States have enacted Old Age Pension legislation, and those who live in such States are able to obtain the benefits allowed them by applying to the State officials.

Very sincerely yours,
Malvina T. Scheider
Secretary to Mrs. Roosevelt

. . .

[undated]

Dear Mrs. Roosevelt,

I want you to know how much we appreciate your aid in speeding up our home loan; we havent it yet, but the appraisers were here and said we should have it the latter part of January. It seems like things changed for us after I wrote you: my husband went to work for the CWA. I had a 2 weeks job at the Registration Office for a Special Election: and my boy has a paper route so we managed to pay up the interest clear to Feb. 27. So we are safe for the present. Then I had a small baby to board for 2 mo. And that was a wonderful help for us. It seems like some gaurdian angle has been hovering over us scence I called for help. I think the work you and our President are doing is just wonderful. I feel as many others do that God gave us Our President and his wonderful help mate. May God Bless you both in the work you are doing. My family join in thanking you for helping speed up the Home Loan and making it possible for those who need it.

Yours Sincerely

Mrs. Geo. Amend

Geo. H. Amend

I wish to join my mother and dad, in thanking you for helping us on our Home Loan. Things are going better at present. I am a member of Troop 3 BSA [Boy Scouts of America] and heard the Presidents message today and you may be assured that we will cooperate with you 100%.

Yours.

Star Scout Troop 3 BSA

[Three pages handwritten]

• • •

January 20, 1934

My dear Mrs. Roosevelt,

My friend—everybody's friend,

I am writing to express my appreciation, of your splendid talk (via radio) urging the passage of the "Old Age Security Act"—each word found a warm response in my heart, for I know much of the neglect and suffering of old age and I am urging that you and your fine husband "OUR PRESIDENT" put forth united efforts to secure the same protection, for all the aged in this great country of ours.

You need not be told of the thousands and thousands, who in many cases have lost their small businesses, which means losing their bread and butter, and are walking into the sunset land with hidden horror in their hearts. The class of people who would starve before they would ask for aid, and yet they are those who have established the civilization, culture, art and morals, of this country . . . Fought and bled for it. Is not the laborer worthy of his hire?

And this opinion, which is not mine alone, is that if there is not provision made for these splendid people— a something that they can accept and maintain their self respect—there will be—and that soon—a tidal wave of suicides that will horrify the civilized world. I know a prominent judge who says "that on an average of once a month some fine man comes to him with the statement that he is going to commit suicide." Yesterday a mother in Tampa shot her three children—to save them from what she had suffered—and then shot herself. Humanities come first. Nor is this condition local—it is

universal. Let us forget, civics, road building, canal
building etc. and divert the funds to relieve suffering
humanity.

Most cordially yours—and may God bless you

Mrs. W. F. Allen

Tampashores, Florida

[One page typed]

*Mrs. Roosevelt gave the radio talk referred to at the U.S. Chamber of
Commerce in Washington, D.C., on January 5, 1934. She began by saying:*

"I do not feel that either to my seen audience or my unseen
audience I have to actually discuss the merits of old age pensions. I think we have come beyond that because it is many
years now since we have accepted the fact, I think, pretty well
throughout the country, that it is the right of old people
when they have worked hard all their lives, and, through no
fault of theirs, have not been able to provide for their old age,
that it is their right to be cared for in the last years of their
life. We did it at first—in what I consider a terrible way—in
poorhouses, but now we have become more humane and
more enlightened, and little by little we are passing in the
various states old age pension laws."

*She then discussed the various ways such a system could be implemented,
saying that she hoped the legislation for the District of Columbia could
become a model bill for the country. She ended by commenting:*

"Such a bill would allow the old people to end their days in
happiness, and it will take the burden from the younger
people who often have all the struggle that they can stand,
and instead of making for bitter relationship—bitter for
the old people because they hate to be a burden on the

young, and bitter for the young because they would like to give gladly and they find themselves giving grudgingly and bitterly because it is taking away from what they can do for the youth that is coming and looking to them for support. For that reason I believe that this bill will be a model bill and pass without any opposition this year."

February 3, 1934

My dear Mrs. Allen:

Mrs. Roosevelt has asked me to acknowledge your letter and to thank you for writing her.

She has always felt that some provision should be made to take care of those who have worked hard during their lives, and through circumstances over which they have no control find themselves in need in their old age. She has endeavored to do what she could toward attaining this goal, and hopes that the day is not far distant when the problem will be satisfactorily solved.

Very sincerely yours,
Malvina T. Scheider
Secretary to Mrs. Roosevelt

• • •

June 14, 1934

Mrs. F. D. Roosevelt,
Washington, D.C.

I know you are overburdened with requests for help and if my plea cannot be recognized, I'll understand it is because you have so many others, all of them worthy.

But I am not asking for myself alone. It is as a potential mother and as one woman to another.

My husband and I are a young couple of very simple, almost poor families. We married eight years ago on the proverbial shoe-string but with a wealth of love. We both wanted more than anything else to establish a home and maintain that home in a charming, quiet manner. I had a job in the County Court House before I married and my husband was, and is, a surveyor. I kept my job as it seemed the best and only way for us to pay for a home as quickly as we could. His work was not always permanent, as surveyors jobs seldom are, but we managed to build our home and furnish it comfortably. Perhaps we were foolish to put all our money into it but we felt it was not only a pleasure but a saving for the future.

Then came the depression. My work has continued and my salary alone has just been sufficient to make our monthly payments on the house and keep our bills paid. But with the exception of two and one-half months work with the U.S. Coast and Geodetic Survey under the CWA my husband has not had work since August, 1932.

My salary could continue to keep us going, but—I am to have a baby. We wanted one before but felt we should have more assurance for the future before we deliberately took such a responsibility. But now that it has happened, I won't give it up! I'm willing to undergo any hardship for myself and I can get a leave of absence from my job for a year. But can't you, won't you do something so my husband can have a job, at least during that year? I realize there is going to be a lot of expense and we have absolutely nothing but our home which still carries a mortgage of $2000. We can't lose that because our baby will need it. And I can't wait until the depression is over to have a baby. I will be 31 in October and I'll soon be too old.

We had such high hopes in the early spring that the Coast and Geodetic work would continue. Tommy, my husband, had a good position there, and we were so happy. We thought surely our dreams of a family would come true. Then the work ended and like "The best laid plans of mice and men" our hopes were crushed again. But now Fate has taken it into her own hands and left us to work it out somehow. I'm happy, of course, but Tommy is nearly out of his head. He has tried every conceivable prospect but you must know how even pick and shovel jobs do not exist.

If the Coast and Geodetic work could continue or if he could get a job with the Bureau of Public Roads,— anything in the surveying line. A year is all I ask and after that I can go back to work and we can work out our own salvation. But to have this baby come to a home full of worry and despair, with no money for things it needs, is not fair. It needs and deserves a happy start in life.

As I said before, if it were only ourselves, or if there were something we could do about it, we would never ask for help. We have always stood on our own feet and been proud and happy. But you are a mother and you'll understand this crisis.

Tommy is competent and dependable. He has a surveyor's license and was level man for the U.S. Coast and Geodetic work in this (Humboldt) county. He will go away from home for work, if necessary, but, dear Mrs. Roosevelt, will you see if you can arrange for a job for him? It sounds impossible, I know, but I am at a point where I **ask** the impossible. I have to be selfish now.

I shall hope and pray for a reply and tell myself that you are the busiest woman in America, if I don't receive it. I am going to continue to work as long as I can and then—an interval of waiting. God grant it will be serene and untroubled for my baby's sake.

Very sincerely, yours,

Maude H. Anderson

(Mrs. B. T. Anderson)

Eureka

Humboldt County

California

[One and half pages typed]

June 23, 1934

Miss Malvina T. Scheider,

Secretary to Mrs. Roosevelt,

The White House

Washington, D.C.

My dear Miss Scheider:

I have read with the greatest sympathy Mrs. B. T. Anderson's letter of June 12, 1934, addressed to Mrs. Roosevelt and forwarded to me by your note of June 21. That note does not make it clear whether you want me to handle the matter direct or give you the information for a reply, but realizing Mrs. Roosevelt's exceptionally sympathetic attitude toward such appeals I am assuming that you may prefer the latter.

During the past few weeks I have been deluged by such appeals. Because of the developmental character of engineering, engineers have been particularly hard hit by the depression, and they are of the white collar class to whom it is particularly difficult to afford relief in a way which does not undermine their own self-respect.

At the present moment I am making every effort to secure an allotment from funds made available a week ago, which will give employment to some thousands of engineers whose cases in many instances are as meritorious and touching as the one so feelingly outlined in Mrs. Anderson's letter. I do not know what the outcome of this effort will be, but if it is successful I will be able to give approximately a year's work to Mr. Anderson, and will be most happy to do so.

I suggest therefore that you forward the enclosed questionnaire to Mr. Anderson, and ask him to fill it out and return it to me. That will put him in line for a job if this new project goes through, and even if it does not there is a remote chance that we may be able to use him on work on which we are now engaged.

I assure you of my deep sympathy and desire to aid.

Sincerely yours,

R. S. Patton

Director

Geodetic Survey

Washington, D.C.

• • •

August 10, 1934

To President and Mrs. F. D. Roosevelt

The White House. Washington, D.C.

Dear Friends:—

This is a letter of thanks. Owing to the presidents kindness in referring a letter (we wrote you last December, 1932) to the Federal Farm Credit Administration, and a consequent telegram from them stating that they would help us, we are still in possession of our home—and have a Federal Land Bank Commissioners loan of $1200 which enabled us to repurchase our farm and by the terms of the agreement, have $200 for repairs on buildings and **do we enjoy repairing**? I'll say we do. We can do all of it without hiring help except shingle the barn. Must hire a little help for that and to say we are improving the looks of the farm is putting it mildly. We've a lot to do yet, but the natural setting of the place is pretty, pines all around—white pine, norway spruce and balsam,—so every thing we do will be worthwhile.

We asked in our former letter if the refinancing program was only for the big farmers—that seemed to us the way it was being applied here,—but we know now that it means others too, and the "New Deal" means something to us.

The CCC boy is home now. He bought a small truck and is working where ever he can, helping at threshing for a neighbor today. The other big boy has work in the woods, and the two smaller ones are helping farm. Randall (15) finished 8th grade and says that now we have the place back he wants to stay and help here, instead of going to Crookston. Just now, while times are hard, perhaps it will be best, as he would go to the Agricultural College at Crookston if he went away to school—and perhaps a year or so later he would get more out of that than now. We will do the best we can to enable him to go later on.

The twins (girls)—joined the 4-H-Club this year and lately they are starting to can. Shall try to can all we possibly can this year as usual.

We are much interested in the building plans of the government and in the new homes being built. We know how happy the families housed in them will be.

We appreciate the efforts made to supply work. Our boy signed up again about 3 weeks ago. He has signed up a number of times, but so far he hasn't been called—he has been more lucky lately about getting work enough to live on anyway. We have all kinds of work on this farm, but very little money to work with and we have to live after a fashion. I mean work like clearing land and plowing new land. One's income is so small that it all goes for living and the work I've mentioned doesn't bring in any cash, you know.

One's efforts have to be concentrated on those tasks that bring in immediate returns and those returns are so small they won't reach to the "cashless" work that needs doing, but we will manage that somehow. We are living on our own efforts, so are much luckier so far than some, who cannot do that. We have the big boys to help us and we feel that all our efforts ought to make our living, and leave the relief for those who have nothing to turn to. Besides, we don't want the boys to give up as long as there's a single thing to do. We do appreciate the fact that the Government is doing so much to help the aged and helpless, and that there are camps for the young men if they can find nothing else to do, but we also feel that if they get other work they should and leave the other work for those who are about to lose courage for lack of work.

This letter is getting long. I must stop and get busy but I did want you folks down there to know that your efforts are helping people, helping people to help themselves and here's one grateful family in Clearwater, Minnesota, who owes you many thanks and appreciation. May God bless and give you all the help you may need and make your work successful in every way. After all—it is God who enables us all to carry on when all else fails, and He will surely not forget us.

With every good wish for your health and happiness and every appreciation of all the help you are trying to give to those who need it so badly—We are sincerely your friends.

I. O. Arney and family
Bagley, Minnesota

Pardon this long letter. We wanted you to know about the help you gave by putting our case in the hands of the Farm Credit Administration. I enclose some pictures which may interest you.

Maude B. Arney

[Ten pages handwritten]

As Mrs. Roosevelt pointed out in a speech,

> "the foreclosure on farms and homes was one of the out-
> standing features of the depression that caused nationwide
> distress. One in every four farms had been lost to the owner
> by the spring of 1933, and half a million were threatened
> with tax sales. In the cities, one million homes were threat-
> ened and homes sold for non-payment of taxes rose to a
> total of 3500 a month. The FCA and the HOLC were
> established by the Administration and by acts of Congress
> to refinance the mortgages of farmers and urban house-
> holders respectively."

*So many people queried Mrs. Roosevelt on these two programs, she devoted
her entire column in the December 1933 issue of the* Woman's Home
Companion *to detailed explanations of how to apply for these loans.*

• • •

[Date-stamped January 2, 1935]

Dear Mrs. Roosevelt,

I am writing you a personal letter that you may advise me
what We shall do: My husband is past 70 years and We
have lived in Idaho for almost thirty yrs. were in Payette
Co. for over 26 yrs. My husband paid over $1000 in taxes
there, and owned property in Baker Oregon, and paid several hundred dollars there also, but during the depression,
We have been reduced to poverty, my husband is a minister, he has been pastoring for quite a number of yrs. But
you know people do not want an old man for minister, my
age is 53. I made application here for relief sewing, and
they took the matter under consideration, and because We
have $70 in the Post Office in Fayette for to pay Doctor in
case of sickness, or in case of death, for Dr. do not go

where they are called, unless people have money to pay for it, neither do undertakers furnish their services without the money is in sight, they have refused to put me on, and because my husband is over 70 years of age they refuse to furnish medical aid, in case We need it, as you will see by the accompaning letter.

Now I do not believe the President realizes the condition of the old people, especially in the west, many old folk who are over 60, are sitting in their once beautiful homes, that a few yrs past were independant, now they are fast being closed out, taxes, interest and the cost of water has accumulated until when the property will be sold it will not pay what there is against it.

There has been provision made for those who under 60, they are elligable to buy the small home, and have a house built and have terms so they can meet it, We went to Fayette to try and get us a loan, but when We met the Govt. apointed man there, and asked him who were elligable, he said all between 21 and 60. My husband asked him, Well what provision has been made for those over 60 and he said the old age pension will take care of them, kindly tell us what We will do until the old age pension becomes a law.

Now Mrs. Roosevelt, We know that you have a great deal of influence, and We also note that you have been using it for good, and expect that you are flooded with letters simular to this one from all parts of the country, as is also the President, We are not making an appeal to you for charity, but that you might use your influence for the old age pension, or some other measure where by those that are "too old" for all the other means of help that are offered, may be honorably benifitted also.

We should be very much pleased to receive a personal reply, at your convenience.

Mrs. T. A. Wayne

With the letter was a copy of a letter from the Idaho Emergency Relief
Administration stating that they only pay medical bills for persons under 65.

[One page typed]

January 2, 1935

My dear Mrs. Wayne:

Mrs. Roosevelt has received your letter. While she is deeply
interested in the question of old age pensions, there really is
little she can do to further necessary legislation. The subject is
being studied by the Committee on Economic Security of the
Department of Labor, to whom all plans are referred.

Very sincerely yours,
Malvina T. Scheider
Secretary to Mrs. Roosevelt

• • •

January 4, 1935

Mrs. Frankling D. Roosevelt
dear madam:

just a few lines from old georgia laddie. I've bin reading
your speaches al along. I agree with you in regard to old age
pensions, $200 too mutch one dollar a day would make a
smoothsailing for many old laddies like myselft. Oh I could
hire me healp to keep house pay my preacher more, give
some stockins to some little girls that passes my home
every day with cold legs, mi I don't know how mutch good
I could do with thirty dollars a months and I would if I had
it you see dear laddie my life work bin raising children. I've
a family of ten of my own eight boys 2 girls and then when
my babie child was fourteen years old my daughter-inlaw

pass a way left five little ones, twins 14 days old. I had to
raise them. They are 16 year now always bin on a farm got
on very well untill 1921 lost my husban sure have had ruff
sailing since have plenty to eat but no money, I started out
in life 50 years a go my husban had a buggy I had a cow
raise my family sent 9 to colage we baught us a farm bilt
us a house, light and water. Now I am 76 years old with
nothing. you smart. Go befor that house that makes laws
tell them to give us old folk one dollar a day we can live and
god will bless you.

Sincerely yours
Mrs. J. C. Wallace
Griffin, Georgia

[Two pages handwritten]

January 9, 1935

My dear Mrs. Wallace:

Mrs. Roosevelt asks me to acknowledge your letter and to tell
you she is very sorry to hear of the difficult time you are having.
She has endeavored to do what she could toward attaining the
old age pension, and hopes that the day is not far distant when
the problem will be satisfactorily solved.

Very sincerely yours,
Malvina T. Scheider
Secretary to Mrs. Roosevelt

• • •

January 15, 1935

Dear Mrs. Roosevelt—

I hope you have time to read these few words of mine.

I have been thinking what a blessing an old people's pension would be to know that we would not be in want in our old age. I am fifty five and I have felt like a convict when ever I have spent a few dollars even for things I needed. I always had the feeling it had to be saved for our future. And I never could be care free and happy.

I have been going around from one store to another trying to save pennies and we haven't any money now. We have raised two boys and the small wages they get they never could take care of us. We have to help them. I think that $200 is too much, as our sons and daughters would want to be supported and young people should work, and thirty dollars is too little. It would take every bit of that for groceries and meat and there would not be any for fuel, clothing, rent or taxes.

With all the good wishes I could ever think of for you and Mr. Roosevelt, from one Mother to another.

Mrs. Mabel Danielson
Jamestown, New York

[Three pages handwritten]

January 18, 1935

My dear Mrs. Danielson:

Mrs. Roosevelt has received your letter. While she is deeply interested in the question of old age pensions, there really is little she can do to further necessary legislation. The subject is being studied by the Committee on Economic Security of the Department of Labor, to whom all plans are referred.

Very sincerely yours,
Malvina T. Scheider
Secretary to Mrs. Roosevelt

• • •

March 15, 1935

Dear Mrs. Roosevelt:

I have read a great deal about you and listened to you on my radio. I cannot do much in politics because all my time is taken up with my home and dependents but I have become interested just recently in propaganda.

It is way beyond me to understand what it really means and this terrible fight between everybody and Mr. Long[1] and Father Coughlin.[2] I can't believe that your talks are what they mean by propaganda because I believe you are honest and sincere in wanting to help everybody.

My husband and I have savings invested in a utility company, my husband says it is a holding one, but for years everybody spoke very highly of it and most everybody had some money in it. I don't know what they have done all of a sudden but it must be something terrible. It would not seem like much to you who are so wealthy and can make so much money but it is a lot to me and I have scrimped, if you know what I mean.

My husband says we have a perfect right to try to defend ourselves even in a depression and that we will not be put in jail. My newspaper prints a lot about it all and I am sending you some clippings especially about how kind you were to compliment a woman who worked for a gas company, of all things. I'll bet she was a surprised girl but then she looks nice and she is no doubt honest and respectable just as if she worked for a laundry or in the city hall. And I can remember that gas companies used to be respectable up to a year ago.

My husband says he has read that the Mayor of New York, he has some kind of a foreign name that don't sound American,[3] wants to stop the gas company because gas is dangerous and smelly and costs so very much but I hope this sweet looking girl does not lose her job. Perhaps her husband is not working just now. And my husband says they are going to make another electric company in New York and if you want a job you will have to be a Democrat and know the Boss and get votes and be a politician. I guess everybody in that city is a Democrat because I have often read of Tammany Hall[4] the name of their city hall maybe.

We liked our President because he has such a kind face and soft voice but he hates the utility business so bitterly and everybody connected with it and it is our bread and butter for my husband has worked for a gas company all his life. He was never in politics only to vote but he says he will be in it next year up to his ears. I can't do a thing with him he is so nasty and sore all the time and writing letters and listening to Mr. Long. He won't listen to Father Coughlin because we are APA's.[5]

I am afraid he will get sassy in his letters like he does to me and then he will be arrested and I have no money to bail him out. There was a Jewish man in our state who got in bad with the NRA for pressing pants too low and another one down South who had to go to the Supreme Court for

---

1–5. Huey Long, populist Democratic senator from Louisiana, created a political machine that controlled his state; he was assassinated in 1935. Father Coughlin, a "radio" priest, with a wide following in the 1930s, used the new medium of radio to express anti-New Deal and anti-Semitic rhetoric. The Roosevelt administration, and PWA chief Harold Ickes in particular, sought municipal reform and the curbing of public utilities. Ickes fought for the preservation of natural resources against exploitation by private interests and helped create national standards for electric-power rates. Fiorello LaGuardia, a progressive reformer, was elected mayor of New York City in 1932. Tammany Hall was the name of the Democratic political machine that began in 1854 and received its death blow in 1932 with LaGuardia's election. "APAs" could refer to either of two groups with the same initials and similar aims: The American Protestant Association began in 1849 and was allied with the American Nativist Party against Catholics, especially the Irish, while the American Protective Association, organized in 1878, was a powerful anti-immigrant and anti-Catholic organization. Both spread rumors that Catholics intended to slaughter non-Catholics as well as hand the U.S. government over to the Pope.

doing something or other. But my husband says his letters are his own personal propaganda because he can't get on the radio or the papers and he has spent more than a dollar for stamps this week. He is fighting mad and there is no living with him.

I honestly don't think Mr. Roosevelt realizes that he is injuring so many women who work and who have saved and lots of them must be Democrats. There don't seem to be any more Republicans anywhere anyhow. Can't we all be fair to each other and stop playing dirty politics all the time and get together in a spirit of co-operation.

My gas and electric bill is not big enough to worry me to death but the price of food is going up and especially meat as you know if you do your own buying, but of course you do not. But if it will help poor people to get work I do not kick as long as it comes in and we can keep the taxes paid and help our folks along.

If the men have all lost their heads and must be at each others throats all the time, why can't we women use a little common sense and work ourselves out of this depression by the old Golden Rule—"Do unto others, etc." and Live and Let Live.

Please read what I have sent to you even if it is Republican for, after all, Jew, Catholic, Protestant or Democrat we got to live and eat. Now maybe I have jumped right into this propaganda stuff and don't know it but I hope I will not be arrested.

With kind personal regards, I am

Very truly yours,

Ada A. Carson

Merchantville, New Jersey

[One and half pages typed]

Enclosed were several clippings from the Philadelphia Enquirer *about a woman heading a gas company, holding companies, and the use of propaganda.*

• • •

October 17, 1935

Dear Mrs. Roosevelt,

Do not think me bold in writing you, but my sister and I want to receive our first Holy Communion and confirmation the 25th of October and have not got the clothes to wear.

We are on direct Relief and they refuse to give them to us. They said they were not issuing clothing. So I thought perhaps by writing to you that you could help me in some way get them, as I have been put off for two years for the same reason. I am thirteen years and my sister is twelve years of age. But both of us are tall and slender.

This is a list of articles we need:

two veils, two white dresses, long sleeves, two white slips, two white undergarments, two pair white hose size 10, two pair white shoes 5-6. If you could tell me where we can get these articles, we would appreciate it very much. Please let me know as soon as possible as time is very short it is only a week from tomorrow. Thanking you I remain

Margaret Flynn
Chicago, Illinois

[Two pages handwritten]

• • •

February 12, 1936

Dearest Mrs. Roosevelt,

I wish you would bear with me and read this letter through. I am a mother of five children, I am thirty years of age. My children are Ethel 11, Roberta 8, Edward 4, Janet 2, and Marilyn 5 months.

I feel deeply grateful to our dear President for my little home. As I know it is his plan that enabled me to obtain this little $4000 house. By paying $31.79 a month on a Federal Housing plan.

It breaks my heart that so many people are trying to interfere in his helpful plan of government. My prayers are rarely said without asking God to help him in every way. I know of many others that also pray for him. I feel sure God will go with him all the way.

As I began to say, I am grateful to him for my home. Before this I lived in two rooms and kitchenette. It was large and I managed alright. But many times stories came to me. People saying how 6 of us were living in 4 rooms. Then Marilyn was expected and I was frantic wondering where I would live. When my sister read about these homes she urged me to buy one. We had no money saved, since Mr. Mernin was only earning $30 a week and had previously been unemployed. Some kind friends came forward and loaned us the necessary down payments to be paid over a liberal period. It goes without saying that many times I doubted the wisdom of going into debt to obtain this house. However it came about that we eventually did own it by Aug. 1, 1935. My 5th baby was nearly due and the expenses were the cause of many fits of hysterics and many heart aches for me. I could have born the worry but due to the fact I was leaving my family to go to the hospital I naturally became more afraid of the great responsibility. Mr. Mernin asked for a raise after Marilyn's arrival and received $3; then too he manages to get some music work since he plays a trombone and he averages about $45 a week. With this money I am paying off $115 a month in debts running to $2000. We applied for a Building loan of $1500 but because of our dependants only received $600, that was Aug. 22, 1935. With that money we paid for an additional room, some necessary top soil, since the house was surrounded with sand, and coke, as we didn't have enough for an oil burner.

I have managed to meet these payments as I should. But I find myself reborrowing and it frightens me, with the children growing up they require so much in clothes, food and an occasional doctor's visit. (We all need dental care, which I cannot afford.)

I keep a nice home, keep my children dressed clean and well dressed. I get in a food and butcher order each Saturday and get butter, eggs and Bordens milk, so that I am sure they eat fairly well. I pay my bills but very seldom have any money to buy anything extra. However I am very grateful to God and never feel I am abused.

What I want to ask you is this. Do you know of anyone willing to lend me the $2000 to pay off these bills (at about $40 or so a month over that period of months it would take, including the proper interest.) This would enable me to stop borrowing every time I needed more than I had to use. It would also make it easy for me to get the children shoes and such when they should have them. To say nothing of the peace of mind it would supply Mr. Mernin and myself. For many night I cry myself to sleep over the worry I have. Naturally doing all my own work and being worried too has been quite a strain on my health and disposition. If you know of a means of this sort I would be forever grateful to you. If you cannot help me it wouldn't make the slightest difference in my very high opinion of you as first Lady of the country. I am sincerely though merely

Helen Mernin
Laurelton, Long Island

[Three pages handwritten]

February 17, 1936

My dear Mrs. Mernin:

Mrs. Roosevelt asks me to acknowledge your letter for her. She deeply regrets that she can make no suggestion as to where you might borrow the money which you need. Unfortunately, because so many people ask, she is unable to lend any money personally.

Mrs. Roosevelt realizes the difficulty of your situation and wishes she could help in some way but I know you will understand that she receives so many appeals it is impossible to do anything in individual cases except where people are in distress and actual need of relief.

Very sincerely yours,
Malvina T. Scheider
Secretary to Mrs. Roosevelt

• • •

February 14, 1936

Mrs. F. D. Roosevelt,
Dear Madam:

I will drop a few lines to you, to let you know how we are situated and what we have to put up with, and to find out if you will help us out.

It is very hard for my husband to get to work, he now

is walking 7 miles to work, through all sorts of weather. He just makes $44 a month on a WPA project. We have to pay big rent, there is 9 in the family now and are expecting another in early Spring. There is a man lives near here, who has a dandy chicken ranch, he was telling my husband about it, he wants to let it go for $350. He wanted my husband to take it. It would be a good proposition and he could make a good living. But he did not have the money, you cannot borrow money here unless you own a lot of property. We thought if you could let us have the money, we would be very grateful to you. We send 4 children to school, and the road has not been cleared this winter. We voted for your husband, for president 4 years ago. And will do what we can to put him in office this election.

If you can let us have the money, we could tell the people of Tioga Co., what Mr. and Mrs. Roosevelt have done for us. We have 7 children, 5 girls and 2 boys. Here are their names in order of their births, their age in 1936

1. Clara Louise, age 13
2. Celia Mae, age 12
3. Edna Irene, age 10
4. Lawrence Leon, age 8
5. Freddie Homer, age 6
6. Cleo Ruth, age 3
7. Doris Marie, age 2

I will close hoping you can help us out.

Yours truly

Mrs. Fred Campbell

Wellsboro, Pennsylvania

[Three pages handwritten]

• • •

February 26, 1936

Mrs. Franklin D. Roosevelt—
Dear First Lady of the White House
I am taking the liberty to ask a favor. I have never asked
for aid before, but my mother Mrs. Chester Harding of
Redondo Beach, Cal. is very ill. Mother and Dad have an
old age pension of $22 per month each, and I understand
they have a county doctor. A gentleman Mr. John Hamilton
a welfare worker called on me to see if I could give some
assistance each week so mother could have someone there
to do for her and dad as they are both feeble. Mother is
78 and my Dad is 80. I would like very much to go to them
but have not the money. I have tried every way to raise
some, and have been unsuccessful. I have a husband who
has been ill for years with nerve and stomach trouble, who
has been a patient in the R.I. Hospital this winter. And
when he is well enough he works then, He works most
time at night on a 13 hour shift which does him more
harm than good, his wages are small. We manage to have
enough to eat and pay our rent. I work some when I can
get it. But we just haven't the money to go and look out
for my mother who writes she needs me. I wonder if you
would loan me $200. That would pay our fares twice or
about $70 a piece on a chair coach and sit up the 4 nights.
I used to live in California years ago. I have a daughter
and 4 grandchildren. Daughter has 3 children, my only
son died last April of a cancer on the brain, and left a little
boy 3 years old. Dr. Carl Rand of Los Angeles operated on
him. He seemed better but died in April and I was unable
to go there. I am heart sick over the whole affair. I do
want to see my mother and do for her. I am sure I could

prolong her life as I am a good nurse and understand food values could cook the food that Mother needs to strengthen her. I do not want to leave my husband here, he needs taking care of also, as he can eat only certain things that he can digest. We used to be in fair circumstances, sickness and trying to help each other until none of us have any thing. You are a mother of a large family, and understand I am sure how I feel. I feel frantic at times when I see how unable I am to do for those that need me. All I can do for them is give them of my strength and encourage them to live. My presence there with my mother would mean much to us both. I will pay you back some day when things get better which they are doing. More people are put to work every day. It is the employer who wants the younger man or woman. The older people are just laid on the shelve. God helping us we can be of use.

Sincerely Yours,
Mrs. Frederick W. Midgly
Eden Park, Rhode Island

[Four pages handwritten]

• • •

June 22, 1936

Dear Mis Roosevelt

I want to thank you very Sincerely for the Intrest taken in my letter and I am mailing you the letter that were sent to me. There seems to be no help no place for them, my sons. It is the one reason I wrote to you as my sons had already made applications to these people and were Regected. My Boys have never ask for Charity only Employment a chance to support their wives and Babys. They are Both College Boys and Ark. Lawyers. We moved here in 1932 from Missouri and when all the Banks closed we lost all we owned. They are willing to go any place where they could get Employment. These men who are lucky enough to get these positions in different Government Projects Employ their wives Family and Friends. And if you are not one or the other you simply have no chance as they tell you thier set up is already made in all these Projects. Husbands and wives Drawing large salerys from the Government when both could live nicely on one with no babys to support while out side a young man, with Better Education—with Babys to feed Just does not have a chance. Their babys would not have Milk had it not been his Milk man told him he would Credit him untill he found Employment. You have been So kind in helping others I thought perhaps you could help My Boys,

thanking You again

Mrs. Maude H. Babb

Little Rock, Arkansas

[One and a half pages handwritten]

• • •

August 30, 1936

My Dear Mrs. Roosevelt

No doubt you will be annoyed at hearing from me but Mrs. Roosevelt, I am at the end of my way and cant see much ahead. I am 65 years old 14th of next month and have fallen arches and pains in my legs untill I cant hardly stand it and I am working on the WPA and have over a year in the school libiary and have to go up 4 flights of steps and I just cant hardly make it and I have no living relative in the world only a brother in law and he has helped me untill a year ago but says he cant now so what am I to do isn't some way you could think of, I love to work but am not able to walk and it hurts me so, and South Carolina does not have an old age pension isn't there some way I could get aid through your help. I almost love you and Mr. Roosevelt. You have helped the whole world so much that I don't see what would become of us poor unfortunate ones should the President not be elected again but I know he will be for he is a grand man and has done more for this world than any other President in my time and if you are the fine woman every one says you are please suggest a way that I can get some help not much just enough to live on as I am not able to work as I am having to do and I do hate to give up. I work 8 hours a day. Please dear don't mention that I have written you but if you will answer my letter and tell me what to do I will apreciate and may God bless both of you and reward you for what you have done for the whole world with best wishes to both.

Sincerely

Mrs. H.

Greenville, South Carolina

[Two pages handwritten]

September 3, 1936

My dear Mrs. H:

Mrs. Roosevelt and her secretary are away and I have been asked to acknowledge their mail. I know that Mrs. Roosevelt would understand your appeal and I am sorry I cannot bring your letter to her attention. However, the only way in which Mrs. Roosevelt could help you would be to refer your letter to the proper authorities requesting that a change in your status be considered. Since you ask that your letter be kept confidential, I will not do this without your consent.

Very sincerely yours,

Administrative Officer

Social Correspondence

• • •

April 22, 1937

Personal—private **Please** read and consider

Dear Mrs. Roosevelt,

Pardon my presumption in troubling you but I am in desperate straits to save my farm and **only** home and **cannot** do so **unless** I can get a loan—a long time loan at a low rate of interest. What I **need** is a long time loan of $2700.00 at **not** to exceed a 4% rate to take up the "Land Commissioner's loan" which I **now** have. (They would **not** give me a Federal Land Bank loan which gives **more** time and a lower rate of interest.)

I've had **little** crop for six years due to hoppers and hot winds. (Had **no** crop whatever last year.) Had to sacrifice nearly **all** my cattle (which was my working capital) in '35 because of **no feed**. Now I have a little start in horses **and** cattle but **not** enough to manage things **quickly**. My land, which I will describe on another sheet, is adequate security for the loan I **need**. I'm **not a beggar** but I am getting old (65) and am **alone** to milk fifteen cows etc. to try to make things go. Have been a widow over thirty-two years and raised and educated my family but these last years have been trying. Money is scarce here. Do you know anyone who would make me this needed loan to save my home?

My farm consists of 320 acres, nearly **all** tillable, one half mile from state highway No. 40, on graded road.

Buildings: six room frame house with three closets and three-quarter basement, small granary and chicken coop, frame barn twenty four by thirty. Has three good wells and about two hundred acres under cultivation. Is ten miles from W. River, the county seat. The land is being farmed this year.

If anyone **will** favor me with this loan on my farm to help me save it I will certainly appreciate it. Will appreciate a reply whether or not favorable.

Mrs. D.
White River, South Dakota

[Two pages handwritten]

May 1, 1937

My dear Mrs. D:

In the absence of Mrs. Roosevelt I am writing to acknowledge your letter. So many appeals for financial assistance come to her that much as she would like to help every worthy case brought to her attention it is not possible for her to do so. The money she has at her disposal for philanthropic purposes has already been pledged and allocated and I am very sorry she would not be able to comply with your request.

Very sincerely yours,
Malvina T. Scheider
Secretary to Mrs. Roosevelt

• • •

November 5, 1937

My dear Mrs. Roosevelt;

First I wish to humbly apologize for the time it will take

you to read this plea for help, as I fully realize you are the busiest lady in all the United States but there seems to be no alternative. My husband and I have no relatives that are in a position to give us a lift and not knowing anyone that could be of assistance, I thought that maybe you, being the Mother of this Country, could at least give me some advice what I should do or whom I could go to.

To make this as short as possible so that I won't waste too much of your time, here is my story:

My mother died when I was a small girl and I was forced out into the world to get my living as best I could until about a little over a year ago when I married a nice young man, thinking that together we could make a home—a thing I had not known since my mother's death. I was working in the WPA Office here and we purchased some furniture with a small down payment and got along fine at first. Then my husband lost his job and last July I lost mine only to find I was to become a mother and was not in a position to secure another position. My husband did secure a job at a very low salary. Just enough to get along. We were forced to let the payments on the furniture go and now they want to take that away as they say they have given us all the time they can. My electric light bill is so high that they will have to shut off the current and I shall have to be in the dark these long, cold, winter nights, as I have no lamps. I did get trusted for groceries until the grocer refused to let me have any more. I can just get enough money for the rent and keep warm and have a little to eat. Have borrowed as much as I can, so I have got to turn to some one. I hate to go on the town and have my plight published. I have got some surplus commodities which help out a lot. As yet I have no clothes for my expected little one and don't know how I am going to pay for the arrival of my little one which is only a month or two off.

I thought if I could get in touch with some one who had plenty of money and who would be charitable enough to give me money enough to keep my home and get some clothes for the baby and ourselves, as both my husband and myself have no shoes but what are worn through the bottom, and pay my light and grocery bill, I think we could mange until I could get another office position or any other for that matter, but I worked my way through high school and Business College and like that work best.

I have a letter from Mr. James P. Quinn, Director of Employment for WPA if you wish to check up on me.

You may think I am out of my mind writing to you like this but circumstances like this can drive one to do most anything. I wish I could get $500. I realize it is a lot of money and any amount would help out a lot, even if I could just get some baby clothes. Maybe we'd be able to find some place to stay if they did take my furniture—my home, which means a lot to me. Can you give me any help or advice? Would it have to be published if I got help from the source you suggest? My husband does not know that I am writing this but something must be done soon. He won't have to know if you cannot help me. He probably wouldn't allow me to do this if he knew but you are the Mother of millions of people and I feel you will understand even if you can't do more. I dislike publicity so I hope you will treat this confidentially and won't do anything that will bring me in the public's eye.

Sincerely yours,

Mrs. J.

Clarement, New Hampshire

P.S. Just one of your humble children. Am 26 years of age.

[Seven pages handwritten]

November 9, 1937

My dear Mrs. J:

Mrs. Roosevelt and her secretary are away, and in their absence I have been asked to acknowledge their mail. I know Mrs. Roosevelt would sympathize with you in your difficulties and would wish it were possible for her to help you, but owing to the great number of appeals for financial assistance which she receives she finds it impossible to help each worthy case brought to her attention. The money she has at her disposal for philanthropic purposes has already been pledged and allocated.

Very sincerely yours,
Administrative Officer
Social Correspondence

• • •

December 1, 1937

My Dear Mrs. Rosevelt:

I don't know why it is, but when I get worried I think of you. I think you are a wonderful woman, when I read of all you do, I never miss reading your column in the **Post** daily, and I read about the young man saying he thought your husband "was a great guy." I look upon him as "The Greatest President." I come from a family of strong Republicans, but Im not one. Im for Franklin D. Roosevelt one hundred percent. He has really done things for needy people. My husband and I are employed on a dairy farm, we both milk 15 cows twice a day. For this we receive $35 per month, are allowed our cottage and a small plot for vegetables. We have three children, age seven, five, and three. We don't know what fresh meats of any kind taste like, its been beyond our reach. Yet my husband tends hogs and raises feed for all the cows, we aren't allowed but very few chickens, and the lady who employs us is against "The New Deal" because it favors the "**Riff Raff** Class." She thinks all people who don't have a lot of land and town property like she has are beneath her, and she hates to have to pay taxes to help out the needy. "It makes my blood boil" but I can't say anything or I'd lose my job.

Its so hard to have to live the way we do, when we use to live better. No radio, we never have any amusement, can't afford it.

Only Our Maker knows how happy I could be if at Xmas time I could have a loan or a personal gift of say $100 or even more so I could get a radio, and a good bed or two and some bed covering, warm clothes for children and husband, and a piece of furniture or two for living room, some paint and curtains, etc. and have a pretty little tree with toys, and have my teeth fixed. We have worked so hard, and yet seems as if we are getting lower and lower.

If someone rich and nice knew **of our** condition and how much we deserve help, they would be glad to make us a loan or gift of a small sum that would help us so much, and make their heart glad at this season of giving. I know rich people aren't in habit of giving to individuals like that but if you could pass my letter onto one may be they could see fit to help us.

I shouldn't bother a busy person like you with this I suppose, but I hope you really will read this letter because I can truthfully say that reading about you and seeing your pictures has made me feel like I can feel free to talk to you. What other President's wife had done that much? I would be thrilled to receive a personal letter from you and would prize it highly and keep it as long as I lived, if you could advise me in any manner I'd appreciate it.

My employer knows all of our worries, but what does she care. All of **her's** fairs well and don't need or want for anything. People like my self are only Riff Raff to her. Thanking you for reading this.

Mrs. Mona Smith

Batavia, Ohio

P.S. If someone rich that you know of can do what I ask to help us out I'll be glad to send snapshots of children, my husband and myself if they would like as I have a kodak. I feel embaressed to come right out and ask for help like this but, looks as if its our only hope of getting on our feet again and we can't go on much longer at this pace.

M.S.

[Ten pages handwritten]

The "My Day" column referred to is that of November 28, 1937. Most of the article refers to that day's visit to Arthurdale, a federal government homestead project in West Virginia. Mrs. Roosevelt ends her column by saying: "A nice little incident happened yesterday morning. While we were waiting for the Congressman [Congressman Jennings Randolph of West Virginia] to telephone, a young man with a large tiger's head painted on the back of his leather jacket, came across the side walk and extending his hand to me remarked: 'You are Mrs. Roosevelt, aren't you?' We shook hands while I murmured that I was, and then he said: 'Tell your husband I think he is a great guy.' "

December 3, 1937

My dear Mrs. Smith:

Mrs. Roosevelt and her secretary are away, and in their absence I have been asked to acknowledge their mail. I know Mrs. Roosevelt would sympathize with you in your difficulties, but she would not be able to do as you ask. Owing to the great number of appeals for financial assistance which she receives she finds it impossible to help every worthy case coming to her attention, much as she would like to do so. The money she has at her disposal for philan-thropic purposes has already been pledged and allocated.

Very sincerely yours,
Administrative Officer
Social Correspondence

. . .

[Date-stamped December 16, 1937]

Mrs. President Roosevelt:

I am writing this letter to you because of three reasons.

First: Because I saw in a newspaper that you person-ally read much of your correspondence; and I failed to believe this but hoped it was true.

Second: Because I wanted to express my appreciation for the fine part you did in appearing on Kate Smith's pro-gram last Thursday evening. I enjoyed the story of the department store girl and had to chuckle at the pronunci-ation you gave to "chiffon." Not that it was incorrect. But just different. I liked you a lot for appearing, though!

Third: Because I want to ask your advice on a serious problem that confronts me. And somehow I feel hopeful of your being able to help me in solving it.

First of all I am a young married man of 27. Two very cute children and a pretty nice wife. We have been married five years. During these five years we have known hard times and have weathered them ok. During these five years my father lost his hardware store, partly due to poor management, and I was put out of work. I got work in another hardware store in another town and a year later, 1935, a better job in a larger store. In 1936 I got a real break and became engaged as a wholesale salesman. And this fall I was given my own territory in Northern Michigan. I earn $47.50 a week. Of this amount, about

$22.50 goes for gas, oil, tires, meals for myself, etc. Then too, out of the remaining $25 I have to keep my car in shape and keep said family going. But we are left with a six dollar a week margin for debts. And debts! That's where my problem comes. During our lean years we accumulated approximately $570 in debts. And every bit of it is due and payable.

What I want to do is to find a loan (no I'm not begging or asking you for a loan) for $600 paying 6% interest and spread in monthly payments over a three year period.

It would be simple if we had security. But we haven't. And I won't go to a gyp finance company and borrow with my firm as signers, for 12% interest over a years time.

Neither of our folks have any capital, nor do we have any rich relatives. And it is only a question now, of a few weeks and somebody will sue and there will go my job, **for sure**!

What I want to find is some one who can afford a loan of this amount for this period of time and be content to trust the integrity and ambition of a young fellow who kept climbing **up** all during these lean years of the depression.

If there is anything you can suggest, or anyone you know who could help, would you let me know. Please?

I do not want a formal typed letter telling me to apply at my local relief office for aid or to the Reconstruction Finance Corporation for a loan. I just want the advice or help you would give your son. There surely must be some one out of this country who can help? Thank you.

Sincerely yours,
Earl Smith
Traverse City, Michigan

P.S. I can, in case it might be needed, furnish figures, facts, statistics, and references by reliable people.

[Four pages handwritten]

. . .

December 18, 1937

Dear Mrs. Roosevelt.

I am sending you with this my love to you and your dear husband and your sons for the benefits we have received through your husband's administration. We have been living on relief and WPA since the storm of 1933. Now my father has been out of work for over four months on account of being sick of his back and can not do hard work. I believe we will not have a Christmas tree this year. My father says that he believes he will have a decent job with the city this coming year because he helped the Democratic party on election day and won. But in the mean time he has no money to buy anything for me or my sisters. I have eight sisters no brothers, one is 18 year old, her name is Margaret, she don't need any toys and another is 17, other 15, other 13, 11, and I am 10 years old, and Helen, 8, Mary Rose 5, and Sylvia 3 for these last ones I wish you could be our Santa Claus and send us a few toys for me and my little sisters also if you have some old clothes of yourself and wish to send them to mother she will fix them for my other sisters. Please, madam, do not say anything to no body because my father don't like for us to ask for anything. I know you have many little children to take care of but you are a very kind lady and I believe you will send my little sister Sylvia a doll, which she wishes to have. Please excuse me for bothering you so much. We all wish you a very happy Christmas to you all with love.

Miss E.J.
Brownsville, Texas

[One and a half pages handwritten]

• • •

March 1, 1938

Dear Mrs. Roosevelt.

I don't know if you will get to read this letter or not but I hope you do.

I first want to tell you I admire you very much, for the kindness you show to the young girls and boys, well not only that but you are an all round good woman, you appear to me as though you wanted to see others happy even if you were unhappy.

I also admire Mr. Roosevelt. I always listen to his talks on the Radio and I think he is doing all in **his** power to help the poor people.

Now I want to tell you about myself. I am not really poor and my husband is a barber we always manage to get along. I have one daughter 16 years old in high school.

I saw you when you stopped at a home on S. Main St. in our town. That is what made me want to write to you. You had such a jolly kind look that day. I know you get lots of letters asking you for things but I am not going to ask you for charity.

I have been in the hospital this winter was operated on and had my gall bladder removed the 3rd day of Dec. 1937. I am not very well yet but can do most of my own work.

Now what I wanted to ask you Mrs. Roosevelt. I wondered if you had a fur coat that you didn't want any more. I need a coat and have always wanted one (a fur coat) but know I'll never be able to buy one. I cant just tell you in words the **thrill** I would get out of wearing one you had worn. Now if you do and would send it to me or any dresses or other coats you have I would be glad to pay the charges on same.

I wouldent want any one in Salamanca to know I wrote you this letter they would think I was crazy, but I'm not Mrs. Roosevelt. I am really on the square and just writing as **friend** to **friend**.

Do you think I am being too bold to write what I have in my mind? If I don't hear from you I'll always feel that you did not get my letter. If you want to send me this I will greatly appreciate it and remember you in my prayers always as a kind woman.

I am

Mrs. S.

Salamanca, New York

[Four pages handwritten]

March 3, 1938

My dear Mrs. S:

Mrs. Roosevelt asked me to acknowledge your letter.

There are certain persons to whom Mrs. Roosevelt sends the clothing for which she has no further use, and she is very sorry indeed that she can not comply with your wishes.

With many regrets, I am

Very sincerely yours,

Malvina T. Scheider

Secretary to Mrs. Roosevelt

• • •

March 4, 1938

Dear Mrs. Roosevelt,

I'm writing you as a poor distressed farmers wife with five children to support and keep in school. I live 2 1/2 miles from school and the children have to walk, (which is O.K.) Glad they are able to walk. Have one boy that we hope will be able to graduate this year from high school. His name is Porter Dunn (if you look over your file you will see he gets a help check from you each school month which is very much appreciated.) The next boy is a Sophomore and the youngest girl is in the eighth grade.

The two oldest children are out of school. The oldest (a boy) works at a shoe factory but the factory has closed down now, and the daughter graduated in 36 but cant get work to do that is very much help. She works in a private home on laundry and house cleaning 2 days a week and 50 cents a day and boards at home. Now you see she cant get along very fast. She has ability to do higher things and is very industrious but the work can't be gotten here. I work away from home when ever I can get any thing to do. You realize how hard it is for the farmer the past several years, I know. We have a farm of 115 acres but have a government loan on it and have a very very very hard time keeping the interest and taxes paid on it. Don't have the home necessities by any means. Now since I've told you just how the conditions are would like to ask you for a personal reply on my question that I am going to ask. Will you please answer it and do the very very best you can by me. Your help will never never be forgotten by me and my family of needy ones.

I need a power washing machine so bad, don't have electricity and will have to get the gasoline engine type and I want to know if you could advise me how to manage a way to get it or if you could help me to pay for one. If I have a machine I might get some kind of laundry work to do to help.

I have heard you would help people that was willing and couldnt help themselves so I'm asking you down deep in my poor weary heart to please please help me.

I have no way now of repaying you but will if I can

ever get where I can. Please answer real real soon as I'm so anxious to know if I can get a machine. The school children are so in need of shoes and other clothing. Could you let me have discarded clothing for them, if so my daughter is a lovely hand to sew will be glad to make them over for them.

I know you have many many things we would be delighted to have to make over. I too have very little to get along with. Others would think they couldn't get along at all on what we do, but I'm so thankful that all are well. Please let me hear from you at once. Thanks for all favors will be so thankful for any and all things you can do.

Mrs. Arthur Dunn and children
Windsor, Missouri

P.S. The Maytag is a good washing machine it costs around $140. That is the kind I'd rather have but will be pleased with any just thought the Maytag a real reliable one.

[Six pages handwritten]

• • •

August 1, 1938

Mrs. Roosevelt, Dear Madam.

I am writing this letter asking for your help. I am eighty-five years of age, a widow, no children, four grand children: at the age of 54 my husband passed away. I took up nursing. I had one child, a son, married, had five children. During the flu epidemic my son died after three days illness, leaving the responsibility of raising the family on his oldest son aged seventeen just graduated from high school. Together we kept the other children in school. all finished with hopes of getting employment—then came **the depression no jobs.** I had to mortgage my home and worked until I was seventy five, then developed arthrytis.

When my oldest grandson and I decided to take out a government loan of $1,000 it would have worked out all right, but he developed T.B. and passed away in less than three years leaving the burden for me to carry. I did it until now. My grandchildren married and their husbands have lost out and I cannot pay the taxes and interest on the property and loan. I have lived here fifty-years and the government will take away my home if I do not pay the taxes which amount to one hundred and twenty dollars. **I cannot raise it** and I am asking you our first Lady of the land, will you please out of your abundence give me enough to pay the taxes for this year. I receive a pension of 30 dollars per month, which I send to the government to pay the loan. I have very few more years to live and I cannot bear to think of losing my home. It's just a small house needs lots of repairs but—it is **home.** I have heard so much of your kindness to poor people. I have put aside my pride and for the first time in my life ask for charity. Will you **please** help me. I can give references as to my honesty, hoping and praying

I am your friend of hope

Mrs. F. M. Vanderford

Carbondale, Pennsylvania

[Four pages handwritten]

August 1, 1938

My dear Mrs. Vanderford:

Mrs. Roosevelt and her secretary are away, and in their absence I have been asked to acknowledge their mail. I know Mrs. Roosevelt would wish me to express her regret that she could not do as you ask. Owing to the great number of appeals for financial assistance which come to her, she finds it impossible to help every worthy case brought to her attention. The money she has at her disposal for philanthropic purposes has already been pledged and allocated.

Very sincerely yours,
Administrative Officer
Social Correspondence

• • •

May 18, 1939

Mrs. Eleanora Rosvelt.
First Lady of the Land;
Dear Madam;

I am totally blind, with a wife and two children. For six years I have had a little stand on the street in front of 1815 7th St. N.W. which is not such a good location on account of so much competition. And during that time I have never missed a day. I have been exposed so much to the weather, that it is going against my health.

I have filed an application to the Vocational Rehabilitation Service for a stand in one of the Government Buildings, which there are thirteen Whites and no Colored. I was told by Mr. Sawyer that on account of my being colored, I could not succeed in getting in.

Knowing of your wonderfull work towards charity and also the blind, I am asking you to please give me aid in securing a stand in one of the Government Buildings.

Because of the great impression you have made among all people especially among our race, I feel happy to ask because I know you will do all in your power to assist me.

May God continue to bless you and your wonderfull

Husband, who I, myself characterize as Moses the second, who has so wonderfully, thus far led the people out of this great depression.

Your most humble servant,
Alexander Clarkson
Washington, D.C.

[One page typed]

June 6, 1939

Dear Mr. Clarkson:

Your letter of May 18th addressed to Mrs. Roosevelt has been referred to this Service for consideration and with request that we make reply.

As you know this Service has been interested in your case for many years and I personally assisted you in 1933 in securing your first stand concession in front of the Phyllis Wheatley Craft Shop for the Blind. Subsequent to that time I assisted you in securing your present concession and it is a matter of record that more recently Mr. Sawyer of our staff has been endeavoring to improve the concession which you now have. It is still our desire to do anything within our power to better your situation.

In your letter to Mrs. Roosevelt you made the statement that on account of your being colored Mr. Sawyer said that you could not be placed in a stand in a Government Building. Mr. Sawyer has denied making this statement and I desire to say that no such statement was ever made on authority from this Service. Such discrimination is not a part of the policy or practice of this Service and our records are the best proof of this assertion.

I regret that you have either deliberately or thoughtlessly made this prejudicial statement. We have many difficulties in establishing blind people in vending stands. Most important of all is the limitation of opportunities in this field which is well demonstrated by the fact that so far we have been able to open only thirteen stands and had to select the operators from a blind population far in excess of that number.

Very truly yours,
H. C. Corpening
Supervisor in Charge
Vocational Rehabilitation Services
for the District of Columbia

• • •

[Copy of attached Braille letter]

October 10, 1939

My dear Mrs. Roosevelt;

Knowing that you are interested in all humanity, I appeal to you for help.

Is there something that you can do to help extend the Braille Project? We have been informed that for a reason of overproduction, this project is to be terminated in an "orderly fashion."

As this is one of the few ways at which a blind person may earn a living, may I be justified in asking your aid?

Very gratefully yours,
Rita D. Oliviera
Works Progress Administration
New Bedford Braille Project
Room 208 Municipal Building
No. 17573
New Bedford, Massachusetts

[Copy of attached Braille letter]

Mrs. F. D. Roosevelt;

I appeal to you knowing you as a most gracious, sincere and undaunted crusader for the relief of the handicapped and underprivileged class.

My appeal is for a continuance of the Braille or Blind Project. I understand this project is to be discontinued in an orderly fashion as our libraries and blind institutions are flooded with uncalled for Braille Literature.

This project is now called non-productive. But I'm sure you can see where it can be made a most beneficial and productive project.

Sincerely yours

Clarkson Temple

New Bedford Braille Project

New Bedford, Massachusetts

October 19, 1939

My dear Colonel Harrington:

The enclosed letters from members of the Braille Project at New Bedford, Massachusetts, were received by Mrs. Roosevelt at Hyde Park. She asks whether there is justification for their fear that the project will soon be terminated.

Very sincerely yours,

Malvina Thompson

Secretary to Mrs. Roosevelt

November 2, 1939

Dear Miss Thompson:

This is to acknowledge your letter of October 19, 1939, to Colonel Harrington, enclosing letters from members of the Braille project at New Bedford, Massachusetts, concerning the closing of this project.

The continued eligibility of WPA Braille projects is now under consideration. We will notify you as soon as a definite decision has been made as to the operation of these projects.

Sincerely yours,

Florence Kerr

Assistant Commissioner

Federal Works Agency

Works Project Administration

Washington, D.C.

The Work Projects Administration, originally called the Works Progress Administration, employed the blind in its Braille project. They transcribed 1.1 million pages of material into Braille by the end of 1937. The advent of World War II, with the subsequent shift in the economy toward the production of war materiel, caused the gradual phasing out of all WPA programs by June 1943.

• • •

[Date-stamped October 31, 1939]

Mrs. Roosevelt:

kind lady just a few lines, I have been looking at your photo on the front page of the monthly book called **Life,** I thought about you 1st as being the 1st lady of the land.

2nd, as a wonderful wife.

3rd, as a model mother.

Mrs. Roosevelt I am asking a small favor of you, I hope that it isnt too much of me to ask of you.

As I am a poor presser in a blouse factory on Broadway, the season is very poor, there is no work at all and I am forced to go on the Social Security Ins. to collect a little money.

I filed my application but I was told that I had to wait a month before I could get my check.

And God above knows Mrs. Roosevelt I will be facing starvation with in a month, work this time of year is so hard to get, I have been picking up odd positions here and there just enough to pay my room rent and to eat or to keep the wolf away from the door.

Mrs. Roosevelt will you please for humanity's sake and for the sake of my poor dead mother open your heart and send me a **little money** just enough to hold me together until I get my check, please do, for God above knows I am in need of it.

I have a little Xmas saving's club but I can't get it until sometime in Nov. before Thanksgiving. I have a few friends but friends are no good without money, it takes money to live in this New York.

When the season opens in December I will send you a beautiful blouse to wear, send me your measure on this paper. I have no parents at all they are dead and I am trying to get along the best that I know how. Mrs. Roosevelt I have told you the absolute truth God knows I have. I saw you last year I believe coming out of the Metro Opera house on 39th and Broadway one afternoon.

Mrs. Roosevelt please for heaven's sake do not expose me, for I do not like notoriety, hoping to hear from you soon. May God bless you and your family especially the good President and his Mother.

Yours truly

Miss J. M.

c/o Pearl Richardson

New York, New York

[Three pages handwritten]

October 31, 1939

My dear Miss J.M.:

Mrs. Roosevelt and her secretary are away and in their absence I have been asked to acknowledge their mail. I know Mrs. Roosevelt would like to comply with your request but I am afraid it will not be possible for her to do so. So many people ask her for loans and financial aid that she is unable to accede to these appeals. I know that all the money she has to give has been pledged and allocated for some time to come.

I am sure Mrs. Roosevelt will deeply appreciate your kind offer to send her a blouse but she does not accept gifts except from her close personal friends. However, I know she would want me to thank you very much for your thoughtfulness.

Very sincerely yours,
Administrative Officer
Social Correspondence

• • •

[Telegram]

January 24, 1940

Mrs. Eleanor Roosevelt:

We recall with pleasure your personal visit to a meeting of the Massachusetts delegation to the Congress of Youth, held in New York last summer.

Your address to that Congress and the many pledges made by the Administration that youth shall not be a lost generation have been considered by us to be an assurance that the government would not shirk its responsibility to youth. For that reason the sharp reductions in expenditures for Social Security proposed in the president's

message at a time when billions are being spent for armaments are all the more shocking.

We cannot help but feel that we have been let down.

The President's proposal to reduce appropriations for
work relief by 500,000 WPA jobs, to dismiss 106,000
young people from NYA, and 65,000 young men from the
CCC is a sad blow to those who had hoped to see a contin-
uation and extension of those progressive policies that
assured for the New Deal the support of youth.

The tragic consequence of this policy is well drama-
tized by the case of Michael Virga. You may not know of
Michael Virga. He is a young Boston boy of 17, facing the
death penalty for killing a shopkeeper in an attempted rob-
bery. Michael was unemployed, could not get into the CCC
and lived with his widowed mother on their $6.65 from
welfare. This case must not symbolize the future of
America's 4,000,000 unemployed youth.

We believe that it is impossible to remain silent when
such a momentous issue confronts the whole nation. We
address this protest to you because we know you as a
friend of the youth movement and one in whom the young
people have placed great trust.

The President, as well as every other authority on
youth problems, has admitted in his annual message to
Congress, that this problem must be solved. To us it
seems obvious that the solution to this problem cannot
be found by any other means than the further expan-
sion of the present public works and relief programs,
and the passage of the American Youth Act,* and

---

*The American Youth Congress, the first mass student movement in United States history,
lobbied for passage of the American Youth Act, which would have provided supplementary
funds for the National Youth Administration, for the purpose of aiding low-income stu-
dents and unemployed youth. Congress never considered the bill, as all New Deal programs
faced the budget ax when federal money was being diverted to war preparation.

especially not by sacrificing social gains to military expenditures.

Therefore, we are supporting the American Youth Act, which was introduced in Congress today. We urge that you join us in this effort to help our generation.

Nathaniel Mills Jr., Chairman,
Alexander Karanikas, Executive Secretary
The Massachusetts Youth Council
Boston, Massachusetts

January 30, 1940

My dear Mr. Mills:

Your telegram of January 24 was received and Mrs. Roosevelt has given it to the President.

Very sincerely yours,
Malvina Thompson
Secretary to Mrs. Roosevelt

• • •

March 28, 1940

My dear Mrs. Roosevelt:

You may recall my letter of February to which you replied that you would like to be able to help me but could not think of anything to suggest. Thank you for your courteous consideration. I wonder if you would be willing to use your influence in helping me to secure one of several commissions to paint portraits for the government? Ex-President Hoover, Secretary Wallace of the Dept. of Agriculture, Dr. Charles Moore, former chairman of the Fine Arts Commission, and probably others are to be painted and it does seem to me that once in a while a deserving and capable person residing in Washington might be given some of this work.

Recently I learned that Secretary [Harold] Ickes had given Henry Hubbell of Florida seven or eight portraits to do for the Interior Department. This no doubt is his prerogative; one of those portraits, however, would have been helpful to a person struggling to uphold high ideals.

Last August I submitted reproductions of my work to Mr. Cammerer of the Arts Commission and wrote to Major Gilmore D. Clark, Chairman of the Art Commission, Senator Barkley, Chairman of the Joint Committee on the Library and Mr. Hoover. I have submitted reproductions of my work to Mr. Le Cron of Secretary Wallace's office and to Edward Bruce, Chief of the Federal Art Project, who informs me that he is only one of several members of the Commission and the best way to get portraits is through influential friends—of these I have few in the government.

I am enclosing some clippings in regard to past exhibitions of my work. I should be greatly obliged and grateful if you felt inclined to take further interest in this matter.

Yours faithfully,

S. B. Baker

Washington, D.C.

Note in pencil in Mrs. Roosevelt's writing: "F.D.R. This man they tell me is a good artist, but getting old. If there are portraits done in the Departments couldn't he be given one or two? I feel sorry for him. E.R."

[On notepaper of the White House, Washington, D.C.]

April 16, 1940

MEMORANDUM FOR WILLIAM H. McREYNOLDS

Will you look this up and see what we can do for the old boy?

F.D.R.

[On stationery of the White House, Washington, D.C.]

April 18, 1940

MEMORANDUM FOR THE PRESIDENT:

I attach your memorandum of April 16th, together with the correspondence you transmitted, concerning the possibility of securing a job of portrait painting for Mr. S. B. Baker, who had written Mrs. Roosevelt.

I have inquired of the Departments and the only tangible prospect so far developed is in Justice. The portrait of former Attorney General Murphy is yet to be painted, and so far as the Department knows, no arrangement has been made to secure this portrait. Justice expressed the willingness to pay the standard price of about $1,500 to Mr. Baker, if it would be satisfactory to Justice Murphy to have him do the work.

I am making further inquiries and will report any new prospects.

Wm. H. McReynolds

This was all returned with the note: "E.R. For your information. F.D.R."

• • •

April 2, 1940

Dear Mrs. Roosevelt:

I have long been one of your silent admirers and feel so keenly that you are carrying the torch for women's rights in the United States, that I am pressed to write to you and present my problem.

In a few months I shall become a mother and must therefore resign from my position with the Federal Communications Commission in another week or so, as it is not the policy of the Commission to grant maternity leave, although this is an exception and not the rule within the government departments. I have but a Grade 3 clerical job at the present time and feel confident that I can with my past experience of six years in the government service, easily obtain another Grade 3 position. However, there seems to be considerable resentment among my fellow employees, especially "we women," in regard to the Commission's policy of not granting maternity leave. In fact, I am besieged with requests not to hand in my resignation and see "what will happen."

I am told by Mr. John B. Reynolds, the personnel man who hired me as a clerk with the Commission, that it is the Commission's policy that I resign. The question that comes to mind is, who is the Commission? Is it the Commissioners themselves, or is it the Commissioners, plus the lawyers, engineers, and clerks that compose the Commission? Have the Commissioners themselves ever expressed any opinion as to granting maternity leave? The fact is, we women question where the Commission's policy originates.

Does it seem unfair to you that in most government departments, even in the WPA, maternity leave is granted, and the Commission should make an exception to this policy? Also, that maternity leave is granted within the Commission to women who have "influence." Also, that leave without pay is granted upon request for a number of reasons, even for disciplinary purposes, but not granted to women who have been given excellent efficiency ratings, who have been trained in clerical work with the Commission, but yet are forced to lose their jobs to have a child and to find employment in new surroundings later.

Dear Mrs. Roosevelt, how can "we women" bring pressure upon the Commission to change their policy and allow us to retain our jobs and be given a few months leave without pay?

Sincerely,
Agnes Taylor
License Clerk
Commercial License Unit of License Division
Federal Communications Commission

April 5, 1940

My dear Mrs. Taylor:

In the absence of Mrs. Roosevelt and her secretary I have been asked to acknowledge their mail. Your letter will be given to Mrs. Roosevelt at the first opportunity after her return to Washington.

Very sincerely yours,
Administrative Officer
Social Correspondence

• • •

May 13, 1940

Dear Mrs. Roosevelt:

I have a feeling I'll be taken for some crank or crackpot before your eyes have even read a few lines of this letter. I hope against hope this will not happen. The President and you our first Lady have done wonders in all types of reclaiming. That of twisted bodies, of slums, of the unemployed youth, of countless other wrecks, so many to mention. But there is one type of a wreck which you may not have heard of. I cannot really classify this type. I could call it a fool. That is the purpose of this letter to tell you of this case and to ask for help in solving my problem.

I am 31 years of age, my name is Albert Kentrus. Married to a good girl and we have two boys, Albert and Ronald. We have been married 9 years. Up until our youngest was born we had led normal lives. In fact all is still normal except myself. I have been working steady for 14 years at a firm called Joseph Hoover and Sons Co, 49th and Market St. Phila. I'm a paper cutter and in the last two years have earned $40 per week. In the past two years I have lost a little time at work but still made enough to live on. I think the thought of making 40 dollars per week made me feel rich and I felt I could do wonders with the money. I felt I could go out with the boys to card games. I began to go to a card game each Friday night. At first I was lucky, made money but then I began to lose and I didn't have the will power to stop. I felt I could get it all back.

We had a bank account of $400 I was able to draw on my own name. This I did until I had drawn all. I couldn't stop now, I kept on playing cards trying to get back my money. My wife found out what happened and we began to have bitter spats. I was ashamed but determined I'd get the money back and then we'd be back where we started. The last 2 years have been a nightmare to me. To my wife a living hell. She loves me and has tried to help me in all I asked of her. We found ourselves in debt. I borrowed money from the banks. But still blindly I kept gambling. I began to play the horses. I began to play a system that never worked. All along I still loved my wife and children and wanted to get on my feet. I began to talk to myself, calling myself all kinds of names for having put my family in such a fix. I finally stopped gambling but inside of me I feel like an old man. I feel broken with no hope of ever getting out of this. I'm carrying a debt that never seems to lighten. I don't know what to do. My wife doesn't realize how bad a fix I put ourselves in. If I could only boil it down to one valid debt which I could pay back at say ten dollars each month I could go back to a normal way of living. Perhaps you can show me what to do Mrs. Roosevelt. I know I must go on living for my family but because of my madness I find it hard to go on. It's a crushing debt and I'm lost. Can you show me the path Mrs. Roosevelt. Please consider.

With loyalty

Albert Kentrus

Philadelphia, Pennsylvania

[Six pages handwritten]

May 16, 1940

My dear Mr. Kentrus:

Mrs. Roosevelt asks me to acknowledge your letter and to say that she is sorry she does not know of any place from which you could borrow the money you need to pay up your various debts, unless you could get it from the Morris Plan Bank or the finance company with which you have already had dealings.

Very sincerely yours,

Malvina Thompson

Secretary to Mrs. Roosevelt

• • •

January 15, 1941

Dear Mrs. Roosevelt,

My father and my husband are to be sent to prison in a few days, and the stigma this will bring to my precious children gives me courage in my desperation, to write to you, yes, as busy as one in your position is.

Please, can't you do something to help us?

My husband and seventy-two year old father have been tried and convicted of misusing WPA funds, by starting the construction of a road which had been dedicated to Marion County, here in Indiana. The State Administrator of WPA, who had developed a keen dislike for my husband, had the investigators build up this case against him on the theory that the road was not within the legal limitations of the blanket county road project.

My husband, Carl F. Kortepeter, was the WPA Co-ordinator of Marion County in Indiana. He directed the many projects which employed as high as 18,000 men. His only thought was to find places to put these men to work.

My father, Guerney G. Derbyshire, owned the land adjacent to the right of way on which the road was started. (Only about a thousand feet of highway was involved.)

Long before my husband was the chief administrator, the same kind of work had been done, and it has been done since his resignation. No question was raised as to the legality of such work until after my husband had resigned from WPA.

The finance division, over which my husband had no authority whatsoever, was responsible for work done within the scope of this project. That division passed and paid all payrolls without any question or objection to the work, which was later to be declared illegal.

This was the "crime" for which my husband has been sentenced for eighteen months in the federal reformatory. He is the sole support of myself and our four children, Max and Paul, eleven and twelve, Nancy Lee, six, and Martha, the baby. My father, perhaps because of his advanced years, received a lighter sentence, twelve months in prison.

In addition to the prison term each one has been fined

$1000. Many people here believe that these men, who are so dear to me, are being used as public examples. WPA here in Indiana, does seem to have a bad reputation, and evidently the Courts believe that the conviction of these two men will satisfy the people and smooth things over.

In the name of our children I write to you. What is in store for us? My children need their father. The debts and disgrace has broken the health and spirits of my father and my husband too, for this constant aching worry has been almost more than they can bear. Many of our former "friends" now avoid us, and our two older children suffer much embarrassment at school.

Thousands come to you, Mrs. Roosevelt, with their troubles and heartaches. I know you cannot help them all, and I have been a long time gathering courage to write to you. Today, these two Bible verses keep running through my mind, and they help make it possible for me to try to reach you.

"Bear ye one another's burdens" and

"There is a Power who cares."

Can't you, won't you, intercede with the President to grant these two men a pardon?

Their whole biography has been full of public service and kindness to others. Justice has failed us, perhaps mercy can still help us to pick up the pieces of our shattered lives and keep our home together.

Thanking you humbly and prayerfully,

Olive Kortepeter (Mrs. Carl)

Southport, Indiana

[Two pages typed]

February 3, 1941

Mr. Howard Hunter
To investigate.
E.R.

[Date-stamped Febuary 7, 1941]

My dear Mrs. Roosevelt:

The letter addressed to you by Mrs. Olive D. Kortepeter under date of January 15, 1941, is returned herewith.

You are advised that upon the filing of the complaint alleging the illegal use of Government funds to improve private property in Marion County, Indiana, the Division of Investigation of this Administration conducted an inquiry to determine the truth or falsity of the report.

The investigation disclosed that Carl F. Kortepeter, then WPA Coordinator for Marion County, Indiana, had directed the use of WPA labor, materials and equipment to construct streets and roads through a private subdivision owned by his father-in-law, Guerney G. Derbyshire, in order to enhance the value of this real estate. Both men were prosecuted and found guilty in December 1939 of conspiracy to divert WPA funds and labor. Mr. Kortepeter was sentenced to eighteen months in a Federal penitentiary, while his father-in-law received a sentence of a year and a day in the penitentiary. This conviction was appealed by both defendants and their appeal was denied.

Mr. Derbyshire was committed on January 25, 1941, after the United States Supreme Court had refused to review the conviction of himself and Mr. Kortepeter, but the latter was granted a stay of execution in order that he might appear for trial in another case in which he is charged, jointly with two other persons, of conspiring to defraud the United States by diverting WPA labor and WPA funds for the improvement of a private subdivision owned by the Eickhoff Realty Company and Charles E. Jefferson, the trial of which was initiated last month and is still in progress.

There is also pending against Mr. Kortepeter a third indictment charging similar offenses in connection with a private subdivision owned by Arthur F. Brown, president of the Union Trust Company of Indianapolis, and Miss E. C. Claypool, owner of adjoining property.

The diversion of Federal funds in the cases in which Mr. Kortepeter is involved amounts to more than one hundred thousand dollars.

Very truly yours,
Howard O. Hunter
Acting Commissioner of Works Project
Federal Works Agency
Works Projects Administration
1734 New York Ave., N.W.
Washington, D.C.

• • •

May 10, 1941

Dear Mrs. Roosevelt:

Please pardon me for the intrusion, by writing this letter to you. Many sleepless nights of worry, and getting my nerves together, gave me the strength to put my plea before you, because I know you have a kind and noble heart, so I feel that even when I will not get result, at least I will get a hearing from you.

Years before I was a prosperous business man, when I lost all I had, being an educated white collar man, and gray haired, I was not able to land on a position, and I was forced to get on the WPA roll. Thanks to our great president, whose kind heart to the poor created this great institution, I been on the roll 3 years, and done some white collar jobs with the satisfaction of my superiors. However all my desire was to rehabilitate myself, and at last by my continuous persistence I got a job, with the San Mateo County Health Department, Redwood City, Calif. I get a monthly salary about $105 average. From this money I have to pay rent. $35 per month and support my family, one sick wife and a son, who is visiting the San Mateo Junior College, not 18 years old, and just passed a federal Civil Service Examination as a third grade commercial radio man.

From my first wife I had another son, who not being 18 years of age, when the First World War started, he enlisted in the American Army, 23 Infantry Regiment Company E, Brooklyn, N.Y. and he was killed in France and is buried near Soisson. My family and myself are well known in the community where we live, and respected. We are of the policies of our dear, good president, who in my opinion, the greatest president we ever had and whose name will go down in history, as a wise and great leader and humanitarian. I wrote to the White House several times and I value the answers I received as the greatest assets I possess.

I advanced all these formalities Mrs. Roosevelt to introduce myself, as I have a great favor to ask from you, if it is not very inconvenient. The request I lay for your kind attention. During the last 5 to 6 years, I was not able and at present time I am not able to buy myself a suit. My suit is getting very worn and shabby, so that I feel bad sometimes to appear in my office, if I will not be able to get hold of a suit. Here, on account I work daily, I cannot turn to any charitable institution. So I ask you dear Mrs.

Roosevelt, if you have any friend, who could spare a second hand suit size 42, no matter what color, only as long as it has no holes in it. I would thank you a million times by doing so, as from my little income I cannot put enough money to side to buy one. I advance that I do not wish or accept any cash money, just a suit and if I could get one, it would make a very happy man out of me.

As for reference, I refer you to my superior officer, Major Dr. Charles C. Gans, who is one of the finest, kindest superior officers any American can have, who has a great many years of military training and who will give you all the necessary information in regard to my person.

May I beg you kindly, to handle my request in a confidential way, I am afraid it would hurt me much in my standing if it would come out, that I asked any assistance from you, Mrs. Roosevelt.

Trust you will find out the true side of my present situation. Please forgive me Mrs. Roosevelt, and I am with a million thanks to you.

Yours very sincerely

Mr. L.

Redwood City, California

[One page typed]

• • •

July 22, 1941

Dear Mrs. Roosevelt:

I know that because you are a person constantly before the public you must receive many letters of complaint, pleas for aid, and those who are simply interested in being heard. I know of several people who have written you in the sincere belief that you could help them; I am writing this in the hope that through one of your media you may be able to help me and those who, through no fault of their own, find themselves outcastes of employment agencies— former Works Projects Administration workers.

Several years ago, like many others my family suffered financial reverses, and we accepted FERA work—but not relief. I have supported my father who is an arrested tuberculosis case and assisted in my mother's support through wages received from WPA work. From November of 1938 to June of 1941 I was fortunate to be on the Administrative Staff, first as Stenographer and later as Occupational Interviewer, receiving when I left $1,440 a year. My record for this period has been excellent, I was dropped from the payroll through no fault of my own and was thankful that I had been permitted to hold the job as long as I had; I desired to try my luck in private industry.

I started July 1, making a tour of every agency handling stenographic, clerical and typing requisitions. The interviewers show their interest in my appearance, my ability to operate a typewriter, stenography and my ambition to continue college even if it meant working at night; yet they are sorry that they can do nothing for me because I have worked for the Works Projects Administration and I will not lie about my work history. I am not ashamed of my work and refuse to live in constant terror that someone might find out that whatever experience I do claim is only a forgery.

I am 26 years of age, white, of good parentage, have good training and good educational background; I am attending Columbia with money saved over a period of five years in order to learn stenotypy—yet I cannot get a job in New York, unless I lie, because I have worked on the WPA. I know of many like myself.

I am not asking for favors or help, nor is this a crank letter—it is the first I have ever written a public personage, but if you could offer me any suggestions I would so very much appreciate your kindness.

Respectfully yours,
Miss Edith Canepa
Woodside, New York

July 24, 1941

My dear Miss Canepa:

Mrs. Roosevelt asks me to acknowledge your letter of July 22. She will try to help you, but it is so difficult for her to find employment for all who write her that she is sorry it is not possible to give you any definite assurance as to a position.

Very sincerely yours,
Malvina Thompson
Secretary to Mrs. Roosevelt

July 24, 1941

Mrs. Florence Kerr
Assistant Commissioner
Work Projects Administration
Federal Works Agency
Washington, D.C.

Dear Mrs. Kerr:

Mrs. Roosevelt asks me to send you the enclosed letter from Miss Edith Canepa, of Woodside, New York. Will you please let Mrs. Roosevelt know whether anything can be done to help Miss Canepa?

Very sincerely yours,
Malvina Thompson
Secretary to Mrs. Roosevelt

August 2, 1941

Dear Miss Thompson:

This is in reply to your letter of July 24, 1941, enclosing a letter from Miss Edith Canepa, of Woodside, New York, in regard to her difficulty in finding private employment due to the fact that she has worked for the Work Projects Administration.

I find that Miss Canepa's record has recently been forwarded to the Washington Office as a possible employee on our administrative staff here. She will be given every consideration once our reductions have been completed and vacancies begin to come up through regular turnover.

Miss Canepa's difficulties in finding private employment in New York City, and her attributing these difficulties to the fact that she has been employed by WPA, is a familiar story from New York City, and to a lesser degree from other parts of the country. It is, I think, a story which has a real foundation. Miss Canepa's suggestion that Mrs. Roosevelt help these workers seems to me a good one. Some eight and one-half million Americans have found temporary public employment on WPA during the past six years. Their abilities and talents represent a pretty good cross section of the American public, and there is no reason why they should be rebuffed by private employers and not considered on their merits as other workers.

Perhaps a discussion of the point in "My Day" would help.

Sincerely yours,
Florence Kerr, Assistant Commissioner
Federal Works Agency
Work Projects Administration
1734 New York Avenue, N.W.
Washington, D.C.

In her "My Day" column of August 15, 1941, Mrs. Roosevelt began: "I have just received a letter which, in itself, would not be so significant, but taken together with various other reports reaching me, is very disquieting.

I am quoting it here approximately as it is written, changing only such things as might identify the writer. [Quotes Edith Canepa's letter.] She then sums up Florence Kerr's letter by quoting the next to last paragraph.

August 18, 1941

Miss Malvina Thompson
Secretary to Mrs. Roosevelt
Hyde Park, New York
My dear Miss Thompson:

I am attaching hereto a clipping covering Mrs. Roosevelt's column of August 15, 1941, which concerns a letter she received from a former WPA worker in New York City. My secretary telephoned the White House to learn the name of the writer of the letter and was informed that Mrs. Roosevelt's mail was in your possession at Hyde Park.

If Mrs. Roosevelt will furnish the name and address of the young lady, I should like very much to offer her employment with the Washington Office of the Work Projects Administration. We are having some difficulty in securing competent stenographers and I feel sure we can use someone with the qualifications and experience the young lady mentions.

Sincerely,
Howard O. Hunter
Commissioner of Works Project
Federal Works Agency
Work Projects Administration
1734 New York Avenue, NW.
Washington, D.C.

August 20, 1941

Dear Mr. Hunter:

The young woman whom Mrs. Roosevelt mentioned in her column of August 15 is

Miss Edith Canepa
Woodside, New York.

Her record is, I understand from Mrs. Kerr, on file in the Washington office.

Mrs. Roosevelt will be delighted, I know, to hear that you can offer Miss Canepa a job and will be most grateful to you for your interest and help.

Very sincerely yours,
Malvina Thompson
Secretary to Mrs. Roosevelt

September 12, 1941

My dear Miss Canepa:

I have been advised by Mr. Howard Hunter's office in the Works Projects Administration that you accepted a position with them on September 4th, and that you are scheduled to report on September 15th.

Very sincerely yours,
Malvina Thompson
Secretary to Mrs. Roosevelt

• • •

Mrs. Roosevelt unfailingly looked at the bright side of life, as evidenced by an article entitled "The Bright Side of the Depression." In the article she highlights the achievements of the alphabet agencies of the New Deal, mentioning the many new parks, swimming pools, and reforestation areas as "bright spots in the depression gloom." Then she turns her focus inward:

"Now for the personal things we have gained. It seems to me that as individuals we have more character because we faced the depression, met our problems and solved them, because we were obliged to try new things, to use our ingenuity, to take our courage in both hands and take advantage of anything which the government offered. None of the government's plans would have succeeded if the people had not made them succeed. In the last analysis we were responsible for our own solution. We were pioneering again for our homes and our country just as surely as our great-grandfathers did. . . . Out of the depression has come to both young and old, I think, a greater ability to meet life and conquer it. With it has perhaps come the realization that man must have faith in the future, faith in himself, faith in some kind of Divine Providence which is willing to help those who help themselves."

Part Three

The War Years

L ong before the Japanese attack on Pearl Harbor on December 7, 1941, President Roosevelt had clearly annunciated how much he hated war: "I have seen war. I have seen war on land and sea, I have seen blood running from the wounded . . . I have seen the dead in the mud. I have seen cities destroyed . . . I have seen children starving. I have seen the agony of mothers and wives. I hate war." In her autobiography Mrs. Roosevelt made her position on the subject clear: "I imagine every mother felt as I did when I said good-bye to the children during the war. I had a feeling that I might be saying good-bye for the last time. . . . At the time of the First World War I felt keenly that I wanted to do everything possible to prevent future war, but I never felt it in the same way that I did during World War II. During this second war period I identified myself with all the other women who were going through the same slow death, and I kept praying that I might be able to prevent a repetition of this stupidity called war. . . . The horrible consciousness of waste and feeling of resentment burned within me as I wondered why men could not sit down around a table and settle their differences before an infinite number of the youth of many nations had to suffer."

As could be expected, the advent of war caused the content of Mrs. Roosevelt's mail to change greatly. However, the change was gradual, as the United States moved slowly to a war footing even before the attack on Pearl Harbor. As early as 1938 frantic families asked her aid in saving relatives fleeing from Hitler's invading armies. Mrs. Roosevelt could have assumed from her correspondence that everyone dealing with the armed forces was unhappy; after all, she seldom got mail from happy people. She heard from men in the armed services who wanted to get out, or at least to get a furlough, as well as from those who could not join the military, usually because of health problems, who wanted to get in. She received letters from men who wanted a different military job or station, men who were AWOL begging for advice, and even from those in military stockades, imploring her that their sentences be reduced. She referred such mail to the Morale Branch of the War Department, explaining that efforts on her part to interrupt the chain of command would do more harm than good.

During the war, African-Americans in their segregated units were expected to sacrifice themselves for a country that did not treat them as equals. Many women wished to be active participants in the war effort, as members of the newly formed WACs (Women's Army Corps), WAVES (Women Accepted for Voluntary Emergency Service), and WASPs (Women Airforce Service Pilots). Mrs. Roosevelt worked to assist minorities and women in taking their place as equals in the fight for freedom then raging. As the war years dragged on, Mrs. Roosevelt faced the painful task of communicating with family members of men who were missing in action or being held as prisoners of war, as well as those who had given their lives for their country.

During World War II Mrs. Roosevelt traveled to England, throughout the Pacific, and in the Caribbean visiting thousands of soldiers, especially the wounded in hospitals. She welcomed the opportunity to meet with them, so she could see not only what the war looked like close up, but also observe how the servicemen were being treated. Her care and concern for each individual revealed itself during her Caribbean trip, when she received countless letters from mothers, wives, sweethearts, and sisters begging her to see their menfolk. She took with her a card file filled with the names and identification numbers of the men she'd been asked to look up, and did visit with them, writing not only to their families back home upon her return but also to the families of countless other soldiers and sailors she had met on her travels.

Mrs. Roosevelt's 1943 trip to the Pacific, an active war zone, remained top secret until she was well on her way. Her "My Day" column of August 17, 1943, began: "This column is being written on the plane just before reaching San Francisco. I am about to start on a long trip which I hope will bring to many women in the U.S. a feeling that they have visited the places where I go and that they know more about the lives their boys are leading. I am going for the Red Cross on this trip, because I found in Great Britain that if you wanted to talk with the boys you had to catch them in their moments of ease and many of those moments are spent in Red Cross Clubs. In addition I want to visit as many of our hospitals as possible, and there again the Red Cross uniform is a familiar sight. . . . I hope that our soldiers and sailors and marines wherever I see them will know how much I appreciate this opportunity to bring them a greeting from their Commander in Chief, and how deeply interested I am in them and their achievements."

The First Lady's "My Day" column dated "August 27th, on plane going to New Zealand," gives the flavor of her trip: "Night before last we reached one of the largest islands we have visited. We had to circle for a time before landing and then change to another plane for a short hop before reaching our final destination, which was great luck for me as the group to which the pilots on this short hop belonged have now made me an honorary member of their organization. Yesterday morning I breakfasted at seven and at eight we started on our rounds and visited two hospitals during the morning. We went to the Rest Camp the Red Cross runs for officers in an old plantation which they have done over and somehow made livable by dint of endless work and ingenuity. Another hospital and one camp in the afternoon and finally a visit to the Red Cross club for enlisted personnel where as many as 8,000 men visit every day. Late in the afternoon at an informal reception I met local government officials and some more officers among them one of my cousins, Commander W. S. Cowles whom I had not even known was in this vicinity. Now I have given you a day's itinerary, and I can begin to tell you some of the things you must want to know and I want to tell you." She then described how well the army and navy nurses were meeting the ever-present challenges of patient care, in which most soldiers suffered from malaria rather than from wounds. She praised the military hospitals that were "manned largely by reserve and volunteer doctors, dentists, surgeons, psychiatrists, many of them the best men to be found in the professions." While Mrs. Roosevelt clearly hoped to reassure those at home of the care and attention their loved ones received, she also couldn't resist the opportunity to mention "a pretty jaunty little lady who lunched with me who flies the transport planes that bring the men in from the front," reminding her audience of the important contributions women made daily in the war.

Regarding her Pacific trip she wrote: "I was always a little sorry when the boys were called together and had to stand in the sun while I made a short speech, because I knew how they hated that. The chance conversations in a Red Cross room, or in a mess hall or in a hospital, I always hoped had some interest for them, and I carried away an endless number of names of mothers, wives, sweethearts and sisters to whom to send messages when I got home. The story has been told—and it is true—of how after my return I telephoned one girl in Washington and told her who I was and that I had a message from her fiancé. She said: 'Don't be funny. Who do you think you're fooling?' and refused to believe that the call was genuine until I sent her a little note."

Mrs. Roosevelt felt especially strongly about the wounded, realizing that while these men were fortunate to be alive, their futures would inevitably be limited to the extent they had to deal with amputated limbs, severe burns, and other disabling injuries. She not only felt keenly the sacrifice these men and women had made for the country, but realized as well the obligation of America in return. If their sacrifice was not to be in vain, all possible steps needed to be taken toward long-lasting peace and freedom.

—CDK

The War Years

November 3, 1937

Dear Mrs. Roosevelt:

One wonders with what feelings, if any, you read of yesterday's mass murder of school children at Lerida by the
criminals with whom the United States, through the
present administration of the neutrality act, is cooperating
in an invasion of the Spanish Republic. Perhaps this news
recalled to your mind the reported sayings of the person
named Mussolini who was recently blackballed as an
habitual murderer in Hollywood but entertained at the
White House, that war is a glorious sport. If that saying is
true, what joy the Roosevelt administration has brought to
that person's brother and to the other Italian fascists in
Spain by refusing to permit the legal, representative
Spanish Government to buy American munitions to defend
itself against invasion, by making such munitions available
to the invaders, by restraining the American Red Cross
from its obvious duty in a friendly republic's time of

trouble, and, finally, by making it impossible for anyone in the United States to offer a refuge here to any of Spain's incredibly wronged children.

Very sincerely yours,
Jean Kerr
Portland, Oregon

[One page typed]

The Spanish Civil War (1936-1939) between the government of the Second Republic and the fascist forces led by Francisco Franco, resulted in many civilian deaths on both sides of the conflict. Franco's military, under his direction, executed thousands of Spaniards during the war and the early years of his regime, which lasted until his death in 1975.

• • •

December 15, 1939

Dear Mrs. Roosevelt:

I am turning to you in a matter which is so close to my heart that I feel justified in ignoring conventionalities and addressing you by letter. I discussed this move with my friend Emma Bugbee, also of the **Herald Tribune,** and she has not discouraged me. The point in question is to rush immigration to the United States of my mother and sister.

I am German born and of Jewish faith. I was assistant correspondent of the N.Y. **Herald Tribune** Berlin bureau from 1926 until the end of 1938 when I emigrated to your hospitable country. I had this measure in mind since 1933 but had postponed it again and again on behalf of my old mother with whom I lived and whom I supported. The idea of taking her along and uprooting a woman of 83 seemed preposterous, on one hand; on the other hand I thought I might be able to spare her, at her age, a life-long separation from me. But when things came to a climax late in 1938 I decided to go, after all, and leave my mother in the care of my sister. I took my first papers out early this year. In March I forwarded an affidavit for my mother and sister to the American Consulate General in Berlin, and they registered their application for immigration visas there.

Unfortunately their registration numbers are so high that it seems it will take several years for them to be considered. In view of this situation I had tried to arrange for them to go to England temporarily; I have good reason to believe that the British Home Office was going to issue their permit early in September—when the war broke out and frustrated this plan. Meanwhile, as you may know, the German Government has intensified their measures against Jewish citizens. According to reports from Berlin they plan to evacuate all Jews from Germany, also from the old parts of the Reich, and send them to a desolate region of the former Polish territory, under desolate and disgraceful conditions, with their place of destination unknown to themselves and their families. Old people would be left behind in Jewish homes for aged people, it is said, which is not much of a consolation considering that in the fall of 1938 homes of this kind were raided and the inhabitants driven on the streets.

The idea of having my sister exposed to the abominable conditions in that so called Jewish reservation, and of the uncertain fate in store for my mother is like a nightmare to me. There are thousands of more or less similar cases. But I think that this individual case differs from the others because, although I avoid signing my stories, the German Propaganda Ministry knows, of course, of my affiliation with the **Herald Tribune;** and I feel that in view of the papers' anti-nazi editorials since September, my family is in an extraordinarily exposed position and the Nazis are quite capable of "taking it out" on them.

In view of this desperate situation I venture to appeal to you, dear Mrs. Roosevelt, asking you from all my heart to take an interest in the case. If you can help me to hurry immigration proceedings for my people I shall be ever so grateful to you; if you find you cannot I feel certain that from the kindness of your heart you will understand my motives and not consider this letter an imposition, but for-give me for having taken up your time and attention for which I am duly thankful.

Please accept my deepest thanks for having allowed me to put my case before you.

Yours very sincerely,
Julie Rothschild
New York Herald Tribune

[One and a half pages typed]

December 21, 1939

My dear Miss Rothschild:

Mrs. Roosevelt is very sorry to hear about your mother and sister and knows how distressed you must be over their situa-tion. She has referred your letter to the State Department, which is all she can do in cases of this kind, and is sure that every pos-sible aid under the law will be given your family.

Very sincerely yours
Malvina Thompson
Secretary to Mrs. Roosevelt

December 21, 1939

My dear Mr. Welles:

Mrs. Roosevelt would appreciate it if you would write Miss Rothschild, whose letter is enclosed, as to what, if anything, can be done to help her family.

Very sincerely yours,
Malvina Thompson
Secretary to Mrs. Roosevelt

December 28, 1939

My dear Miss Thompson

I have your communication of December 21, 1939, transmitting the enclosed letter from Miss Julie Rothschild of the *New York Herald Tribune* concerning the cases of her mother and sister whom she wishes to bring to the United States from Germany.

The cases of Miss Rothschild's relatives as well as many others which have come to the attention of the Department are very appealing. Unfortunately, however, there is nothing that may be done under the existing laws and regulations to expedite the issuance of visas to them.

Miss Rothschild's letter indicates that she is not a citizen of the United States and therefore is not eligible to file a petition for her mother. The parents of American citizens are entitled to preference under the law but no special provision is made for the parents of alien residents of this country or for sisters. As non-preference applicants, Miss Rothschild's mother and sister will have to await their turns within the non-preference category of the quota of their native country according to the dates of their registrations which I understand were made last March. On the basis of such registrations I fear that it will still be a considerable period of time before they may expect to receive final action on their pending applications.

I regret exceedingly that I am unable to offer any suggestions with a view to expediting action on the cases of Miss Rothschild's relatives but I assure you that their cases will be accorded final consideration as soon as the circumstances permit and that all evidence submitted in support of their applications will be carefully examined. The consular officer handling their applications is, as you know, responsible for ascertaining the facts pertaining to the applicants and for taking proper action on their cases.

Sincerely yours,
Sumner Wells
Undersecretary of State
Department of State
Washington, D.C.

January 2, 1940

My dear Miss Thompson:
I received your kind letter of December 22 and also copy of a State Department letter dealing with the cases of my relatives. As things are there is nothing for me to do but to wait and hope for the best.

May I ask you to transmit my very sincere thanks to Mrs. Roosevelt for having given her benevolent attention to the matter? I appreciated it very much indeed. And please accept my very best thanks for all the trouble you took on my behalf.

Sincerely yours,
Julie Rothschild
New York Herald Tribune

In 1951 Eleanor Roosevelt visited Israel, interested in seeing how the country dealt with the mass of Jewish immigrants pouring in from all over the world. She asked Ruth Gruber, who in 1944 had accompanied one

(Above) Eleanor Roosevelt on the U.S.S. *Sequoia*, working on her correspondence.

All photos courtesy Franklin D. Roosevelt Presidential Library, unless otherwise indicated.

EARL SMITH
BOX 228
TRAVERSE CITY,
MICH.

DEC 16 1937

Mrs. President Roosevelt:

I am writing this letter to you because of three reasons.

First: Because I saw in a newspaper that you personally read much of your correspondence; and I failed to believe this but hoped it was true.

Second: Because I wanted to express my appreciation for the fine part you did in appearing on Kate Smith's program last Thursday evening. I enjoyed the story of the department store girl & had to chuckle at the pronunciation you gave to "chiffon". Not that it was incorrect. But just different. I liked you a lot for appearing, though!

Third:
            Because I want to ask your advice on a serious problem that

(Above) A typical letter sent to Eleanor Roosevelt, dated December 16, 1937.

(Above) Eleanor Roosevelt and her secretaries at the White House. Her social secretary, Edith Helm is standing, and her private secretary, Malvina Thompson Scheider is on the right.

(Above) Homeless man crouching in doorway. During the Depression almost one out of two U.S. households endured underemployment. Lack of income forced many, including the elderly, to a life on the streets.

(Above) Children of Rural Rehabilitation Client, on a plantation in Arkansas.

(Above) Migrants from Oklahoma, looking for work in the California pea fields, 1935.

(Top) Farmer and sons walking in the face of a dust storm, April 1936.

(Bottom) Eleanor Roosevelt visits a Works Progress Administration project to convert a city dump into a water front park, Des Moines, Iowa, June 8, 1936.

(Above) Eleanor Roosevelt visits a Works Progress Administration nursery school, Des Moines, Iowa, June 8, 1936.

(Above) Eleanor Roosevelt, observing conditions first hand during her visit to San Juan, Puerto Rico, March 1934. She asked to be shown areas such as this street, and gathered a crowd of observers on the way. **Courtesy AP/Wide World Photos.**

(Top) Mail comes by "Pony Express" to men of an antiaircraft crew in Saar Valley, Germany, March 16, 1945.

(Bottom) Eleanor Roosevelt eating lunch with G.I.s, Australia, Sept. 9, 1943.

(Above) September 1942, gasoline rationing: the busiest spot on the Pennsylvania Turnpike. Eastbound motorists stop at this service station because it's the last chance to fill up before entering the gas-rationed area.

(Above) The six plane factories of the Douglas Aircraft Company have been termed an industrial melting pot, since men and women of 58 national origins work side by side in pushing America's plane output. Miss Amanda Smith is employed in the Long Beach Plant of the Douglas Aircraft Company.

(Above) May 1942, the tradition of Betsy Ross is being kept alive in this quarter-master corps depot where a young woman worker assists in the creation of American flags for military activities.

(Above) September 30, 1944, Eleanor Roosevelt visits Emergency Refugee Center at Fort Ontario, Oswego, New York, where 982 refugees from war-torn Europe found haven. They shipped out of Naples, Italy, aboard the *Henry Gibbins*, in a convoy shadowed by German U-boats. Elinor Morgenthau, wife of Secretary of the Treasury Henry Morgenthau, is in flowered hat behind Eleanor, who's signing autographs after a service at the camp synagogue.

(Above) She's a mother and a grandmother, she works at a U.S. Arsenal tapering
shells for 50 mm anti-aircraft guns and she loves listening to news broadcasts.
Eva Smuda, 55, who came to America from Poland at the age of 3, has one son
in the Army, and a son, a daughter, and a son-in-law working with her at the
Frankford Arsenal. March 1942.

(Above) Eleanor Roosevelt at the Gila River, Arizona, Japanese Relocation Center, April 23, 1943.

thousand survivors of the Holocaust to a temporary refuge in the United States, to show her around. After visiting a refugee camp, Ms. Gruber reports, "[s]he [Mrs. Roosevelt] suddenly looked sad. 'Is anything wrong?' I asked her. 'I wish I had done more for the Jews.' I put my hand on hers. 'You did whatever you could. Government policy did not make refugees our top priority. Nearly every leader in Washington insisted, First, we must win the war. Then we can take care of the refugees. They didn't realize that if they waited there might not be any refugees to take care of.' She shook her head. 'I should have done more.' "

• • •

June 14, 1940

My dear Mrs. Roosevelt:

Among my circle of acquaintances there has been a great deal of thought and conversation given to the plight of children in war-torn Europe. Unfortunately, thought and conversation of this type usually comes to no action, due to a lack of unity and coordination.

We feel, however, that if you, as a leader of thought among women in America, were to give this some thought in your column "My Day," some organization against which people can have no prejudice, might arise.

Sincerely yours,
Jean Bevan
New York, New York

June 19, 1940

My dear Miss Bevan:

I was glad to have your letter and I appreciate your interest.

The question of taking refugee children is of grave concern to many people. Congress has been asked to take up the question, as it requires legislation, and the State Department and Congress are working together on it.

As soon as a policy is formulated, we can call together all people interested, both individuals and groups, to carry out whatever is decided, but until the government acts there is nothing individuals can do.

I have this question very much at heart and will do all I can.

Very sincerely yours,

Eleanor Roosevelt

Many schemes for the rescue of refugees were promoted in the early years of the war. In February 1940, the Alaskan Development Bill was introduced in Congress by Representative Frank Havenner, a Democrat from California, and Senator William H. King, a Democrat from Utah, assuming that Alaska could easily absorb refugees. Top Alaskan officials, as well as the U.S. State Department, remained adamantly opposed to any such plan. This and similar bills never made it out of committee, with the result that European refugees found no haven in the United States during World War II.

• • •

July 15, 1940

My dear Mrs. Roosevelt:

I am writing you in regard to the refugee problem which is confronting us in the U.S. at the present time. I, like lots of Americans, am deeply interested in this matter. I do not believe that we should assume the responsibility of caring for England's refugees. If she didn't have Canada and Australia to look to it would be a little different. In view of this fact, I think we should turn to our own destitute in America, and all of these people who have so much to offer foreigners, help some of our own orphanages. They sure could use some extra cash. I believe that "Charity begins at home."

Any country that has faced a depression for ten years and still has ten million unemployed, certainly doesn't have any business looking for aliens to care for. We cannot any more afford to enter this war in sympathy than with arms. If we do we are going to pay the price.

I am for tightening down on the Immigration Law. In my estimation that is just as important as any preparedness program.

What we need most of all is more red blooded Americans who can stand on two feet and demand that in this country Americans come first. That's just the trouble right now, there are too many aliens holding jobs that Americans should have.

I am not a crank as you might suspect, but just one honest to goodness American who is sick and disgusted with this foreign element in the good old U.S.A.

More power to you in your work for Americans, I am,

Respectfully yours,

Mrs. J. Barngrover.

LaVerne, California

• • •

July 17, 1940

My dear Mrs. Roosevelt:

Earlier this week a group of American men in the Philippines sent a cable to Secretary Hull and a number of women felt that they would like to send you the similar one which follows:

WE HAVE JUST CABLED SECRETARY HULL REQUESTING SUPPORT FOR BRITAIN ON THE BURMA ROAD AND A STRONG ATTITUDE ON THE FORMOSAN CONSULATE AND SHANGHAI MARINES QUESTIONS. THOUGH

UNINTENDED BY THE PRESIDENT, WE BELIEVE HIS STATEMENT OF THE
SIXTH INSTANT REGARDING THE MONROE DOCTRINE IS INCREASING
THE AGGRESSIVE JAPANESE ATTITUDE. KNOWING YOUR COURAGE, WE
REQUEST YOU TO PUBLICIZE THE PLEA OF THE WOMEN OF THE ORIENT
FOR COURAGE IN MEETING AGGRESSION. THIS MAY BE THE LAST
CHANCE. IF CHINA FALLS, OUR ONLY FRIENDS ARE GONE AND THE
WORST MAY HAPPEN HERE.

After securing several scores of signatures but before the actual cable went off to you, Secretary [of State Cordell] Hull's fine statement against the closing of the Burma Road reached us by UP wire, and so we did not send you the cable.

But we do want you to hear by this Clipper mail[*] of the sentiment among American women here in the Philippines against any form of appeasement toward Japanese aggression. The results in Europe of the appeasement policy have been all too apparent to leave any shred of hope that a similar policy might be effective in the Far East.

American women, of whatever political affiliation, have learned to look to you as an unofficial helper in high places. May we count on you to make whatever use possible of our humble petition as you meet American women on the other side of the Pacific, whether it be through your column, through your platform addresses, or through your personal conversations? Other threats to the American Way of life will doubtless arise in the not too distant future and then we trust that you will release parts or all of our most sincere petition.

---

* Pan American World Airways China Clippers inaugurated intercontinental airmail service in 1935. The planes flew from San Francisco to Manila via Honolulu, Midway, Wake, and Guam. The graceful planes were named after the far-ranging sailing ships of the nineteenth century.

For your taking such a splendid part in our national life, we do wish to thank you!

Sincerely yours,
Mary Graham and others
W.R. Babcock and Company, Inc.
Importers and Exporters
Manila, Philippine Islands
July 30, 1940

My dear Mrs. Babcock:

Mrs. Roosevelt asks me to acknowledge your letter and to tell you that she will do what she can in the matter about which you write.

Very sincerely yours,
Malvina Thompson
Secretary to Mrs. Roosevelt

Also in the file: two slips of notepaper indicating that Mrs. Roosevelt asked the president to read the letter. It was then returned to her.

• • •

December 9, 1940

Mrs. Eleanor Roosevelt
Washington, D.C.
Madam:

Although I know that there are many, many thousands petitioning you, I use this last chance left to me, because it concerns the dearest one, a human being can possess: A mother,—my mother.

I am of Austrian descent, wife of a physician, who due to his scientific work has got a call to come to this country, where he has been teaching at New York University for almost two years. A photocopy of an article in the *New York Times* concerning my husband is enclosed.

My parents who during the World War 1914-1918 were driven from their home by Russians lost at this occasion everything they had. My mother never really recovered from the physical strain she suffered during the wartime period. In 1935 my father died. In 1938 my mother underwent a serious operation and still lying in bed, she had to witness the arrest of my husband who immediately after the Nazi invasion in Austria had been imprisoned for three months. Despite her illness she shared with me the hardships and the undescribable troubles of that time until my husband has been released due to the generous intervention of the American Medical Society. Finally for the second time in her life she was forced to leave her home. She went to Belgium where from she was to join us in this country. But unfortunately in the meantime Belgium was invaded by the Germans. My mother tried to flee to France but after having spent many weeks on bombed roads and in open fields, and having lost everything she possessed she had to return to Belgium, where she now lives in great need because of the conditions in that country.

This is briefly the story of my mother.

And now to the core of the matter. My mother, Mrs. Helen Flintenstein, Antwerp, Isabella Lei 52, registered for immigration to this country as early as June 1938. About a year ago the American Consul in Antwerp wrote us, that my mother would get her visa in the spring of this year. But the Nazis occupied Belgium before she could leave it. We bought a ship ticket for her two months ago, and the representative of the American Export Line in Antwerp informed the American consul, that a ticket is lying to my mother's disposal in Lisbon. Finally she has been told that at present time only on an order from the State Department in Washington a visa can be granted her, although she met all demands required by the immigration laws.

Please imagine, Madam, that I am her only child, that she lived with me in one home for almost my lifetime, that she has not even one relative in all Europe, since I am here and her family has lived in this country for two generations, that she therefore is quite abandoned and helpless.

Please do not mind my boldness, it comes only of desperate filial love.

You have my deepest gratitude for anything you can do in my mothers behalf.

With the expression of my most sincere veneration

Very respectfully

Emily Borak

Jackson Heights, New York

[Three pages typed]

July 16, 1940

Dr. Jonas Borak,

Jackson Heights, New York

Sir:

The receipt is acknowledged on July 15, 1940, of your undated letter enclosing evidence of support furnished by you in behalf of the immigration visa application of your mother-in-law, Mrs. Helen Flintenstein.

Owing to the present emergency, the consequent lack of direct communication with countries outside of Belgium and the difficulties in the way of obtaining transportation facilities from this country to the United States, it has been necessary to suspend temporarily the issuance of immigration visas. Further consideration of the visa case referred to in your letter under acknowledgement must, therefore, be deferred for an indeterminate period of time.

Very truly yours,

Louis Sussdorff, Jr.

American Consul General

Antwerp, Belgium

Accompanying these letters was the following article from the New York Times *dated July 4, 1939, headlined "Austrian Radiologist Here a Fugitive From Nazis:"*

Dr. Jonas Borak, noted Viennese radiologist, arrived yesterday on the French liner Paris as a refugee. He has been invited by New York University to give a number of lectures. He traveled on a German passport, which he said he had obtained in Vienna from an unnamed Nazi official whose mother he had once cured of glandular cancer.

Dr. Borak was in prison in Vienna last month and his suicide was reported here erroneously on March 17. The scientist said he had been arrested originally because he had written an article attempting to prove by cranial measurements, skulls, photographs and genealogies that there was no such thing as a Jewish race.

Dr. Borak said he spent eighty-eight days in four prisons and was released after the American Medical Association asked the Nazi secret police about the rumor of his suicide. He got through to Antwerp, where the United States Consul gave him a non-quota visa after reading a letter in which Dr. Albert Einstein wrote: "He is one of the world's most unselfish friends of humanity."

January 8, 1941

Dear Mrs. Roosevelt:

Referring to the letter addressed to you by Mrs. Emily Borak, 35-06 Eighty-Eighth Street, Jackson Heights, New York, New York, concerning her desire to bring to the United States her mother, Mrs. Helen Flintenstein, I take pleasure in advising that our consular officer at Antwerp has been requested to submit a full report on the case. Immediately upon the receipt of a reply, I shall communicate with you again.

Sincerely yours,
[illegible signature]
Department of State
Washington, D.C.

The name Helen Flintenstein does not appear on any lists maintained at the United States Holocaust Memorial Museum, either of survivors or those killed in the death camps. According to the German census of October 1941, there were 17,242 Jews in Antwerp. Beginning in May that year all Jews had to wear the yellow star. Large-scale deportations started in 1942, with most deportees being sent to Auschwitz; the last deportation from Antwerp took place in September 1943. An archivist at the Joods Museum van Deportatie en Verzet, Mechelen, Belgium, found no mention of Helen Flintenstein in any of their lists.

• • •

POSTAL TELEGRAPH

NEW YORK NY 1941 JULY 29 8 PM

MRS. F D ROOSEVELT

HYDE PARK NY

MADAME TO HELP SAVE TWO VALUABLE LIVES FOR THIS WORLD PLEASE CONSIDER THIS CASE STOP ISRAEL SCHENKEL FIFTY SIX AND

WIFE LOTTE BOTH CHEMISTS AUSTRIAN REFUGEES OF HIGHEST INTEGRITY
AND MORALS STOP JEWS OF IMPECCABLE BACKGROUND WITHOUT ANY
RELATIONS IN OCCUPIED EUROPE ASK ME THEIR ONLY DAUGHTER FOR
INTERVENTION IN WASHINGTON WITH FOLLOWING WORDS STOP EVERY-
BODY HERE IN MARSEILLES MANAGES THROUGH RELATIVES IN UNITED
STATES TO SECURE SENATOR'S INFLUENCE IN WASHINGTON ONLY WE TWO
ARE LEFT TO STARVATION OR SUICIDE STOP SICK AND STARVING THEY
WAITED 3 YEARS FOR VISA STOP NOW IT WAS READY AND GRANTED FOR
JULY FOURTH BUT NEW IMMIGRATION LAW PROHIBITED MARSEILLE
CONSUL TO WRITE THEM OUT MADAME PLEASE IMAGINE STATE OF MIND
OF THESE POOR HUMAN BEINGS STOP THEY FLED FROM HITLERS AUS-
TRIAN ANNEXATION 1938 TO BELGIUM AND WAITED FOR UNITED STATES
VISA STOP JUST BEFORE ANTWERP CRASHED ACCEPTED MR SCHERMANS*
BOOK OF THE MONTH CLUB SPONSOR FOR AFFIDAVIT. HITLERS BELGIAN
ANNEXATION 1940 SENT THEM FLEEING TO FRANCE TO CAMP DE GRIS
STARVATION AND INCREDIBLE MISERY NEW AFFIDAVITS NEW WAITING
FOR VISA NO PASSAGE MONEY NO VISA GRANT TILL FINALLY JULY FOURTH
STOP MADAME I CAN PROVE THEIR INTEGRITY I CAN GET NEW SPONSOR
AFFIDAVITS I CAN TRY TO BORROW THE PASSAGE MONEY BUT I CANT
SPEED UP OR FAVORABLY INFLUENCE WASHINGTON STOP PLEASE HELP
WITH ADVICE WHOM TO SEE AND WHAT TO DO STOP IT WOULD BE ONE
MORE OF THE INNUMERABLE ANONYMOUS GOOD DEEDS OF A GREAT LADY
STOP RESPECTFULLY ELAINE BECK.

[Note on top left-hand corner: Copy sent to State Dept., 7-30-41.]

*Israel Schenkel, born December 14, 1886, of Austrian nationality, appears on
the list of one thousand Jews taken from Drancy, France, to Auschwitz in
Convoy 21, departing Drancy on August 19, 1942. S.S. Heinrichsohn sent*

---

* Those seeking to enter the United States needed an "affidavit" of support from a U.S.
citizen. Harry Scherman founded the Book-of-the-Month Club in 1926 with his partner,
Maxwell Sackheim. The Scherman Foundation, incorporated in 1941 by Harry Scherman
and still active, provides grants to groups involved with environmental issues, family planning, human rights, and social welfare.

"the usual cable, addressed on the day of departure of each convoy to Eichmann in Berlin." (The term convoy here refers to trains.) According to the Auschwitz Chronicle, *on August 21, 1942, one thousand Jews arrived at Auschwitz from Drancy. One hundred thirty-eight men and 45 women were admitted to the camp and given numbers; these would have been selected on the basis of those most able to work. The other 817 deportees were killed in the gas chambers that day. Lotte Schenkel did not appear in the records.*

• • •

[On stationery of Western Union]

MRS. ELEANOR ROOSEVELT=

WHITE HOUSE WASH DC=

I AM TO BE MARRIED THURSDAY NOVEMBER 20TH ALL PLANS FOR THE WEDDING HAVE BEEN MADE WE CHOSE THIS DAY BECAUSE OF ITS SPECIAL SIGNIFICANCE MY FIANCE PRIVATE ALAN M MARK AND I HAVE BEEN GOING TOGETHER FOR SEVERAL YEARS WE WISHED TO BE MARRIED WHILE ALAN WAS IN COLLEGE BUT OUR PARENTS THOUGHT WE WERE TOO YOUNG HIS PARENTS SELECTED HIS 24TH BIRTHDAY WHICH IS NOVEMBER 20TH AS A SUITABLE DATE. LAST YEAR THEY WERE BOTH KILLED IN AN AUTOMOBILE ACCIDENT THEREFORE THIS DATE WHICH THEY PICKED HAS GREAT SIGNIFICANCE AS IT IS THE ONLY DAY WE CAN BE MARRIED AND FEEL THAT HIS PARENTS ARE WITH US. MY WEDDING DRESS IS READY THE INVITATIONS ARE OUT TONIGHT ALAN WIRED TO SAY THAT AT THE LAST MINUTE HIS LEAVE HAD BEEN DENIED THIS HAPPENS DESPITE THE FACT THAT HE IS A PRIVATE IN GOOD STANDING AND HAD BEEN LEAD TO BELIEVE HIS LEAVE WOULD BE GRANTED. IN THE LAST EIGHTEEN MONTHS ALAN, WHO WAS AN ONLY CHILD HAS LOST HIS PARENTS HAS TAKEN OVER HIS FATHERS BUSINESS THEN TURNED IT OVER TO A STRANGER IN ORDER TO ENTER THE ARMY. FOR YEARS WE HAVE BEEN LOOKING FORWARD TO OUR WEDDING DAY. I AM SURE THE ARMY DOES NOT WISH TO IMPOSE GREATER HARDSHIP THAN NECESSARY ON ITS SELECTEES. I TURN TO YOU BECAUSE I KNOW YOU ARE INTERESTED IN YOUNG PEOPLES PROBLEMS AND HAVE HELPED THEM

PRIVATE ALAN M MARKS ADDRESS IS SECOND STUDENT TRAINING REGIMENT
INFANTRY SCHOOL FORT BENNING GEORGIA I HAVE EVERY CONFIDENCE THAT
YOU WILL HELP US AND THAT WE SHALL OWE ALL OUR FUTURE HAPPINESS
TO YOU HOPEFULLY YOURS=

PHYLLIS BLAUFARB CENTRAL PARK WEST NEW YORK CITY.

November 11, 1941

MEMORANDUM FOR MAJOR M.D. TAYLOR:

Mrs. Roosevelt has referred the attached telegram to me.
Will you please look the matter up and reply directly from
the War Department, saying the matter has been referred
to you by the White House.

Many thanks.
Edwin M. Watson
The White House
Washington, D.C.

November 19, 1941
Miss Phyllis Blaufarb,
New York, New York.
Dear Madam:
Your telegram of recent date, addressed to Mrs. Roosevelt,
has been referred to the War Department with her request
that you be informed regarding a furlough for your fiancé,
Private Alan M. Mark.

A radiogram has been received from the Commanding
General, Fort Benning, Georgia, in response to one from this
office of November 17th, reporting that a furlough for a
period of ten days has been granted Private Mark and that
he left Fort Benning on November 17, 1941, for New York.

Very truly yours
Major General
The Adjutant General

• • •

April 30, 1942

My Dear Mrs. Roosevelt,

Please forgive me for taking the liberty for making the following request of you, but I'm certain you'll recognize and understand the spirit which motivates my writing to you.

Ever since Dec. 7th 1941, I have tried unsuccessfully to enlist my services in the armed forces. Being 36 years of age, the Army would not accept me, as I have not had any previous military training. I therefore volunteered at my Draft Board for immediate induction, and on April 7th, was sent to Governor's Island for induction and selected leader of the group. Unfortunately, I was rejected and placed in class 1B for "insufficient vision," being otherwise in good shape physically. I have since tried the Navy, applying for a commission in the Morale Division, but turned down there also for insufficient vision.

Feeling that a man's talents and efforts at this time should be given over in the service of the government, I have again tried and failed to find an opening in some governmental department where my talents could be of use.

In the past eight years I have been in the singing profession, doing solo singing on radio shows, also acting as singing master of ceremonies in hotel floor shows, including 3 engagements in the past 4 years at the Shoreham Hotel in Washington. I also had the proud pleasure of recording the campaign songs for the Democratic National Committee in President Roosevelt's campaign for re-election in 1936.

Prior to 1934, I was engaged for eight years in the real estate and insurance brokerage business, and in assisting my brother in conducting his law business, studying law with him at the same time. Prior to that I was employed in the office of Mr. Henry L. Stimson for six months as a law clerk. I have also had several seasons experience as a sports and social director in summer resorts, and feel capable of writing philosophical and morale building articles.

I feel greatly disappointed, Mrs. Roosevelt, that I have not found an outlet in which to give of my service to the government, particularly as I do not have the heart nor desire to do any singing during this great period of trial, and knowing your great penchant for assisting people, my purpose in writing to you is to appeal for some advice, suggestion or recommendation as to how or where I can be of some service.

I assure you of my gratefulness, Mrs. Roosevelt, for any consideration you may give this request.

In high esteem,
Respectfully
Bruce Cummings

[Six pages handwritten]

May 4, 1942

My dear Mr. Cummings:

Mrs. Roosevelt has asked me to thank you so much for your courtesy in writing. She is appreciative of your efforts to enter the Armed Forces, but as your eyes prohibit this she feels you should go on with your profession as people need to be entertained now.

Very sincerely yours,
Malvina Thompson
Secretary to Mrs. Roosevelt

• • •

May 2, 1942

My dear Mrs. Roosevelt

I have been tempted to write you so many times during these long agonizing months but hated to be an extra occasion for you to write or read another letter. However, today I felt I could not hold back any longer. In the strangest way I feel that I know you and that you will fully forgive my bothering you.

My only son Ignatius Sargent is a class mate of your son Franklin at Groton, known to him as "Possum." He left us for overseas in command of a flying fortress shortly after Pearl Harbor. His little wife, 23 years old, who is going to have a baby, heard from him by phone from Java about 6 months later—he had been in combat and was sick in the hospital with malaria. I tried to contact him myself but couldn't. Last we heard was from Australia Easter Day, it was a great relief. Today I got my first letter, such a sad lonely letter—he was sick at the time. What I want to ask you is there any possible way in which I could contact him by cable or telephone, are the letters getting in to Australia—is he getting our news? And is there any chance of his coming home on furlough; he is gone over 4 months now. I used to see your boy Franklin often during the first 4 years of his schooling and twice I read to him in the infirmary where he was sick with sinus. I am so sorry to see that he has been so much in the hospital of late. However, dear Mrs. Roosevelt, you have him near you and you see him and I hope God will continue to keep him safe.

Very Sincerely and hopefully
Mrs. Theodore W. Chanler
New York, New York

[Four pages handwritten]

May 18, 1942

MEMORANDUM FOR MRS. ROOSEVELT:

In response to your memorandum of May seventh I contacted the War Department concerning Lieutenant Sargent, Air Corps, and attached hereto is their suggested draft of reply for your signature.

                    Edwin M. Watson
                    The White House
                    Washington, D.C.

                         [undated]

Mrs. Theodore W. Chanler,

New York City, New York.

Dear Mrs. Chanler:

I can well understand your concern over the absence of your son, Lieutenant Sargent, as my sons are not all with me and I never know when they will be ordered to or from our combat zones.

The War Department states that you should be able to reach your son by cablegram, although there may sometimes be delays in transmission. The delivery of mail has been difficult because of the wide dispersion of our forces around the world, but constant efforts are being made to improve the mail service.

There is always a chance that your boy will get a leave to return home for a few days, although we all know that the needs of our country's service must come first in time of war.

In many ways, war is more difficult for mothers than for any one else. It is our important task to bear with the uncertainty and set an example of fortitude to those around us.

                    Very sincerely yours,

The above was significantly amended by Mrs. Roosevelt, who took out

*personal references, made it less condescending, and added a more signifi-
cant offer of help:*

Dear Mrs. Chanler:

I can well understand your concern over the absence of your
son, Lieutenant Sargent.

The War Department states that you should be able to reach
your son by cablegram, although there may sometimes be
delays in transmission. The delivery of mail has been difficult
because of the wide dispersion of our forces around the world,
but constant efforts are being made to improve the mail service.

There is always a chance that your boy will get a leave to
return home for a few days. If you wish to send me your cable, I
will try to send it for you.

> Very sincerely yours,
> Eleanor Roosevelt

• • •

August 24, 1942

Dear Mrs. Roosevelt:

For the first time since my arrival here at Ft. Lewis last
November, I attended a USO Camp Show. The show was
excellent but I failed to enjoy it for this reason. The officers and their wives and guests filled not only the entire
middle section of the theater but a large part of the two
side sections (occupying the best seats) so that the enlisted
men were crowded into a very small portion of the theater,
many of them standing, a great many more **turned away**
for lack of seating or standing room.

Since it is my understanding that these shows are for
the purpose of entertaining young men either drafted or
enlisted in the service I was quite upset to find that officers

who have the money and privilege of leaving camp for their entertainment were depriving these boys of seeing the show.

I have discussed this with young officers wives and they tell me that this situation exists time after time and that the Commanding Officer of the post reserves a section of seats each time for a large party.

Don't you agree that this situation needs remedying? I for my part shall never attend again and hope that you may intercede in behalf of the enlisted personnel of the various camps.

Sincerely,

Mrs. John K. Orr

Ft. Lewis, Washington

[Two pages handwritten]

September 8, 1942

My dear Mrs. Orr:

Mrs. Roosevelt has asked me to thank you very much for your letter. She is interested in what you say and will try to help remedy the situation.

Very sincerely yours,

Malvina Thompson

Secretary to Mrs. Roosevelt

September 18, 1942

Dear Miss Thompson:

Mr. Taft has given me your letter of the 8th, with copy of a letter addressed to Mrs. Roosevelt from an enlisted man saying that the officers at his post take all the best seats at the USO-Camp Shows, freezing out the enlisted men.

This is a most deplorable thing and we make every effort to remedy these situations when we hear about them. However, we all agree that the general principle of giving the Post Commander responsibility for handling local situations must be adhered to, and I think there are very few posts where the Post Commander is not cognizant of the dangers in this sort of situation and already taking steps to prevent them.

If Mrs. Roosevelt would care to give me the name of the post, we could draw the matter to their attention in a general way without any personal references.

Yours Sincerely,

F. H. Osborn

Brigadier General

Director

Special Service Division

Services of Supply

War Department

• • •

September 28, 1942

Mrs. Franklin D. Rosevelt,

Dear Mrs. Rosevelt:

I am from Kentucky, Edmonson Co., and I came all the way here to try to see you personally and talk with you on a very serious proposition. You are a mother as I and I'm sure if I could only see and talk with you, you would understand just how I feel. Now may I explain to you what I wanted so much to do in person. I have a Son who has been in US Army service 3 years and almost 3 months. He is only 19 years old now and is a high school graduate. He sailed 5 days after war was declared. And he stayed in Iceland 4 or 5 months was sent away from there but cant tell

me where he is. Any way Sept 10th he was walking Guard
and the P.X. was on the corner of his post. He went in and
drank a coca cola. While he was in a Lt. comes in and
reported That he wass off his Post. They tried him The
same Day gave him 5 years and a D.D. Mrs. Rosevelt It
was a minor thing and I Think It was entirely too much
Don't you? And I gave Senator Barkley The Letters I had
from him also one I had from another soldier over there
and one from a Chaplin. They all think he was given a Raw
Deal and no Justice in it. What I'm Trying to ask you to Do
get in touch with the adjutant general before these papers
are approved of in Washington and Try to get It cut Down.
If only you could under stand how I feel today and what a
Grand sweet child he has always been. He is too young to
be across, should be Dishcarged and at Home but I pray
God It wont Be a D.D. Im trying to write this on a Joggy
old Train as I travel back toward Kentucy. Will you please
please write me a personal letter May God Bless you and
may this awful war soon come to an end.

Yours.

Mrs. Elzona Ray

Vine Grove, Kentucky

or you can address me this way I'm Senior Cook at the Dr.
and nurses mess at Fort Knox.

Mrs. Elzona Ray

Station Hospital Nurses Mess

Fort Knox, Kentucky

October 5, 1942

My dear General Cramer:

Mrs. Roosevelt has asked me to send you the enclosed letter
from Mrs. Elzona Ray, concerning the sentence imposed on her
son, Private James H. Ray, New York, New York.

Mrs. Roosevelt is sending it for your information and for whatever consideration you may wish to give Mrs. Ray's letter.

When you have finished with the enclosed letters, their return will be greatly appreciated.

Very sincerely yours,
Malvina Thompson
Secretary to Mrs. Roosevelt

October 7, 1942

Dear Miss Thompson:

General Cramer directs me to acknowledge receipt of your letter of October 5, 1942, inclosing a letter to Mrs. Roosevelt from Mrs. Elzona Ray, concerning the sentence imposed on her son, Private James H. Ray, together with the letter of Private Ray to his mother.

No record of trial of the case has been received in this office. When it is received, your inquiry together with Mrs. Ray's letter and her son's, copies of which have been made for the purpose, will be given careful consideration, and you will be advised of the final action taken in the matter.

Very sincerely yours,
James E. Morrisette
Colonel, J.A.G.D.
Chief, Military Justice Division
Office of the Judge Advocate General
War Department

• • •

October 11, 1942

Dear Mrs. Roosevelt:

I don't feel I have any right to write you this letter, but, knowing you from your personality and understanding of this younger generation, I write this letter not as a soldier of our beloved country, but, as a young married man who is encountering a little difficulty.

Let me begin from the start. I enlisted in the Army on June 15, 1940, was assigned to the glorious 1st Division. On May 5 of this year I was fortunate enough to be chosen to attend the Officers Candidate School, at Fort Sill, Oklahoma. After completing six weeks of school I was confined to the station hospital. Since then I have had an operation on the right side of my knee, on the cartilage. During this time I met an Army nurse. Before we knew it we were in love, next thing we were married. We were married one week ago yesterday, Oct. 3, 1942. Since then we, my wife and I have had to carry on a "sneaky romance" or honeymoon. Now my trouble, Mrs. Roosevelt is this, my wife is afraid to tell her superior of this, and I want her to. But, she says if she does they will transfer her and I am the one who wants to be transferred. I love her very dearly and she does me. This afternoon we had quite an argument over all this.

Mrs. Roosevelt, as a mother, wife and friend of this generation, I ask you in all sincerity and appreciation what or where can we do or go to help alleviate this condition. I know you are a busy woman and I am not supposed to write to you or any one else on matters of this nature but it can't be avoided. I love this country of mine and am willing to **die** for it, but all I ask is that my wife be given some satisfaction to have a peace of mind so we can see each other as any married couple may do.

If you, Mrs. Roosevelt, can help us I will appreciate it and be ever so thankful for it that it can't be put in writing. My wife doesn't know of this, so again I would appreciate it if it were kept in confidence.

Hoping you will be able to help me, I remain.

Respectfully Yours,

Corp. E.M.W.

Lawton, Oklahoma

P.S. My wife's name is S. I am writing this when out on a pass. I have to return to hospital in the morning. I will always pray for you and my beloved President. My home is Brooklyn, N.Y., so, Mrs. Roosevelt you will understand my **forwardness and audacity** if you will call it such, as it seems to be a New Yorkers trait and habit. Thanking you again and God Love and Bless you and yours.

[Five pages handwritten]

Mrs. Roosevelt asked the War Department for advice, which was as follows:

October 27, 1942

My dear Corporal W.:

Mrs. Roosevelt made inquiry concerning the problem confronted by you and your wife and she has been advised that neither of you committed any breach of War Department regulations.

I quote the following from a memorandum sent to Mrs. Roosevelt by the War Department:

"As far as the War Department is concerned, it is not necessary for either a soldier or a nurse to secure the permission of his or her superior for getting married.

"The question of their staying together is not at all different from that which every young married couple must now face. Both Corporal and his wife have given themselves to the Government service, and each of them is subject to the necessities of his branch. It would obviously be unwise for the War Department to attempt to arrange assignments in such a way that husbands and wives in the service could be kept together.

"Perhaps you could re-apply for officer candidate school when you are released from the hospital, secure a commission, and attempt to save as much of your pay as possible so that you and your wife will have something to begin with after the war."

I am writing you this letter as Mrs. Roosevelt is now in England and the date of her return is uncertain.

Very sincerely yours,
Administrative Officer
Social Correspondence.

• • •

[Note on top of letter in pencil in Mrs. Roosevelt's hand: "FDR, what if anything can be done about this letter? ER"]

December 5, 1942

Dear Mrs. Roosevelt:

I am writing this letter to you as a plea from a heart sick born American; even tho' I don't deserve being called an American, never the less, **I am**.

I don't know how to phrase this letter, but believe me, I would not write to you unless I knew I would get the 1/2 break from you.

I should have wrote this letter to War Department, but as you know a war is on, and I may be misunderstood, **especially the likes of me**.

Believe me in this letter goes the heart and soul of a man that made a mistep, why I did I shall explain. Around 1923 I enlisted in the American Army. I was stationed at Schoffield Barracks, Hawaii. I was married and a father of 2 children. I was legally separated from my wife. I did not reveal this to the Army authorities. At the same time my mother died, and I was a very heart sick man. Any way I found myself in the Army. After 1 year service I started to break out with boils, and styes, and my left leg gave me continual pain, also I had dizzy spells. I was under medical treatment but I did not respond to the treatments. I was a worried man. My brother sent me a headline from the press stating my wife had fallen from a 4 story window and was found naked and injured, at the same time he told me my children were in very dire circumstances, being separated from my wife and children my first great desire was to get back to them. I asked for a furlough and it was granted to me. I got back to my children and found my wife a cripple, and the kids in need of medical and all sorts of treatment.

I found myself in a position that I did not have the heart to leave them, even tho' I did not live with my wife again. I endeavored to find a home for them, as their mother was an immoral person and crippled.

All this time I was in ill health myself in a hard pressed state which I can't explain in this letter. I found a girl to take care of the kids. Then I went to a hospital, the Eye and Ear and had a double Mastoid operation for 2 years one of my ears drained, and I had a difficult time to recuperate from this operation, then when I felt a little better I suddenly lost the balance of my body, the internal ear collapsed. After 5 years treatment in Allegheny General Hospital, I recuperated enough to start thinking of what I done to my country **by not reporting back to my post**. Then at this present time I am again under medical treatment for some type of arthritis. I am now taking injections of Collodiel Sulphate.

Now I realize I done wrong, I find myself that I can't get work, every plant I go to ask for work they ask for finger prints. I shy away from the job, knowing I shall **be disgraced** when I am found out.

Mrs. Roosevelt what shall I do? Can this terrible thing be straightened out? I never meant to go against my country, I would rather die first.

Whatever shall bear out of this letter, I shall knowingly believe in your help and wisdom.

Whatever is in store for me I shall be awaiting, but I am not guilty of **desertion wilfully**.

Very respectfully,

Vernon L. Smith

Pittsburgh, Pennsylvania

P.S. Incidentally the girl that had taken my children and helped them is now my wife. The children's mother is dead.

Believe me Mrs. Roosevelt, I shall rest content knowing you will help me some way, as I also believe our great President can give a break to a lowly little guy like me.

I am not totally disabled, but just enough pain all the time that it sets a guy off his best.

I will gladly and willingly go back to fight and die for my country. I am still a better man than the enemy.

January 25, 1943

MEMORANDUM FOR: MRS. ROOSEVELT

I asked my Liaison Officer with the War Department to look into the matter set forth in the attached letter and he suggests that you may wish to include substantially the following in your reply:

Since receiving your letter requesting advice concerning your military status I have taken your case up with the War Department. I find that a man who is a deserter at large from the Army should report immediately to the nearest Army post and turn himself in. Since you have been in desertion for more than three years you will be given a physical and mental examination, and if you are further qualified for military service, you will be restored to duty and processed through the nearest reception center. If you are found physically disqualified, you will be given an other than honorable discharge from the Army.

Edwin M. Watson

The White House

Washington, D.C.

. . .

[Undated]

[On stationery of the United Service Organization. Printed at the bottom of the page, "Idle Gossip Sinks Ships"]

Dear Mrs. Roosevelt,

This is probably improper and unfair to bother you with my troubles, but you seem like a lady who can help a fellow and I am about to the end of my rope.

There is nothing of importance about me to warrant my writing to you. I am not wealthy or influential but only God almighty knows how miserable I am.

Four months ago I joined the naval service with the best of patriotic intentions. I signed almost half my pay a month over to the purchase of a war bond a month and I wanted to get started fighting the Germans. You see I am of the Jewish faith which gives me two strikes against the Japanese and **four** against the Nazis.

When I left home I not only left the city I love, my folks, and all that every one else gives up but I had nothing of my former life to take with me. The other fellows either drink, smoke, gamble, or a million other things that they did at home. My pleasures back home were the hills and woods and farms of Buck County where I hoped to get a piece of ground for my self someday. Three of the happiest years of my life were spent in a small agricultural school in Buck's Co.

Please can you help me? All I ask is a chance to go back East. They can give me half pay, put me in the North Atlantic patrol all winter or have me scrub the City Hall decks but I want to be back East. Back East where I would be happy again, knowing I am doing my duty to "Uncle Sam," fighting the Nazis, and have that wonderful feeling that I would have a chance to get to see my folks and the things I love even if it would be a few days out of the year.

I was sent to school here but I became sick and nervous so the doctor took me out of school at my request, leaving me an apprentice seaman who can be placed on any duty.

Please do not laugh at me like they do here and I do hope this letter will not get me into trouble, they may ship me anywhere for the devil of it, then I would really go off the handle.

I will enclose a picture of myself when I was seventeen and also a letter from my ma. She is getting older very fast and when my brother joins that will make three in the service and no one home.

Please again will you help me?

Very Sincerely yours,

Thank you

Benjamin F. Bershtein A.A.

General Detail

U.S. Receiving Station

San Diego, California

P.S. Will you send the picture and letter back to me? The letter I have to read some more and the picture reminds me of a better day and things to come.

[Three pages handwritten]

December 21, 1942

My dear Mr. Bershstein:

Mrs. Roosevelt has your letter and is so sorry she can not be helpful. The White House can not ask for transfers for men in the

Services and any attempt to use influence would do you more harm than good.

Very sincerely yours,

Malvina Thompson

Secretary to Mrs. Roosevelt.

• • •

[undated]

Dear Mrs. Rosevelt,

We were Sent here from the post given above for a training course at the Caterpiller and Tractor School here in Peoria, for five weeks.

We have orders which states that every man would be paid 15 days in advance for expense.

When we arrived here, the Capt. Long who is in charge of us, told us that he would have to Send in to Chicago Ill for our money since there is no finance here. Meanwhile the Sergeant made arrangement at a Colored Restaurant for us to eat until Our Ration Money came in, this place, all type of people come in and hang out, it is a very rough place, and the food is none too good, in fact the Colored People don't have a place for good people to eat in, here in this town.

This town is so fixed that we as Colored Soldiers are not wanted in white restaurants we have been stoped from eating in many of restaurants around by the white, and realy the colored people have little or nothing to offer us. We as American Soldiers feel that their should be something done about the wellfair of our Colored Soldiers while Attending School here in this town. Due to the fact that we have to get two of our meals out in the Street we Spent our personal money for food in a white restaurant where they

Served us willingly for more than one week, but Stoped us through our Sergeant here. Now as Spending our Personal Money in order to get good food, we were thinking that when Our Ration money came in Captain Long would give us our personal money back, which we needed for personal use Such as Keeping neat and clean.

Captain Long's regulations here is to pay each man in advance $10 a week, we were here 13 days before our money came in and according to Capt Long's regulations here, by the last day of Nov 1942, we should have had $30 which would have paid us up for the days we had been here and give us one week in advance. This would have been fair according to his regulations here.

But he only payed us $15 Capt Long States that he is holding our money so we will have some left when we leave here.

Mrs. Rosevelt, I am a private and have been a deacon of a Baptist Church for 7 years and if I didn't think that we need your attention on this matter I wouldnt take up your valuable time.

I feel that the money the government is giving us for food is ment to be Spent for food. I also believe that what ever the alowence is, that it is a plenty to keep a man from having to eat lite as we do. We are given $10 for food, this $10 has to last us 8 days and Captain Long is talking about cutting this down to five dollars a week, every 8 days and we have to buy 2 meals a day.

Mrs. Rosevelt, I hope you don't think I am just a fault finder, because I am a proud solder and am trying to make good.

But I do think As American Soldiers we Should have a little better care than we are getting here and from what I've red and heard of you I know that you wont let us be treeted this way. I may be gone when things are better

Arranged here for the Colored Soldiers, but I would be Satisfied to know that my comrades who Are to come here after I'm gone are treeted better than what we are.

Mrs. Rosevelt, Since you are the only one that I knew could and I believe will help us, as helpless Colored Soldiers Striving to play our part in this war, will you please See that Something is done for our benefit. On the reverse Side of this sheet I have a list of Colored Soldiers and their Serial # as a witness that this is actual facts I'm bringing to you. Thanking you in advance for your kind Consideration, please answer my appeal. May God ever continue to Bless America and may it also be some day that we the Negro Soldiers, can Enjoy some of America's Freedom.

Pvt. Louis E. Chavis, Company A

and

Pvt. Eddie C. Fitten, Company A

Pvt. James R. Davidson, Jr., Company B

List of witness
Pvt. Joseph C. Jones
Pvt. Robert Barksdale

[Four pages handwritten]

Note attached: December 21, 1942
Referred by Mrs. Roosevelt for attention of Secretary of War, copy with names deleted

It was precisely this kind of situation that Mrs. Roosevelt had in mind when she delivered speeches and wrote articles during the war years:

"Where the Negro is concerned, I think they have a legitimate complaint. We have expected them to be good citizens and yet in a large part of our country we haven't given them an opportunity to take part in our government. We have, however, made them subject to our laws and we have drafted them into our army and navy. We have done better than ever before, I think, in really integrating some of them with their white brothers in the various services. It has been an uphill fight, however, and the tendency has been to keep them in the menial positions performing the kind of services which are needed but which do not give an opportunity for glory or for compensation to the same extent that other services might do."

"Over and over again, I have stressed the rights of every citizen: equality before the law, equality of education, equality to hold a job according to his ability, equality of participation through the ballot in the government. These are inherent rights in a Democracy, and I do not see how we can fight this war and deny these rights to any citizen in our own land."

• • •

December 17, 1942

Mrs. Eleanor Roosevelt,
The White House,
Washington, D.C.
Dear Madam: Re: Louis Edward Olivera, A.S. 2nd/class, Commander
Service Force, Subordinate
Command Pacific
I hope you will find time to help me in my need.

In June of this year we had a campaign for 1000 recruits for Hero's Day—the day of Hero's Parade when World War #2 Heros honored our city of Portland with their presence.

The night before Hero's Day, my little 15 year old brother came home about 8 pm white faced and serious and

announced that he'd enlisted in the Navy. He had told
them he was 18 and changed the age and birth date on a
working permit he'd just obtained and on a copy of birth
certificate with a typewriter to "verify" his 18 years,
thinking that was all necessary. He told Mother she **had** to
sign for him and if she didn't he'd get in trouble for
"forging" and signing to a lie. Even then he was wishing he
hadn't acted so impulsively but felt it was too late. The
boy's father is not living with the family and has not been
for some years, and we have other smaller children. My
mother and I did not know what to do, so I called the
Recruiting office—giving no names, but merely asking as a
point of general information what happened if a minor
lied about his age. The Recruiting officer said he'd get a
Dishonorable discharge and could not at any future date
when he was of age enlist in the Navy for lying. He also
said if the Navy found out his true age he'd automatically
be dishonorably discharged **even if his mother signed if
his age was a lie**. I swear this to be God's truth.

Mom was frantic and went over to ask some questions.
She was told he would be sent to a training school at San
Diego for 6 weeks, and would be given "an Aptitude" test
and sent to a Naval School for extensive course—possibly
in Virginia where many of the younger boys are trained
for a couple of years in Mechanics etc, as various fields are
open. The Officer said the younger boys were often in
school two years or more. So Mom, anxious about the
child, and torn between the feeling he was too young and
yet not wanting to expose him as a liar and forging his age
and signing to a false statement which he and I had feared
and impressed upon her would be serious as we thought it
was, signed, but they did not ask if he was 18, or even
mention his age, but just as I said told her it was for Naval
Course in Mechanics or aviation, etc, and asked her to
sign. Of course going to school and learning a good trade

is all right and sounded good for a child, but she signed only because he was so scared of exposure and I was too and nervous, and merely signed thinking it was a release or consent for School in the States for a couple of years.

My Mom is a wonderful woman who has brought up 9 children alone, working in canneries, sewing nights, and sacrificing and overworking all her life. But she does not read English and talks with an accent. She really didn't know what it was all about and I am to blame because I was anxious not to get him into trouble, and a "dishonorable" discharge sounded so awful, and I was nervous and panicky and so was mom and we were confused. Moreover, I must confess I wasn't as close to the boy as I should have been. You know how older sisters are—especially those who work—I guess he thought me "bossy" and I'm afraid I was as I stuck my nose in and advised Mom to sign and we'd have time to think, and I'd find out more and then we'd know what to do.

Instead, after 6 weeks basic, that kid was sent overseas. Mom and I are nervous wrecks. He'd never been away from home before and we got a tragic letter from him in September saying—and I quote, "Dear Mom: I hope you won't think me silly or a big baby, for telling you I go in hiding places and cry until I have a headache, I am so homesick. I am going to my Commanding Officer today and see if they won't let me go home, I'm so young. . . ." Since then we haven't heard from him. We expected to hear the results, but no word.

Mom has worried and cried and not slept and lost weight until she is ill and on the verge of a nervous breakdown. It's disrupting everything at home and causing anguish and heartbreak for she's working out days to keep busy and keep from thinking, and evenings has children to feed and house to keep and sewing and etc and still can't sleep when she goes to bed though worn out as she worries until she is so nervous and so am I that we jump on the kids for everything from taut nerves and can't stand their innocent average children's antics etc, and I know they're bewildered and becoming resentful of our going to pieces yet I know I don't mean to and just can't help it and Mom must feel worse over her baby.

I wrote months ago to his C.O. and told them the truth. The first letter to the C O at Basic, Co. 42, San Diego (Training School) received no answer. I wrote the President and the Secty of the Navy once before but by the time I got the papers ready the letters came back, and we didn't hear from him since Sept. We sent several boxes of candy and cookies which never came back but letters did. I just sent him his Christmas present yesterday as didn't know where to write until I wired the Secty of the Navy Sunday and he wired back collect the boy had been transferred (still a new address) and mail addressed to him at: Commander Service Force, Subordinate Command Pacific, c/o Fleet Post Office, San Francisco would ultimately reach him.

As a mother, you know the anguish my Mom is going through in having a 15 year old—I beg your pardon, he was 16 on November 5th, last month—overseas.

Could you please PLEASE lend him back to her even if only on a Christmas. Honestly, she's in such awful shape I fear a collapse or nervous breakdown and she keeps pushing herself and working to forget and is too rundown and I'm terrified as it is evident either her mind or her health or both will snap. Christmas makes it worse she'd hoped so to hear from him or have him home for furlough. Another thing, the Recruiting officer that night (the one she talked to before signing and who said it was for schooling) said before he was transferred from the San Diego School to Virginia he'd be home on a few days furlough as they also always did before they transferred. The child has never been home or able to contact us, since on ships 6 weeks after except for the one letter, between the Cygus and the LaPerla.

It's not that we don't want to do our part. My Mom puts everything she can spare into bonds (always did since they started but more than she can spare since the kid is overseas and she is so worried) and so do I. A brother of 22 (married and with a 2 month old son) is in the Army, but as he's old enough to be in we and he are willing and glad, and my fiancé, who will be my husband after this week, is an Instructor for Army Air Corps cadets, training them at Mesa del Rey, and has graduated several classes for advanced training. Louis is a mere baby.

I hope that Charity and Humanitarianism and Human Interest will prompt you to wire to contact his Commanding officer at the first chance and recommend his discharge. If you cannot do that, please would it be asking too much to bring peace and a chance for a regaining of health to our Mother by at least giving him a furlough so she could see him and know he's well and then I believe, and so does Mr. Green (prominent local attorney with Boesen Green and Landye) and Judge Long, and my doctor that Mom will be much different and not worry anymore, and also Louis will get over his homesickness and possibly even be anxious to get back into the service.

Again, I pray you will be kind enough to recommend his discharge to the Secty of the Navy until he is at least a year older, or if that is impossible, at least give him a furlough as soon as you can get him in. It will mean so much.

Thanking you, and may God bless you in your wonderful guidance and direction of OUR CAUSE,

Dorothy Olivera
Portland, Oregon

[Four pages typed]

December 28, 1942

My dear Miss Olivera:

Mrs. Roosevelt asks me to acknowledge your letter of December 17. She is very sorry there is nothing she can do, except to send your letter to the Navy Department for consideration. However, she hesitates to do this without your permission.

Very sincerely yours,
Malvina C. Thompson
Secretary to Mrs. Roosevelt

This letter was returned to Miss Thompson with this handwritten note on the bottom: "Would appreciate it if she could do that with her recommendation for release. Other former service men, Navy and Army both pictured in papers released 14 to 16 yrs old. Thank you. Dorothy Olivera Fehl"

Louis Edward Olivera, born November 6, 1926, died January 28, 1995, served in the U.S. navy, lived in Portland, Oregon, and was buried in Willamette National Cemetery, Multnomah County, Oregon, on January 31, 1995.

• • •

December 19, 1942

Dear Mrs. Roosevelt,

I am only one of many thousands of soldier privates, writing to you in the hope of getting help from you. Having tried every other means possible I am asking for your help in solving a problem which means everything in life to me. I am handicapped greatly by a defective speech which always fails me at the wrong time and is always causing me embarrassment. Born of American parents, and having graduated from an American High School, it seems to me that I should have an equal chance in life as everyone else, if it is possible.

I have tried to go to an Institution for stutterers and stammerers in Indianapolis, Indiana for a long time but something has always gone wrong. I borrowed the money once when in civilian life and was all set to go but I found that the Railroad Company I was working for wouldn't grant my leave of absence. Then I loaned the larger part of the $360 I had borrowed for this purpose to a very good friend of mine who is now helping me pay it back. A few days later my company offered me the leave, but it was too late. The friend had already spent all the money and now I'm still paying on it but it is about paid out now.

I have appealed my case to several Army officers but I've never gotten much satisfaction, only that they might make me limited service and give me a special job in radios. But I'm not sure this has gone through yet.

I graduated from Scott Field School of Radio Dec. 12 with an average of only 77% which I know isn't my best. I never asked a question in school, what I learned I picked up in my own way. I'm sure I could have qualified for the Officers Candidate School which they offer here but I know I could never make the grade, handicapped as I am.

I have a girl back home like all other boys do. She wrote me about a month ago telling me she was coming to see me. But I had to write and tell her not to, that I might leave at anytime to forestall her coming. I knew to bring her on the field would mean a lot of talking and introducing her to my friends. I can be talking to a person and right in the middle of my talking, my speech will leave me and I just stand gasping for air, therefore you see I don't do too much talking.

I've got to go to this institution, because you see my life is being wrecked. I've thought of many ways to go but they don't seem to work out. If I had the money to go, sometimes I think I would go AWOL and go to it. No punishment would be to great for me if I could rid myself of this terrible handicap. I've even thought of suicide, I would probably be better off dead. But when I think of mother and dad and brother and sister back home I try to dismiss these things from my mind immediately. I know they love me as I do them and I wouldn't want to hurt them for anything in this world. I hope I never have to. Because I want to do this in my own way and the right way.

Do you see this means my whole life to me. No one seems to realize the seriousness of my condition. All I want is an equal chance in life and I am appealing to you for help. I hope there is something you can do for me.

I am due to be shipped out of Scott Field in a week or so but my mail will be forwarded if you do get this letter and can do anything for me.

To give you a description of myself, I am six feet three, weight about one hundred ninety and I never have any trouble getting a girl if I want one. But at present girls mean nothing to me because of this handicap I can't seem to have any fun or enjoyment with them; I am twenty two years old.

Hoping you can help me in solving this problem I will be awaiting your answer.

Sincerely yours,
Herbert A. Cox
Scott Field, Illinois

P.S. It would only take approximately four weeks to rid me of this handicap. At a charge of $360. I would give $10,000 if I had it.

[Three pages handwritten]

December 28, 1942

Dear Mr. Cox:

I have your letter and I am afraid the Institute is not telling you the truth. It is a long tedious process to get over stuttering. You can help yourself very much, and perhaps you can go to a good doctor and let him tell you what to do and do it faithfully. You should speak slowly and stop talking if you feel nervous.

Very sincerely yours,
Eleanor Roosevelt

• • •

February 5, 1943

Dear Mrs. Roosevelt

I am asking you a big favor as I do not know just how to go about it or who to write to. So I am bringing my problem to you. My daughter has been going with a soldier for approx 2 years. He has been in service 6 years. So he has led her to believe that he wants to marry her but at times he says he thinks they should wait a while longer. He has asked her to come down to camp and on 2 occasions she made a trip of 3 days each with a friend to Augusta Ga., to see him. Now this week he has been transferred to Kansas City Mo. And she is to go out there to visit him. These trips cause disturbances in the home and she has to work and he knows it. She has promised him that she would come. Now I been told that he was married but **cannot** prove it to her and she does love him and he tells her that I upset her although he doesn't know that we suspicion him. I don't want to hurt her nor do I want her disgraced and I would appreciate it very much as it would

mean intirely on her future to know if he has an allote-
ment concerning a wife and child. I am only interested in
my 23 year old daughter and no one else. Neither am I
trying to cause him any disgrase. I think you know just
what kind of a position we are facing and she is the kind
that would consider it should it be true. Now I am writing
this request to you as it depends entirely on my daughter's
future. Please give this your consideration as she would
not do anything that isn't just right in her mind. Thanking
you for your time, I am,

Respectfuly.

Mrs. V. B. Coffey

Atlanta, Georgia

The Soldier in-Volved address:

Sgt. Jimmie Blissett

Camp Gordon Ga.

[Four pages handwritten]

· · ·

*The original letter referred to below was not in the file. It was written by
Mrs. Wilton Gates of Washington., D.C. Mrs. Gates enclosed a transcript
of a court martial and two photographs. Her husband's name was Private
Wilton S. Gates, Fort Bliss, Texas.*

March 4, 1943

Hon. Robert P. Patterson

Under Secretary of War

War Department

Dear Judge Patterson:

The President suggested that I send you this since you are a
lawyer, and also familiar with the necessity for military discipline.

I read this through last night and while I realize that in the Armed Forces men must learn what complete obedience means, I do think that officers when they are entrusted with the exercise of that type of authority, must look upon it as a trust and when a situation such as this comes up, I feel the officers haven't used their authority properly.

I also realize that we haven't been able to train officers for a long enough period and we certainly haven't been able to train boys long enough to have our youth understand what complete obedience means and for a boy to be given a sentence of dishonorable discharge and ten years imprisonment for the type of thing which is brought out in these court martial proceedings, seems to me nothing short of criminal.

None of these boys are shown to have previous bad records so I take it for granted they were confined for minor offenses in the prison. The officers practically dared them to have the courage to keep on in spite of what he told them, in their refusal to work. They evidently felt though they were late in not permitting the last twelve boys to go into breakfast and singling them out in rather an unfair way, I can not imagine that going out to work for the day without any breakfast would not also seem unfair.

The whole tone of the court martial, I think, savors of untrained officers who haven't learned to prevent situations such as these, or of men who have been spoiled by having the power.

Will you please return this whole file to me as I promised to send it back to the woman, with the photograph.

I realize you may not be able to do anything about it but somehow men's lives at this age do seem to be important and I boil when I think of what seems to me complete injustice.

Very sincerely yours,
Eleanor Roosevelt

March 15, 1943

Dear Mrs. Roosevelt:

This is in further answer [previous answer not in file] to your letter of March 4, concerning Wilton S. Gates.

As a result of the action of the Board of Review in the Judge Advocate General's Office,[*] the sentence was reduced to five years and the execution of that part of the sentence ordering dishonorable discharge was suspended. Thereafter, on May 4, 1942, the case was examined for clemency and in view of the report of the United States Disciplinary Barracks, clemency was at that time denied.

The record showed that Gates had been in trouble on various occasions before he came into the service. He had an unhappy childhood because his Father died when he was quite young. He was sent to Boy's Town, Nebraska, where his Mother had him admitted at her own request for forging her signature to a Government check belonging to her. After he was there for about eight months he ran away and subsequently appeared before the juvenile court for the forgery. He was placed on probation and later discharged on the condition that he join the Civilian Conservation Corps. He did this, but the local police report indicates that he deserted the Civilian Conservation Corps and was induced to return. After three months of service there he was honorably discharged. He left school in the eleventh grade at the age of 18 to be married. Two months after he married he enlisted in the Army and, with his wife's consent, gave his status as single. The psychiatrist reports that he has a history of emotional instability.

Gates was previously convicted by a special court-martial

---

[*] Each military department had a Judge Advocate General Corps, composed of attorneys, to deal with civil and criminal legal problems, such as contracts, court-martials, and employment questions.

for desertion at Fort Bliss, Texas, on July 31, 1941, which was terminated by surrender at Will Rogers Field, Oklahoma on September 30, 1941. His conduct in confinement on his present sentence has been excellent.

Unfavorable consideration of his clemency application was based in part upon the short length of time which he had spent in confinement which afforded insufficient opportunity for observation of his progress in rehabilitation. As it is believed that sufficient length of time has elapsed to permit more accurate conclusions, the Commandant of the Disciplinary Barracks has been requested to furnish a progress report for the purpose of reconsidering the case for clemency. Similar action is being taken in the case of all of the co-defendants with the exception of one who was also convicted of assault with intent to commit sodomy and whose dishonorable discharge has been executed.

In view of your interest, I will be glad to advise you of whatever further action may be taken in this case.

Sincerely yours,
Robert P. Patterson
Under Secretary of War
War Department
Washinton, D.C.
March 19, 1943

My dear Mrs. Gates:
Mrs. Roosevelt has asked me to send you the enclosed copy of a letter from the Under Secretary of War.

Mrs. Roosevelt will be glad to let you know if she hears further.

Very sincerely yours,
Malvina C. Thompson
Secretary to Mrs. Roosevelt

April 15, 1943

Dear Mrs. Roosevelt:

On March 15th, I wrote to you that the Commandant of the Disciplinary Barracks had been requested to furnish a report on the case of Wilton S. Gates and three of the other men who were convicted with him. This report was requested for the purpose of reconsidering clemency in these cases.

The reports have now been received. In the case of Gates it appears his conduct in confinement has been good. As I stated in my earlier letter, he had a history of emotional instability. It is now reported that he is suffering from epilepsy manifested since childhood, and there is a reasonable presumption that the malady contributed to the commission of the offense for which he was convicted. Under all the circumstances, action is being taken to remit the unexecuted portion of his sentence and restoring him to duty. He will then go before a Medical Board to determine whether in view of this condition he should be retained in the military service or should be discharged on account of physical disability.

The conduct of one of the other prisoners has been good, and consideration is being given as to whether the remaining part of his sentence should be remitted entirely or in part. The other two prisoners have not had good prison records, and it is not felt that any action should be taken in reference to their cases at the present time.

As you know, the problem of enforcing military discipline is an important one. It is particularly difficult in an Army whose soldiers have nearly all recently come from civil life. The War Department is fully conscious of its responsibility and is doing everything within its power to handle this problem. Your interest in these cases is appreciated.

Sincerely yours,
Robert P. Patterson
Under Secretary of War
War Department
Washington, D.C.

April 17, 1943

Dear Mrs. Gates:

Since writing to you on March 19, Mrs. Roosevelt has received a further report from the Secretary of War, copy of which I am enclosing.

Very sincerely yours,
Malvina C. Thompson
Secretary to Mrs. Roosevelt

May 28, 1943

Mrs. Eleanor Roosevelt
The White House
Washington, D.C.
Dear Madam:

Knowing how busy you are, I hope you find time to read our little note of appreciation for what you've done. We can never thank you enough and will always remember with grateful hearts the help and consideration received from the "First Lady" of our land.

Private and Mrs. Wilton S. Gates
Washington, D.C.

• • •

March 26, 1943

Dear Mrs. Roosvelt—

You may never read this letter, But hope you will. My Son
Pvt. George. H. Dalrymple was reported to me by War Dept
Washington. D.C. as Missing in Action, in North Atlantic on
Feb 2 1943 due to the Sinking of a Ship by enemy. He left
Taunton Mass. From Camp Miles Standish was in Enge-
neering Corps.

And is on casualty list. I can't seem to hear anything
more about it.

What Ship? The Navy Spokesman didnt Seem to know
whether convoyed or not. 850 lost in North Atlantic. I want
to hear more so much and particulars, its awful not to
hear, I Just hoped that you would help me to know in Some
way—

I am so grieved not to know About it—

If possible let me hear more

I am heartbroken

Thank you

Respect—

Mrs. George Dalrymple

Franklin, North Carolina

[One and a half pages handwritten]

March 31, 1943

My dear Mrs. Dalrymple:

Your letter of March 25th has been received and I know Mrs.
Roosevelt would want me to express her sincere regret that
she cannot be helpful in supplying information other than that
which has already been given to next of kin in cases such as
yours where boys have been reported missing in action. When

additional information becomes available, it is first given to the families of the boys who have been reported missing and unfortunately, Mrs. Roosevelt has no way of obtaining such information prior to notification given by the Departments concerned.

Much of the information, such as the names of ships, strength of convoy, etc., must remain secret until such time as it would be useless to the enemy.

I know Mrs. Roosevelt would want me to convey to you her deepest sympathy in the sorrow which has come to you.

Very sincerely yours,
Administrative Office
Social Correspondence

• • •

May 23, 1943

Dear Mrs. Roosevelt:

I am enclosing a letter to you from my only Son. Believing that you will not use this letter against him, but in some way a honest man will be sent to this camp to investigate the conditions there. Being a mother I just can't sit blindly by and see everything that is fine and decent crushed out of my only child. To say nothing of the other mother's sons.

Thanking you for any help you can give, I am

Yours truly
Sarah F. Normant
Newport News, Virginia

[One page handwritten]

May 18, 1943

Dear Mother:

As you know I've never had any hate in my heart for anyone regardless of race or creed. Since I've been in the Army I've seen hate and I've learned to hate and distrust. It is one of the worst states of mind to ever allow your self to retreat into. These people, poor whites, and there attitudes towards Negro "men" is abomnable. They think we're primative iliterate children.

We have boys here who can hardly get around but yet the officers say it's in the mind. The Army to most of us has become a joke, a farce, which makes our hearts bleed when we think of what is happening to our boys over seas. Suppior numbers is our only chance. Requesting transfers is impossible—the morale is to low among much of the soldiers of all races. Some boys who have just come from Australia say that Negroes aren't fighting they're slaving.

Mother you and Doctor Greene, both, seem to think that my side is a joke. It isn't and never has been it's about to run me out of my mind. I've got to decide on whether to stay here and go crazy or take an chance letting them find me. I cant stand this torture much longer. They say there's nothing they can do. I've just got to suffer. Yet they want to subject me to strenuous work. I cant do it anymore. Whatever I decide, if Im wrong forgive me. You have done all that a mother could do for a son and I love you, and Daddy too. Pray for me Ma, I've forgotten how.

Love

Your son

[on stationery of Quartermaster Detachment (CLD), Camp Claiborne, Louisiana]

May 27, 1943

Dear Mr. McCloy:

The mother of a boy at Camp Claiborne, Louisiana, has sent me his letter, of which the enclosed is a copy. It seems to me to ring true.

Eleanor Roosevelt

(Dictated but not read by Mrs. Roosevelt)

[Stamped "Confidential"; declassified on Feb. 27, 1975]

July 26, 1943

Dear Mrs. Roosevelt:

Under date of May 27th you referred to me a copy of a letter you had received in which complaint was made of the treatment of Negro soldiers at Camp Claiborne, La. Your correspondent inclosed a letter from her son in which indications were given that he was suffering from forms of race discrimination. In addition, the soldier indicated that he is suffering from an unstated physical condition which has not been treated by the medical authorities.

Since the name of the soldier is not given, it has not been possible to investigate his complaint of inadequate medical attention. However, an investigation was made at Camp Claiborne to determine if the reported race discrimination exists and to ascertain the cause of the alleged bad morale among Negro soldiers.

I now have the Inspector General's confidential report on this matter, and I believe the best way to give you the information is to transmit to you the pertinent extract from the report. It is enclosed herewith.

There has arisen a tendency in the Negro soldier to believe any wild story of discrimination or abuse. The story will spread like wildfire and the Negro soldier has been so

sensitized by references to his abused position that he is prepared to believe anything and does. The Negro press has been
quite careless in reporting and playing up accounts of alleged
mistreatment. By no means all the blame can be traced to the
Negro or the Negro press and even though I firmly believe the
Army is far ahead of the country generally to realize the many
difficult Negro problems, there is room for great improvement in
our handling of the Negro in the Army.[*] General Marshall has
recently issued a strong directive to the Army commanders
which should initiate a much closer attention to the handling of
those matters by the responsible Army officers.

The problem is a national one but the War Department is
making every endeavor to see that the general condition of
Negro troops in the Army is improved and that causes of friction
between them and the white troops are removed. Unfortunately
the steps which one side feels would remove the trouble, almost
invariably stimulate trouble from the other side and a solution in
one part of the country in a particular situation can rarely be
applied generally.

Sincerely,

John J. McCloy
Office of the Assistant Secretary
War Department
Washington, D.C.

[Inspector General's report, *marked "copy"*]

Camp Claiborne has a strength of 40,778 white troops and 8,480
negro troops. More than 50% of the negro personnel are being trained at
the Engineer Unit Training Center. The remainder are with the Third
Army Troops and with the Station Complement. The 103rd Infantry
Division (white) is stationed at this camp. Except for a relatively small

---

[*] President Harry Truman ordered the desegregation of the military in 1948.

number of negro troops with the Station Complement, all negro organizations are quartered in contiguous areas. General observations and the records of past incidents, indicate that a relatively low state of discipline exists among the negro units of the Engineer Unit Training Center. No serious mass breeches of discipline have occurred for several weeks. Additional negro engineer regiments are to be activated in the near future which will tend to increase racial problems. On 1-2 May 1943, there were three mass raids on exchanges by negro enlisted men, during which several hundred dollars worth of merchandise was removed and exchange equipment damaged. There were disturbances of a similar nature on other dates. It was reported that on other occasions attempts have been made by negro enlisted men to overturn busses; that busses were stoned and windows broken by groups of negro enlisted men and that white civilian drivers have been without cause threatened, abused and vilely cursed by negro personnel. On one evening a large crowd of negro enlisted men gathered at the service club used by negro men, in protest of alleged mistreatment of a negro enlisted man by a white officer. A mutinous spirit prevailed and the crowd was slow to disperse when directed to do so by high ranking officers. A CN (tear gas) candle was set off by authorities during this demonstration. The extent to which negro troops from the III Army units and from the Station Complement may have participated in these disturbances was not determined and guilty persons remain unpunished. It is believed that directives should be issued effecting greater emphasis on disciplinary development in the training programs of these negro units.

The plan for the use of camp military police in connection with threatened or actual race disturbances appeared to lack adequate and strong centralized control. The strength of the camp military police, particularly as to negro personnel, was not considered sufficient. A conference was held with the Commanding Officer, Second Security District (La.), Eighth Service Command, relative to these matters. That officer visited Camp Claiborne with a view to effecting necessary coordination. He has stated that he will recommend that 50 additional negro military police be authorized.

Other than the limited and extremely overtaxed recreational and entertainment facilities in the city of Alexandria there are but few places in the general vicinity where clean recreational facilities can be found for white or negro troops. Much can be done to improve conditions in this camp relative to recreational facilities and entertainment programs; enlarged and improved motion picture, service club, and athletic facilities, to include construction of swimming pools, are highly desirable. These projects should be given high priority when engineer troop labor is used on construction projects as a part of their engineer training. Priority should also be given to projects for the general benefit of the camp as a whole. Separate suitably equipped officers' clubs have been established for white and negro officers. No discrimination was noted in matters pertaining to exchanges, guest houses, religious matters, Red Cross, or Army Emergency Relief. Exchange facilities appear adequate. The same general type of facilities is available to guests at the Guest House for negroes as is available to guests at the Guest Houses for white persons. Greater congestion and overcrowding, however, exists at the former. Relations among white and negro chaplains are harmonious. Records show that three times as many Red Cross cases per capita are handled for negro personnel as are handled for white personnel. Official records show that during the period, 1 January–19 June 1943, 61% more per capita was loaned to negro personnel than to white personnel by the Army Emergency Relief.

• • •

May 25, 1943

My dear Mrs. Roosevelt,
I am writing this letter on behalf of my brother
Private David Levine—aged 31
Camp Hale, Colorado
He was inducted March 31, 1943 and having volunteered for the Mountain Infantry, commonly known as

the Ski Troops, he was sent to Camp Hale Colorado on April 14th.

On May 5th it was suddenly discovered that his wife had developed Acute Leukemia, and he was granted an emergency furlough that he might be at her side. Her's is a fatal illness and there is no hope of recovery. This is the opinion of two of the leading blood specialists of the country. They have also given us to understand that there is no telling when the end will come, but in all probability it will be a few months.

As my brother had entered the army leaving at home a perfectly healthy wife,—this has been a terrible shock to him. And so he has felt compelled to ask the army for a transfer to a nearby camp, as to be over 2000 miles away at such a critical time is inconceivable to him. He feels that it would be impossible to return to Camp Hale and carry on his duties with the physical and mental fitness that is required. Certainly he would be of little use to his division in such a state of mind. Believe me, Mrs. Roosevelt, it is not that he wishes to shirk his duties as a soldier, but only to carry them out at a reasonable distance from his wife so that when death occurs, he shall be sufficiently near to arrive in time for the funeral, which in our faith is at sundown of the same day. Surely with such a feeling in his heart, the army could find him a better man, if this transfer were permitted.

All of the facts may be verified with the Red Cross Field Director at Fort Hamilton Brooklyn, N.Y. The Red Cross has been doing their utmost to effect his transfer. But it seems that while all army officers contacted agree his case merits the transfer, the abundance of red tape involved is so mountainous that they cannot cut through it. Finally a Major at Fort Hamilton advised him to wire the Adjutant General's Office in Washington D.C. for a hearing. For with specific instructions from the personnel there he could be acceptable at Fort Hamilton.

Today, he sent that wire—I, his brother having seen all the difficulties he is encountering, have doubt as to his receiving this hearing,—and so I am writing to you Mrs. Roosevelt, because I feel that you who have championed and have won so many lost causes, can sympathize, can understand, and can cut through the red tape.

Please forgive my writing all this to you, but my Mother, Father and all of our family, are desperate with worry over the health of my brother David, should he have to return to Colorado under these tragic circumstances, and his emergency furlough expires within a week.

Anything you can do Mrs. Roosevelt, any advice you can give, or any assistance you can render will be deeply appreciated.

Sincerely,

Irving Levine

Kew Gardens New York

[Four and a half pages handwritten]

June 9, 1943

MEMORANDUM FOR MISS THOMPSON:

In the attached letter addressed to Mrs. Roosevelt, Mr. Irving Levine requested assistance in securing a transfer for his brother from Camp Hale, Colorado, to the vicinity of New York City. The basis for the request was a report to the effect that Private Levine's wife is suffering from a fatal illness, and that she is not expected to live much longer.

I have had this matter taken up with the Adjutant General, and orders have been issued temporarily transferring Private Levine from Camp Hale to Fort Hamilton, New York. At the same time, an investigation is being conducted by the Red Cross to substantiate the statements of Mr. Irving Levine, and if they are found to be correct, Private Levine will be permanently transferred to Fort Hamilton.

I have written to Mr. Levine giving him this information. However, he probably has already received the information, since the Adjutant General telegraphed his brother on May 26 telling him of his transfer.

B. W. Davenport
Major, General Staff,
Assistant Secretary, General Staff
Office of the Chief of Staff
War Department
Washington, D.C.

• • •

Dear Mrs. Roosevelt.

I am turning to you for help as I dont know who else I can go to. Being a woman and mother you'll understand where other won't what Im up against.

I have 2 children a boy of 3—also a baby 11 months old. My husband Nils P. Dahl is in the service since Jan 1–43.

Since Pearl Harbor, and he being an Norwegian, he has wanted to do some thing for the war effort. He is mechanically inclined, and knows about Diesel motors he tried getting a job when in Defense plants also ship yards, were he would be of most use, but was turned down not because of his knowlidge but because he wasn't a citizen.

So due to some misunderstanding with the draft board he got in the service. That would be very well had I been well and had other means of support.

But after the baby I got Phlebitis in my leg and am handy capped, since, beside heart trouble, and other ailments Since he's gone I havent the time to get any treatments as it would have to be in a clinic my baby has been more sick than well, all winter.

He had a janitor job before he left and because I had no money or even the strength to move I have tried to keep it up so as to have a roof over our heads. All winter I had the tenants helping me out seeing I was sick they didn't want to see us put out. I feel I can't do this much longer and as things are don't know what I can do. As I cant go out and pay rent for an apartment out of the allotment money I get.

Now Nils was home on a furlough from Camp Hale Colo. And saw how he had left us. He went to General Motor Inc. and asked for a job so they told him if he could be released from the service there is a job waiting for him.

Mrs. Roosevelt if he could be released until such time when he really will be needed it would give me a chance to get my strength back also get some treatments, so that in time he can go back and do his part for our Country and us. But as things are at present I beg of you to try and help us out Im not asking only for my self but the children as I can't give them the attention they need feeling like I do; the boy has to be kept in because I can't be out with him and when left alone runs out on the streets;

Every thing Im writing is true and could be investigated not only on my say so But there are the War, also Hospital records So Please see if some thing couldn't be done for us. In Ref. To my husbands release

Sincerely
Ann Dahl
New York, New York

[Two and a half pages handwritten]

July 29, 1943

MEMORANDUM FOR MISS THOMPSON:

In the attached letter addressed to Mrs. Roosevelt, Mrs. Nils P. Dahl requests assistance in obtaining a dependency discharge for her husband. She described at length the financial difficulties which she and her children have been facing as a result of the military service of her husband.

I have had this matter looked into very thoroughly and it has been decided to grant Private Dahl a dependency discharge in order that he may return to civilian life and better support his wife and children.

B. W. Davenport
Major, General Staff
Assistant Secretary, General Staff
Office of the Chief of Staff
War Department
Washington D.C.

• • •

[Letter marked "Forward"]

Dear Mrs. Roosevelt.

A few days ago I read your column where you told of receiving the news that your son was safe. The same day we received from the war Dept the terrible news that our **only** son Lieut. Richard Dilley was killed July 21. Nothing more. He was such a wonderful son. He had worked his way thru four years college graduating as a Civil Engineer in Jan before his country took him in Aug. just 2 years ago. He had been in England almost a year and every letter how kind the people there were and how he loved the country. He spoke especially of one dear lady who took him into their home and how dear she was to him. Is there anyway I could find and write her. He thought so much of his major, can I someway get his name so I could write him. Our dear boy was with Co B- 829 Engr. Bn. I hope you will never have to know what our sorrow means it is almost too much. His every hope was coming back to what he hoped was a home founded on a permanent victory.

Mrs. Edna Dilley
Kansas City, Kansas

[Two and a half pages handwritten]

August 10, 1943

Dear Mrs. Dilley:

I am deeply distressed to hear of your sad loss and while I know there is nothing I can say which will help, I do want you to know how deeply I sympathize with you.

I will try to find out from the War Department the name of the Colonel and perhaps some of the men in his company may know the name of the woman who was so kind to your boy.

It is hard for a mother to lose her son but knowing that he was willing to give his life for his country and for his fellow men should make you proud. I hope God will give you the strength to bear your loss bravely.

Very sincerely yours,
Eleanor Roosevelt
August 14, 1943

My dear Mrs. Dilley:

Mrs. Roosevelt has obtained the following information and asks me to pass it along to you:

"The War Department records show that Major Christian

Hanburger has been the commanding officer of the 829th Engineer Battalion since its activation on May 24, 1942. This officer's address is APO 644, c/o Postmaster, New York City."

> Very sincerely yours,
> Malvina C. Thompson
> Secretary to Mrs. Roosevelt

• • •

September 28, 1943

Dear Mrs. Roosevelt:

We were told you helped so many Mothers who have sons in the service so I thought maybe you could help me. I have a son serving the U.S. Army somewhere in the South Pacific. He has never been home since he was inducted in the Army June 19, 1941. He has been serving in the South Pacific for one year. (In Guadalcanal, New Georgia Islands and New Caledonia).

A few months ago we got a letter saying he was in the hospital, we don't know what the matter is, but from the hints he gave he has the tropical Malaria. (He said in one of his letters that he saw you a short time ago in the hospital visiting the boys.) We have a very close friend who has been close to our son, and he says more boys die from the tropical fever than they do of bullets. We can't understand why our President leaves our boys over there to die, because if they are brought back to the states there is a possible chance for them to survive. Our boy has been in constant fight almost all the time since he has been over there.

I was in poor health when my son left and am getting worse as time goes on. We have been doing every thing we can toward the war effort and intend to keep on doing so, but we do hope and pray that you will do all you can to see that our son can be shipped home as soon as possible. It will be deeply appreciated.

Respectfully yours,

Mrs. Selma Sulser.

Kaskaskia, Illinois

Our son's address:

Pvt. Forrest J. Sulser

c/o P.M. San Francisco, California

[Two pages handwritten]

[undated]

MEMORANDUM FOR MISS THOMPSON

Several days ago you referred to me the attached letter from Mrs. Selma Sulser, who stated that her son, while confined in a station hospital in the South Pacific area, had seen Mrs. Roosevelt. You asked that we determine Private Sulser's condition.

A radio report has just been received to the effect that Private Forest J. Sulser, Eighth General Hospital, c/o Postmaster, San Francisco, California, has been hospitalized for malaria. His condition is not serious and at the present time he is in a convalescent camp. It is expected that Private Sulser will return to duty in the near future.

B. W. Davenport

Major, General Staff

Asst. Secretary, General Staff

• • •

October 1, 1943

Dear Mrs. Roosevelt:

Knowing of the interest which you take in the families of the members of the armed forces of the United States and the diligence with which you put forth efforts to aid and comfort them, I am appealing to you personally.

My wife's first cousin, Major Charles Roy Kerr has been reported missing since 2 January 1942 in the Philippine Islands. This has caused anxiety and anguish to the family and, in fact, it was the primary cause of the death of his wife. At present, settlement of the estate is held in abeyance pending the end of the War.

There are enclosed, for your information, a copy of a somewhat flamboyant account of the suicide of the spouse of the above mentioned cousin, as published in the local Akron, Ohio newspaper, together with a copy of the last letter received from Major Kerr, dated 1 January 1942.

I feel that knowing the circumstances involved in this case, you will use every power at your disposal to ascertain whether the man in question is alive or dead.

Very truly yours,
Newell Keith Woods
Csp (G), USNR
Yukon, Florida

[1 page typed]

Copy of the report, appearing in the Akron, Ohio, newspaper:

Doctor Missing—At Corregidor—Wife Suicide
Anniversary of Corregidor came and went and still no word came of her physician husband, a major in the U.S. Army. Mother's Day

brought a telegram and for a minute hope flared, but it was from a nephew in the marines.

So late yesterday, worn with months of waiting and worrying, Mrs. Jessie Kerr, 61, sister of Mrs. Mary Malboeuf, went to the basement of the Malboeuf home where she has been staying for several months and hanged herself with a piece of clothesline.

The sister, a teacher at the Immaculate Conception School across the street, found her when she returned with an armful of groceries, just before dinner. In an upstairs room, Mrs. Kerr's grandniece, Mary Catherine Doyle, 7, ill with the measles, had been calling for her aunt in vain.

CALLED TO SERVICE—Dr. Charles Kerr, a practicing physician at Chenoa, Illinois, was called into active service as a member of the army reserve, early in 1941. He was made a major and was stationed at first at San Antonio, Texas. He sent word for his wife to join him there, but before she arrived, he was summoned to San Francisco and from there was sent to a hospital in Manila and later at Corregidor. She never saw him again.

For months, the wife carried on her daily duties at her Illinois home. "But the rumble of the trains through the tunnel and even the swarming of the starlings got on my nerves," she told her sister when she decided to come to Akron last September.

LISTENS TO NEWS: "My sister spent many hours listening to war news on the radio, and haunted the Red Cross and wrote to the War Department constantly for news of her husband. But she had never been able to get a word," Mrs. Malboeuf said today. "She got so she couldn't eat and brooded deeply over the war news. Yet she read stories to Mary Catherine all day yesterday, and prepared the child's lunch before she went down to die."

A note was found, giving instructions as to her burial. Dr. R. E. Amos, Summit County Coroner, in passing a verdict of suicide said his investigation revealed that Mrs. Kerr had attempted suicide a week ago by hanging herself with her apron strings but they broke before she was strangled.

Copy of the last letter received from Dr. Charles R. Kerr:

January 1, 1942

Dear Aunt:

Well, was a good boy last night and stayed in. Rebuilt a box for my extra stuff yesterday PM. Some different temperature than a year ago, although I used a blanket several nights (out doors). You'll know more of what is happening than I, as we don't get radio reports any more as the battery radio they had, petered out. One I had is useless as no electric current, so I've boxed it up with all my nice white clothes.

You'll have to conjecture on location, as letters aren't supposed to carry location etc., as one can see. Am all right, can add, up to now. Sent Jessie a radiogram Xmas, asked her to drop you a line. Not much one can write. So Jap planes have been able to have uninterrupted tours of the island, Cook's Tour, so to speak, but reckon that'll be changed before long. Hope our politicians and great statesmen get wise to themselves sometime and find that bluff is a very thin bat and their grand ideas of greatness won't always suffice.

Hope this reaches you some day. Recon returning supply ships will carry mail, might as well.

Won't be surprised if before long that the Japs will find their air tours of the islands not the happy uninterrupted cruises they have been.

This is dry season. That helps out but makes military operations possible while the wet reverses things. Well, I'll write again one of these days.

All ok,

Roy

Happy New Year

Charles R. Kerr

Major, MC

Manila, P.I.

October 26, 1943

Mrs. Franklin D. Roosevelt
Re: KERR, Charles Roy (Major)
The White House Washington, D.C. Inq: WOODS, Newell
Keith Csp (G), USNR
My dear Mrs. Roosevelt:
This is in reply to your letter of October 7, 1943, initiated
by Newell Keith Woods, regarding Major Kerr, who,
according to the latest information was serving in the
Philippines at the time of the surrender of Corregidor.

We have checked through official channels in an effort
to ascertain any available information regarding the
present status of this officer and the only record we have is
that he has been "missing in the Philippines" since the surrender, May 1942. His emergency addressee, whom he has
listed as his sister-in-law, Mrs. Mary Malbeouf, of Akron,
Ohio, was notified May 19, 1943.

As you probably know, at the time of the surrender
of Corregidor, all men who had not previously been
reported deceased, wounded, or prisoners of war, were
considered "missing" until such time as will permit the
War Department to determine what has happened to
them. There is, of course, a limitation in the amount of
information that can be obtained as to the whereabouts
or welfare of a "missing" man. Inquiries are no longer
being sent to the International Red Cross Committee at
Geneva. Because it is necessary to go directly to the
enemy for information concerning "missing" men, it has
been realized that such inquiries further endanger the life
of the serviceman. Also, because of the tremendous
volume of work that is being handled at International
Headquarters, individual inquiries hinder the release of
lists of prisoners of war.

Lists of men who are prisoners of war of the Japanese

government are still being received. To date this officer's name has not appeared on any list, but it is possible that it may in the future. War has so disturbed communications that it is usually a matter of months after a man is captured before his name can be forwarded by the belligerent and cleared through the International Red Cross at Geneva. This is particularly true in the Pacific Area. We do not wish to raise any false hopes, but on recent lists of prisoners of war have appeared the names of some who had previously been reported "missing" in the Philippines since May 1942. Because of this, the War Department has not made final determination on many "missing" men. We are very sorry we have no other information for you at this time. However, if we can be of further assistance, please do not hesitate to call upon us.

Yours very truly,
Charlotte Johnson
National Director
Home Service
American Red Cross
National Headquarters
Washington, D.C.

November 1, 1943

My dear Mr. Woods:
In the absence of Mrs. Roosevelt and her personal secretary, I am sending you copy of communication received from the American Red Cross concerning your letter to Mrs. Roosevelt.

Very sincerely yours,
Administrative Officer
Social correspondence

The Japanese attacked the Philippines on December 8, 1941, one day after

Pearl Harbor. General Douglas MacArthur withdrew to the island of Cor-
regidor, near Manila. A pro-Japanese government was formed, but many
Filipino guerrilla fighters joined the American forces. In Bataan, the forced
"death march" of 70,000 American and Filipino prisoners of war from
Marivales to San Fernando resulted in the death of thousands.
MacArthur's forces triumphantly returned to the area in October 1944.
The U.S. military tried the leader of the Japanese forces, Lt. Gen. Homma
Masaharu, and executed him on April 3, 1946.

• • •

October 2, 1943

Dear Mrs. Roosevelt—

I do hope you don't think this is an imposition on my part,
but knowing how you feel about fair play, I do think you
won't mind my writing to you about the following case that
has just come up, and perhaps you may be able to do something about it.

My husband is in the Anti-Aircraft Artillery at Camp
Stewart, Georgia. I, too, work in a defense plant here in
Buffalo to help the war effort.

Being of Jewish faith, my husband and his fellow men
of the same faith in his battery naturally expected to get
the two days off on our New Year's as it is customary to
attend services on those days. Not only did their Capt.
refuse to give them any time off, but picked the five Jewish
men, of a lot of eight men, and gave them K.P. duty, the
duty ending at eight o'clock so that they were unable to
attend services at camp at 7:30 p.m.

Every other battery gave their men from 2 to 5 days off
for the holidays. I do believe this is an outrage, and something should be done about officers taking so much upon
themselves. It is very evident that this officer dislikes

Jewish people, and the thought of racial prejudice, in time of war, is too horrible to think about.

We must all stand together, regardless of race or creed, if we are to win this war, and such practices must be stopped.

Please Mrs. Roosevelt, see what can be done about this, as I don't feel too happy about it, and receiving mail from my husband whom I love better than life itself, full of bitterness, has upset me, very much.

Thanking you for bearing with me, and hoping you may be able to do something about this outrage, I remain,

Sincerely

Mrs. Ruth Shapoff

Buffalo, New York

My husbands address is Pvt. I. Shapoff, Batt. A.
Camp Stewart, Georgia

[Three pages handwritten]

October 19, 1943

My dear Mrs. Roosevelt:

The alleged discrimination against members of the Jewish faith stationed at Camp Steward, Georgia, has been investigated by the Commanding General, Antiaircraft Command. The investigation shows that members of this organization of Jewish faith were informed that they would be free to attend religious services on 29 September, 30 September, and 1 October. This information was posted on the bulletin board and also announced to the Battery by the organization commander. All Jewish enlisted men of the organization who applied for permission to attend the services were given this permission, including four of the

five men detailed on kitchen police duty. The fifth man did
not request permission to attend services on 29 September
and was kept on duty. When he did request permission to
attend services on 1 October that request was granted.
This investigation was conducted by a commissioned
officer who is himself an orthodox Jew.

It seems clear in this case that no intentional discrimination against Jewish enlisted men occurred. The soldier
who missed service on the 29th was either ignorant of the
method of obtaining the necessary permission or inatten-
tive to the announcement made in his organization.

The writer of the attached note has apparently
received a one-sided version of the affair. You will know
best how to reply to her letter on the basis of the information given above.

Sincerely,

John J. McCloy

Office of the Assistant Secretary

War Department

Washington, D.C.

*On October 20, 1943, a letter was sent to Mrs. Shapoff quoting the first
paragraph of the letter above.*

• • •

October 22, 1943

My Dear Mrs. Roosevelt:

I have been praying for help and guidance in this time of
grief and tragedy, and the thought came to me that I could
appeal to you for help.

My nineteen year old daughter met and fell in love
with a soldier while he was stationed near this small town.

She is a Western Union operator and they met when he came to the office. He seemed to be a very nice and respectable boy. He came to our home often while here. They planned to be married when he got a furlough that he was expecting. But instead they got orders to go overseas and left immediately before my daughter knew she was going to be a Mother. He is in England still unaware of the fact for she hadn't told anyone till she told me this week. I feel that I must help her, she has no one else. Her father is dead and her brother, my only son is in service and he must not know for he would be so grieved.

She is sure he would marry her if he had a chance. I feel that it would be right for him to have a chance since he is fighting for the things dear to him and that would prevent a tragedy in three lives.

Please Mrs. Roosevelt, if there is anyway possible for a marriage to be performed under these conditions. I will be ever so grateful if you will please inform me as to how to go about it.

Very Sincerely yours,
Mrs. B. H. Deere
Milan, Tennessee

[Two pages handwritten]

[On notepaper of the White House, Washington, D.C.]

November 9, 1943

MEMORANDUM FOR COLONEL MCCARTHY:

Mrs. Roosevelt asks if there is any way such marriages can be performed by proxy.

Malvina C. Thompson
Secretary to Mrs. Roosevelt

November 23, 1943

Some time ago you referred to me the attached letter concerning proxy marriages and said that Mrs. Roosevelt would like to know if there was any way in which such marriages could be performed.

The Judge Advocate General tells me that the validity of a marriage by proxy will be governed by the laws of the place where the marriage is celebrated. A search has revealed that there is no state statute specifically authorizing such marriages, and there is an almost complete lack of court decisions passing upon their legality. In view of lack of authority on this subject, the Judge Advocate General feels that he cannot state the effectiveness of a marriage by proxy. Also, in view of the fact that the rights of a "wife" to dependency benefits and the rights of a "widow" to six months' gratuitous pay and a pension are involved, the Judge Advocate General has expressed the opinion that the War Department should not attempt to suggest any plan for the accomplishment of such a marriage, nor to comment on its legal effectiveness, nor to approve the marriage in any way.

The Adjutant General has suggested that the prospective mother submit a statement alleging that a named enlisted man is responsible for her pregnancy and that she desires to marry the soldier. The statement should be accompanied by a doctor's certificate showing her physical condition. When these papers are received by The Adjutant General, the soldier's commanding officer would be asked for a report as to whether or not the soldier acknowledges in writing responsibility for the pregnancy, and whether or not he is willing to be married to the prospective mother. If the soldier admits responsibility and is willing to be married, he will be returned to the United States and granted a furlough for the purpose of marriage. Of course, the return of a soldier will depend on the military situation in the place where he is serving and the availability of transportation.

B. W. Davenport,
Major, General Staff
Asst. Secretary, General Staff
Office of the Chief of Staff
War Department
Washington, D.C.

• • •

[Date-stamped January 7, 1944]

My Dear Mrs. Roosevelt:

I am writing you, asking a favor because I know you attend to the little things of life. I remember you so well in the last war where your cheer meant so much to our wounded boys—you will not recall me but I might introduce myself as the mother of Lt. Com. Buzz Carroll who gave his life to save others in Liscombe Bay tragedy and has been recommended by Captains Crommelin and Rowe for the Congressional Medal of Honor. He saved 12 boys and I am so anxious to get in touch with as many of them as I can, for thru them he lives.

No one but you would trouble to find out if it were possible thru the Navy Dept. and perhaps I am asking too great a favor but I am making a scrap book for Buzz's children and do so want some of those names. In this terrible conflict, we are so overwhelmed with grief that the small worth while things are forgotten but some how I feel that nothing is unimportant to you if it helps lift the burden of the other fellow.

If not possible to get this information in Washington

perhaps they could direct me how to go about it and I shall spare no pains to secure it. Most cordially and gratefully,

Elia R. Carroll

St. Joseph, Michigan

[Three pages handwritten]

[Date-stamped January 31, 1944]

My dear Mrs. Roosevelt:

I am in receipt of a communication from your secretary, who enclosed a letter from Mrs. Elia R. Carroll, of St. Joseph, Michigan. Mrs. Carroll would like to know the names of the men of the USS LISCOME BAY rescued by her son, Lieutenant Commander Wells Worth Carroll, United States Naval Reserve, who is now in the status of missing in action.

The senior surviving officer of the USS LISCOMBE BAY is being requested to furnish the Navy Department any information he may have concerning these men. When his reply has been received, you will be informed accordingly.

Mrs. Carroll's letter to you is returned. My personal sympathy is offered to her in her anxiety.

Sincerely yours,

Ralph A. Bard

Office of the Secretary of the Navy

Washington, D.C.

The U.S.S. Liscombe Bay, *CVE-56, was a small escort carrier, basically a freighter hull covered with a flight deck; the sailors referred to these ships as Combustible Vulnerable and Expendable. The* Liscombe Bay *met its fate in its very first battle, at Tarawa, Gilbert Islands, in the South Pacific. After a seventy-six hour fight, the Americans secured an atoll at a cost of*

980 marines and 29 sailors. The next day a Japanese submarine torpedoed and sank the Liscombe Bay, *causing the loss of an additional 644 men of the navy.*

• • •

January 25, 1944

Dear Mrs. Roosevelt:

March will mark the first anniversary of the Battle of the Warsaw Ghetto—the first act of armed resistance waged by the entire Jewish community of Poland under the Nazis.

This heroic spirit of a people, that voluntarily chose a soldier's death rather than be slaughtered as slaves, that took up arms against the mightiest military machine of our time in order to maintain its human dignity, shall remain as an outstanding episode in the annals of mankind.

Thousands upon thousands of the heroic defenders of the Warsaw Ghetto paid with their lives for their daring. Tens of thousands of those who remained—men, women and children—were slaughtered by the Nazis in cold blood when the armed resistance was broken. The Jewish ghetto was set on fire and obliterated. The Jewish community of Warsaw has ceased to exist. Thus, March will mark the first anniversary of a Nazi crime that congeals our blood.

"Ghetto Speaks,"which is published by the American Representation of the Jewish Underground Labor Movement of Poland, and voices the thoughts and sentiments of the Jews locked within the ghettos of occupied Poland and throughout subjugated Europe, deems it a duty to dedicate its March issue to the anniversary of the heroic resistance and to the memory of the fallen heroes.

We are seeking to obtain as many messages as possible

for this issue from prominent liberals and leading person-
alities of the United States and Great Britain. Regardless
of size, these messages will help pay tribute to the memory
of those who died fighting for our common cause, as well
as aid in the condemnation of their murderers.

We are taking the liberty of asking you for such a
written statement. With your kind cooperation, we hope to
make the special March issue of "Ghetto Speaks" a true
expression of the prevailing sentiments among leading
Americans and Britons. Even a wire, bearing your signature, would be of great assistance.

Thanking you most sincerely in advance for your kind
cooperation and prompt response, we are,

Very truly yours,
Emanuel Nowogredsky
American Representation
General Jewish Workers' Union of Poland
New York, New York

[One page typed]

February 7, 1944

My dear Mrs. Roosevelt:

I have taken the liberty of drafting for your possible use a reply
to the request from the American Representation of the General
Jewish Workers' Union of Poland for a message from you for the
March issue of their magazine.

Sincerely yours,
Cordell Hull
Secretary of State
Washington, D.C.

The following was enclosed with the above letter:

My dear Mr. Nowogrodsky:

I am glad to send you the following message for publication in the March issue of "Ghetto Speaks":

It is a common experience when every day horror is piled upon horror until the senses weary, to wonder if we have lost our power to feel. Our greatest inspiration and our strongest faith is drawn from the brave and pitiful people whose spirit is all they have. The Jews of the Warsaw Ghetto were such people. It is trite, perhaps, to say what is true, that they died for all of us, that we must live for them. But it is the kind of truth that is too soon forgotten. Only truths that ask little of us are easy to remember. My message to you, therefore, is what I tell myself, "Let us not forget."

Sincerely yours,

February 10, 1944

Dear Mr. Secretary:

Thank you very much for drafting the message to the General Jewish Workers' Union of Poland. It is much better than any I could have phrased.

Very sincerely yours,
Eleanor Roosevelt

• • •

July 18, 1944

Dear Mrs. Roosevelt

As perhaps you may remember I wrote to you just after you left here that I had been visiting the U.S. Navy hospital

Mogile 4 for several months, but that the permit to go there had been cancelled. You very kindly answered my letter, and thought that I should try again to get in. Doctor O'Connor also advised me to do so; but I did not meet with success.

However I turned my thought to inviting men to dinner on Saturday afternoons. Have had ninety six so far. They have all seemed to enjoy themselves and I have had some very pleasing letters from some of our guests.

One thing that has made me rather sad is that so many of them have told me that the doctors advise the poor war torn men to "Go to town." "Go and get drunk." Some of the lads did this and unfortunately some of them did things when drunk that they would not have done when sober, even to murder, with the result that they have returned to their native land as prisoners on three, five, ten, or even fifteen years service debarred of all rights and pay. What a return for service in this horrid battle field. One young man said to me "Mrs. Kibble will I want to kill men when I get home? It haunts me for I have to kill every Jap I see when he may even be asking me for bread." Yet in spite of this Doctors tell the men to "Go and get drunk." To my sense it is almost as bad for them to do that, as for the unfortunate man to do dreadful things when under the influence of what the doctor told him to drink. Can anything be done to prevent it?

Not one man but many told me of these things and it is unfortunately not only your doctors but the New Zealanders also who so advise.

May I once more say how much good your visit did here. Nearly everyone I know said that you had made us understand America better.

Thanking you for your patience in reading this and hoping for the return of your husband in the forthcoming election.

I remain

Sincerely yours

Mrs. Alice Mary Kibble

Auckland, New Zealand

[One and a half pages typed]

[*Handwritten note at bottom of page*]: "I am a naturalized American Citizen. Would like to return but do not see my way to do so but— we shall see."

August 24, 1944

My dear Mrs. Kibble:

Mrs. Roosevelt has asked me to thank you so much for your letter of July 18th.

Mrs. Roosevelt appreciates your writing and will do what she can to remedy the situation.

Very sincerely yours,

Malvina C. Thompson

Secretary to Mrs. Roosevelt

August 31, 1944

Dear Mrs. Roosevelt:

I have your note of August 24th enclosing a letter from Mrs. Alice Mary Kibble who has written to you concerning conditions in New Zealand.

I think that the advice given by the medical officers to the combat weary men may have been misinterpreted and perhaps the enlisted men have been a little too zealous in carrying it to the extreme. One of the great problems which have confronted the officers who are running the rest camps to which battle weary soldiers return, is to relieve the tension which men build up on the battlefield. It is hard to get these individuals to relax and to forget the experiences which they have undergone.

It may be that the officers who have given the advice to which Mrs. Kibble refers, have gone too far in their attempts to secure this relaxation and I will bring this to the attention of the officers in that area.

Sincerely,

[name handwritten only, illegible]

Office of the Secretary

War Department

Washington, D.C.

• • •

September 1, 1944

Mrs. Eleanor Roosevelt.

Washington, D.C.

Dear Friend.—

I am writing you, for information in regards to my Son, in the 7th Army. He has been in Africa, Italy and is now in France. While in Italy he was taken up with a 12 year old Italian boy, who lost all his folks, in air raids. For 3 months he followed the Army, where ever it went, to be with my Son John R. Hill, and would not leave him, even when the air raids was perty warm. So my Son says he wants to send him home to us to take care of. Could you tell us, how to go about it to get him here. We are willing to give him a home. As our boy wants us to. Any information you can give us will be appreciated. Our Son had to put the boy in a orphans home in Italy, before he

went to France in August. The boys name is Bingio Bar-
batts.

Please answer.

Yours Truly,

Mrs. Lillian Hill.

Wild Cherry, Arkansas

[One and a half pages handwritten]

September 4, 1944

My dear Mrs. Hill:

Mrs. Roosevelt has received many inquiries from persons
desiring to care for or adopt European children and has advised
the writers to communicate with the U.S. Committee for the Care of
European Children, 215-4th Avenue, New York 3, New York.

Very sincerely yours,

Administrative Officer

Social Correspondence

• • •

November 3, 1944

My dear Miss Thompson,

May I refer to your letter, October 31, advising me to write
to Mrs. Roosevelt instead of having a personal interview
with her, as she is so very busy just now.

Thanking you in advance for transmitting to her the
enclosed letter, believe me

Very sincerely yours

Anna Soubbotitch

Doctor in law

(wife of the former Yugoslav Minister at the Court of St. James)

New York, New York

November 3, 1944

Mrs. Eleanor Roosevelt, Honorary President of the American Friends of Yugoslavia

Dear Mrs. Roosevelt:

Yesterday I received your secretary's answer to my letter which was deposited at your home on Washington Square, N.Y.C. on October 26.

I am deeply grateful realising, that, even in so extremely busy days, you are willing to give up some of your time for the cause of the people and children of Belgrade.

My plea is: to be of help in sending the most urgent, the **most desperately needed** first aid **medicines** to the people of the destroyed, but liberated capital of Yugoslavia–Belgrade. The most needed medicines are sulfa drugs and aspirins. From Bari (Italy) a plane could reach Belgrade in two hours, and the funds of the United Yugoslav Relief Fund could be made available for the purchase of these medicines.

Of course, I realise, that the argument could be raised: that the case of Belgrade is only one among hundreds. As evidence against such possible arguments, I am enclosing a list of facts concerning the "Battle Belgrade" which shows the kind of exceptional destruction which was the fate of Belgrade—in addition to the heavy bombardment of our capital by the Allies on Easter 1944, and the most cruel bombardment by the Germans on Easter 1941.

Before the war, Belgrade had nearly 300,000 inhabitants. During the war, refugees from the whole country sought shelter in Belgrade, and according to information received through the International Red Cross, 120,000 orphans and homeless children were sheltered in Belgrade and vicinity.

All these children and adults, who survived the bombardments, are now without shelter, homes, fuel, winter clothing and even without the most common medicines. An urgent cable from the International Red Cross announced the **complete lack of medicines** already some months ago.

Thousands and thousands are now shivering in the severe and icy winds which blow over Belgrade during the month of November. These people are weak and undernourished, especially the children, and their resistance against colds, gripps and pneumonia is far below the minimum.

Therefore the most urgently needed aid is help in medicine like sulfa drugs, aspirins etc. Help in food, clothing etc. will go the normal way through the normal channels of relief to the liberated countries. We are sure that this kind of help (clothing, food etc.) will come to our people as soon as the destroyed lines of communication are, to some extent, restored to normalcy, so that aid can come through either from the liberating Russian Army, or the Red Cross, etc.

It is quite evident, that during war medical aid is very slow in reaching its destination by normal channels; far too slow for so many urgent cases for whom days or perhaps even hours may prove fatal.

As I already pointed out, from Bari it would take a plane only two hours to reach Belgrade.

Half of the shipping space of a small military plane (just a few cases of sulfa drugs and aspirins) would suffice to save the lives of tens of thousands, who otherwise are condemned to die during flu and pneumonia epidemics on the very morning of their liberation.

I cannot imagine that this request,—for the use of **one half of** the shipping space of **an airplane**, which, if granted, would facilitate the salvation of thousands of lives,—could be rejected. Especially not after it was officially announced

(*New York Times,* November 2) that the United States are in possession of 74,500 crafts of all types.

Neither can I imagine that such a request could be rejected in view of the fact that these poor and shivering people in Belgrade are the **same** courageous and enthusiastic people whose pressure brought about the revolution of March 27, 1941, which, in its turn, brought Yugoslavia into the Allied camp instead of letting her become another of Hitler's stronghold in the Balkans.

Dear Mrs. Roosevelt, I appeal to you as the Honorary President of the American Friends of Yugoslavia, to take this urgent matter of saving so many human lives into your own energetic hands, and to intervene through exceptional channels in order that this most urgently needed consignment of medicines may be shipped immediately.

I appeal to you not as an official or semiofficial, but as one of these people of Belgrade, who, indeed, are my people, to whom I belong with every inch of my being, and whose sufferings are my sufferings too.

I appeal to you because I can see these hundreds of thousands feverish and exhausted pairs of eyes looking toward us for help.

Anna Soubbotitch

New York, New York

[Three pages typed]

[*On top of this letter in Mrs. Roosevelt's writing is: "Find out what is going now through Red Cross and Army and then tell her."*]

Honorable Basil O'Connor

Chairman, American Red Cross

Dear Mr. O'Connor:

I am enclosing a copy of the appeal Mrs. Roosevelt has received from Dr. Anna Subbotitch for first aid medicines for the people of Belgrade. Will you let Mrs. Roosevelt know what is going through to these people?

Sincerely yours,
Malvina C. Thompson
Secretary to Mrs. Roosevelt

In a letter of Nov. 20th, Mr. O'Connor of the Red Cross reported back to Mrs. Roosevelt that the "composition of the medical program would depend on the recommendation of the Joint Relief Commission at Geneva and would be subject to the approval of the Anglo-American Blockade authorities." Much aspirin had been sent and 1100 more pounds was in the process of being purchased. "Due to transportation difficulties, only about a third of supplies shipped from this country have reached Yugoslavia."

Honorable Herbert Lehman
United Nations Relief and Rehabilitation Administration
Washington, D.C.
Dear Governor Lehman:
Mrs. Roosevelt asks me to send you a copy of the appeal she has received from Dr. Anna Soubbotitch, for medicines for the people of Belgrade, and to ask you what is going through to Belgrade now.

Very sincerely yours,
Malvina C. Thompson
Secretary to Mrs. Roosevelt

An answer by R. F. Hendrickson, dated Nov. 24th, indicated that the United Nations was "not authorized to undertake activities in any area while hostilities are going on. Will go in when it is determined by military commander that hostilities no longer exist."

November 14, 1944

Honorable Henry L. Stimson
Secretary of War
Dear Mr. Secretary:
Mrs. Roosevelt asks me to send you a copy of a letter she has
received from Dr. Anna Soubbotitch, appealing for medicines for
the people of Belgrade. Mrs. Roosevelt would appreciate information as to what supplies are now going through to the people
of Belgrade.

> Very sincerely yours,
> Malvina C. Thompson
> Secretary to Mrs. Roosevelt

November 18, 1944

Dear Miss Thompson:
Your letter of November 11, 1944, enclosing copy of a letter from
Dr. Anna Soubbotitch has been received by the Secretary. He
has asked that Mrs. Roosevelt be advised that the question of
relief supplies for Yugoslavia, as for other liberated areas, has
been receiving the active attention of the War Department for
some time, and that General Wilson and the other military
authorities in the area are fully advised of the difficult situation
obtaining in Belgrade and other parts of Yugoslavia.

The Combined military forces have made plans to furnish
relief and rehabilitation supplies, including a substantial quantity
of medical supplies, to the Yugoslavs; and, as soon as military
operations and conditions permit, these supplies will be moving
into the afflicted areas in appreciable volume.

> Sincerely yours,
> John W. Martyn, Administrative Assistant
> War Department
> Washington, D.C.

All of these replies were sent by Malvina Thompson to Dr. Soubbotitch.

November 13, 1944

Dear Miss Thompson,

I have your letter from December 2nd and your note from December 3rd by which you were kind enough to send me on behalf of Mrs. Roosevelt the answers to letters from the Administrative Assistant of the War Department, the Acting Director General of the UNRRA and the Chairman of the American Red Cross in connection with the matter of urgent medical relief for the suffering people of Belgrade. Thank you very much, indeed. I am enclosing herewith a letter addressed personally to Mrs. Roosevelt, which I beg you to forward to her.

Very sincerely yours,
Dr. Anna Soubbotitch

[One page handwritten]

November 13, 1944

Dear Mrs. Roosevelt,

It is with the deepest appreciation that I am thanking you for all your understanding, sympathy and intervention in connection with the desperate condition of the poor people of Belgrade.

Through the answer of Miss Malvina Thompson and the letters from the Administrative Assistant of the War Department, the Acting Director General of the UNRRA, and the Chairman of the American Red Cross—she was kind enough to send me—I understand that the U.S.A. authorities omitted nothing to help wholeheartedly this unfortunate people of mine.

In all their distress it will doubtless be a moral relief for them to know that it was not through the lack of understanding, sympathy and readyness to help by the great democratic America that no help at all reached them from the day Belgrade was liberated up till now.

I beg you to accept the warmest appreciation on behalf of the suffering people of Belgrade, for your and your great country's sincere friendship.

Gratefully yours,
Dr. Anna Soubbotitch.

December 20, 1944

My dear Dr. Soubbotitch:

Thank you so much for your letter. I have given the one to Mrs. Roosevelt which you addressed to her.

Very sincerely yours,
Malvina C. Thompson
Secretary to Mrs. Roosevelt

• • •

[Date-stamped December 1, 1944]

Dear Mrs. Roosevelt:-

I'm a member of the 124th General Hospital in England, and have been here about three and a half months, and have been in the service twenty-six months.

My wife who is living at Rockford, Illinois is seriously ill and has been in the hospital almost three months, she is pregnant and is expecting the baby in February, but the doctors are afraid they will have to take the baby in the early part of December with a caesarian section. She has a rheumatic heart condition that is causing all of her trouble, and is so weak that it is impossible for her even to write to me. If she is this weak, I hardly know how she'll be able to come through a caesarian operation. Her doctors brought her to the hospital because they wanted to have oxygen handy in case she needed it.

I've received cables from my wife's doctors through the Red Cross stating how seriously ill she is and that her heart showed signs of failing. It also stated that the doctors recommended my presence, and said that it would help her so much if I were there.

I made a request for an emergency furlough and it was approved by our Detachment Commander, and also the Commanding Officer of our hospital. The request with the doctors letters and cables was then sent to our base headquarters and there turned down. My wife was in the hospital before I came over-seas, and I had an emergency furlough so that I could be with her.

Mrs. Roosevelt, I've heard so many times of how you've helped people, and I'm hoping and praying that you'll be able to do something for me and make it possible for me to be with my wife the early part of December. They haven't told my wife that they were trying to get me back for that time because they didn't want to worry her, or to let her know just how bad she is. I just have the feeling if I could be there that I'd be able to pull her safely through this, and that they might save the baby.

My wife's doctor is Dr. Charles Leonard, Gas Electric Building, Rockford, Illinois. She also had a baby specialist, a Dr. Heinemayer, and a heart specialist.

Please do everything in your power to get me back for the first or second week in December. I just have to be there to help her, I try to do my work, but it's just impossible to because my mind is with my wife, and I just have to be with her.

Sincerely,

PFC William J. James, Jr.

124th General Hospital

Medical Detachment

New York, New York

[One page typed]

December 11, 1944

MEMORANDUM FOR MISS THOMPSON:

I have the letter addressed to Mrs. Roosevelt which was forwarded to me the other day regarding the possibility of bringing Private First Class William J. James Jr, to the United States to be present when his wife will have an operation this month.

I have been informed that the Theater Commander who is cognizant of the local military situation and in the best position to determine the local situation has been delegated the authority to return military personnel to the United States. It was suggested that Private James be advised to contact the local field director of the American Red Cross, who, it is understood, will have the case investigated and pass on the information to the appropriate commander for his consideration. Under the circumstances outlined, I am told that the War Department is reluctant to initiate any action for the return of a soldier to the United States or to intercede in behalf of any individual.

A. K. Oulie

Major, General Staff Corps

Acting Assistant Secretary, General Staff

Office of the Chief of Staff

War Department

Washington, D.C.

December 13, 1944

My dear Mr. James:

Mrs. Roosevelt asked the War Department about the possibility of your being allowed to return home to be present when your wife will have an operation this month and I am enclosing a copy of their reply.

Mrs. Roosevelt wishes you good luck and sincerely hopes all will go well with Mrs. James.

Very sincerely yours,
Malvina C. Thompson
Secretary to Mrs. Roosevelt

. . .

February 7, 1945
Dear Mrs. Roosevelt:

(I enjoy very much reading your daily column.) What do you think can be done in trying to get **more** food to our boys in German prisons? From all reports something needs to be done just as soon as possible. There are so many collections taken for other persons overseas—why can't we get more food to our boys through the International Red Cross? We can't let them starve. I have a son who has been **missing for eight months.** If he is living he may be a German prisoner. I can't get any word from him.

Don't you think this can be done? Please answer and let me know what you think about it. Thanking you,

Very Sincerely,
Mrs. Myrtle Gates
Akron, Ohio

My dear Mrs. Gates:

Mrs. Roosevelt asked the Red Cross about the possibility of getting more food to the men who are in prison camps in Germany and I quote in part, from their reply:

[I]n a cooperative effort between the U.S. Army, Navy, State Department, and various other government agencies, and the American Red Cross, we are shipping huge quantities of food parcels to the International Committee of the Red Cross in Switzerland for our prisoners of war. We have a very sizable reserve supply of food parcels in Switzerland and until very recently, supplies of food were moving regularly and promptly from Switzerland to the prison camps in which Americans were being held. Now, because of the almost complete breakdown of transportation facilities within Germany, and because of the state of chaos which seems to exist there, food

packages are being moved from Switzerland to the prison camps in Germany under great difficulties and with less promptness and regularity. Extraordinary efforts are being made to overcome these difficulties, but it would be a mistake to minimize the seriousness of the situation prevailing at this time.

Very sincerely yours,

Malvina C. Thompson

Secretary to Mrs. Roosevelt.

• • •

February 12, 1945

SOMEWHERE IN GERMANY

To: Mrs. Eleanor Roosvelt

White House

Dear Mrs. Roosvelt,

It makes me proud to be the one chosen to write this letter to you from among so many fellows.

We are living in a small town with roofs that leak like a sieve but don't mind it at all because it's for something worthwhile "The American Way of Living." We have seen quite a bit of what used to be German towns and it seems that the Artillery boys are doing a good job of taking them off the map.

This letter is being written because the boys were discussing the subject of fruit cake and there being none around for quite a while we have decided to write to someone in order to taste one that has the American taste to it. Each man placed three names in a helmet and your name was the one lucky enough to be drawn. The boys doubted that we will get one but in all fairness to them I still wrote this letter to keep my end of the bargain. I know you would not let them down.

We did have a little fun here the other day. Some of the boys found a horse so we went through all the trouble of fixing a saddle for it and when we finally finished the dog-gone horse wouldn't do anything but walk so will use him when we run out of beef. The boys wish you and your husband good luck and God speed.

Sincerely yours,
Pvt. Henry Lehman
c/o Post Master
New York, New York

. . .

February 23, 1945

My dear Mrs. Roosevelt,
After receiving a very despondent letter from my sister in the Women's Army Corp. I did not know how I could help but I decided to appeal to you.

By quoting from her letter, I believe you will understand her state of mind much better than if I attempted to describe the circumstances.

"I don't know how to begin this sad letter. I should start from my transfer to this filthy, dirty WAC detachment. I am so unhappy. I am afraid I am going to do something I'll regret. The place is Brooks Field, Texas, about six miles from San Antonio. It sounds good, doesn't it? You should see it. When I got here Sunday, I wanted to turn and run. This company is so lax it is terrible. My wall locker is running away with roaches. The floor in here looks like it is never scrubbed. The company commander is too lazy to care. She hasn't even talked to me yet. Every other place I have been the company commander talks to you and tells you their policies. All I have done since I've been here is cry. I haven't eaten much. In two years I have never felt so bad as I do now. I have been a good girl up to now but if they don't give me a transfer, I swear you or my family will never see me again. What am I going to do? Get pregnant, that's the only way out, outside of losing my mind, which a girl who came in with me has already done. She is in Big Spring, Texas and they have her in a straight jacket. I'll give them three weeks to transfer me."

This letter was written on February thirteenth and she had arrived at Brooks field on Sunday.

On February seventeenth she wrote another letter:

"I am going to try, if they don't transfer me, to get out on my flat feet. If not, I guess I'll have to take the last way out. Get pregnant. I guess that sounds awful coming from me because I have been a good girl. The army hasn't changed that. But it looks as though it will, that's how desperate I am. I just can't stand it here. Tell ma to pray for me. Maybe everything will come out all right then.

"Here it is Saturday night. I used to have so much fun.

When that stops in the army, one's life almost does. When you have fun it makes you forget. I am working fourteen hours a day, then the next day off; but they have a million things for us to do."

We are so very worried about her. We are appealing to you as a great, understanding woman and as the mother of a daughter.

Can you help her? A transfer would be so welcome. But from the tone of her letter, she seems on the verge of a nervous breakdown. It would be better for all if she could get a discharge. And her letter certainly is not a recommendation for any other girl to join the Women's Army Corps. We have heard about the WAC's having many girls who do become pregnant. Could it be that they do get into such trouble in order to get out?

Mrs. Roosevelt, please help us and her and all the other girls in the same predicament.

We have heard so much about the good you have done for the colored people and we have confidence in you. Thank you for whatever you can do.

My sister's address:
Corporal Natalie C. Sheppard
Squad D
Brooks Field, Texas

Very sincerely,
Sarah Hodson
Baltimore, Maryland

[Six pages handwritten]

Mrs. Roosevelt referred the matter to Oveta Culp Hobby, Director of the Women's Army Corps, who investigated and sent the following letter:

Dear Miss Thompson:

The investigation indicated that conditions and facilities affecting morale, discipline, messing, housing and general administration of WAC personnel at this station compared favorably with like conditions and facilities at other Army installations.

The enlisted woman who had voiced the specific complaints was interviewed and several explanations for her state of mind advanced. She had been but recently transferred from another installation. This transfer had necessitated her separation from a very close friend, another enlisted woman who had served with her throughout her entire military service. This separation and the recent death of her fiancé, in action, were no doubt partly responsible for her state of mental depression.

Furthermore, the woman in question apparently has not been in the best of health and this fact may have influenced her desire for a discharge from the service. It was the recommendation of the investigating officers that the enlisted woman be given further medical attention to determine whether or not her physical condition is such as to warrant a discharge. The final disposition of this case will depend upon the recommendations of the medical authorities.

From the information received on this case, I am led to believe that the complaints of this enlisted woman concerning general conditions at Brooks Field were without foundation and that her reactions were probably the result of circumstances of a personal nature which were disturbing to her state of mind.

Thank you for your interest in bringing this matter to my attention.

Sincerely,
Oveta Culp Hobby
Director
Women's Army Corps

• • •

March 2, 1945

My Dear Mrs. Roosevelt,

Before I begin, I want to apologize for this intrusion, and then I shall announce myself. I am Mrs. J. , a poor Greek woman from the island of Crete: the island which is widely known for its bravery and sacrifice for freedom. I am one among the millions here in America who has lost every loved one in that struggle.

I thank God for being here in this wonderful country and that my eyes have not seen the cruelty and hardships endured by our Families.

As a humble mother of America, I come to you, now, with my problem. I have a son who loved going to school immensely, but I could not afford to send him to college due to financial circumstances. He worked during the evenings at the railroads, and went to school during the day. This continued for a period of three years. Unfortunately, he was taken into the service a year before graduation, but he was not sorry, for he wanted to serve his country.

He was sent to school at Fort Benning, Georgia where he labored strenuously to finish his schooling. Unfortunately, the week before graduation, the class went on maneuvers, and my son fell off a bridge, injuring his leg. I thank God that he wasn't killed. He remained at the hospital for approximately three months, after which he experienced more maneuvers. He worked hard again, finally receiving his commission. He was immediately sent to Camp Roberts, California where he is training the new boys, out in the barren, open, land. His leg has begun to ache again, but he refuses to mention it for fear of being called a "sissy."

He literally cries himself to sleep every evening, especially when there is a change in the weather.

You, too, are a mother and know the pain in a mother's heart. You can thoroughly understand my feelings as a mother. I am asking of you, a favor for the first time. I don't want my son to be discharged, if it is possible, I'd like for him to be given a job perhaps in Washington where his leg will not bother him any more. I believe he is well qualified.

Please let me have this one request. I can repay you only through my prayers. May all the good you have done for the poor return to you in blessings.

Please forgive me for having done this, but I am a mother. This between you and me for no one knows but God, now **you,** and I.

Respectfully,

Mrs. N.

Address:

Lt. N.S.

Camp Roberts, California

[Four pages handwritten]

March 2, 1945

Dear Mrs. N:

I have your letter and I sympathize with you and all our citizens of Greek origin who have lost their loved ones in this war. It is very sad to have lost all your people.

I can understand your pride in your son and also your anxiety. I am afraid, however, there is nothing I can do about a transfer for him, as these matters are entirely in the hands of the military authorities and I could not interfere. If your son is suffering from the effects of his injury he should report it to the

Army doctors and I hope that he will do so immediately. He will not be considered weak, but very sensible, for doing so.

I hope that his condition is not serious and that he will entirely recover from the injury.

Very sincerely yours,
Eleanor Roosevelt

• • •

[Date-stamped March 3, 1945]

Dear Madam:

I am writting to you in regards of my brother Sgt. James N. Haughey, New York City, N.Y. I realize that it is quite a job keeping track of all our boys and what each has done and I also know that there are several other boys who has went through the same as my brother and also given their lives in many cases but I want you if you will be so kind to look into his case. He has been over seas 2 1/2 years and has went through Africa—Sicily—France—Germany and sence Africa he has had malaria and has been taken out of action and put in the hospital several times. He took his squadron through Sicily without losing a man but entering France he was the only one who was saved out of 2 squadrons and this outfit—16th Inf. 1st Division was wiped clear out. Jim hasn't complained about any of this but his letter Jan 21 he had Trench foot[*] the last we heard and has been shipped from one Replacement Center to another and he hasn't had any mail sence November. He is discouraged I can tell by his letters. He has been in service 3 years the 14th of November and has never had a furlough. He was sent over after 6 months here in the

---

[*] Trench foot, which afflicted many soldiers, is a condition of the feet produced by prolonged exposure to water.

States and he went in the November before Pearl Harbor. He was very nervous when he left Germany and put in the hospital in France and very seldom wrote—saying it was his nerves. He was operated on the right side had boils taken off of his right knee and had infection in his right hand. Their outfit went through quite a lot and his best buddy was sent back to the states for malaria and now has a discharge from service (which he deserved). Jim was very happy cause he got back to the states and if he knew I was writting this he wouldn't want it but I can tell by his letters he's very discouraged and homesick and so in hopes he'll be able to get a 30 days furlough and I'm sure it'd help his moral out a lot if he could only get back **once** to see the folks and his wife. I realize I'm asking for quite a lot but it's only for his sake as I'm afraid he'll crack up if he has to go on or doesn't get mail very soon. Please look into this for me and I wish to thank you for taking your time and my name and address isn't important it's just Jim's health and life I'm asking for.

Thanking you I am
Jim's Sister

[Three and a half pages handwritten]

• • •

March 3, 1945

Dear Mrs. Roosevelt,

My address has changed again and you can see I'm in a new organization (new to me.) The location is somewhere in the Marianas Islands. Of all my Army travels, this was by far the most interesting and fastest though uneventful.

The trip from Honolulu didn't make me sea sick as the one from the Solomons to Hawaii. During the former we ran into a storm that litterally swept me off my feet and I didn't dare to watch the water. This time, most all the way, I couldn't see it.

The book I mentioned some months ago is developing satisfactorily. These trips occupy a great deal of space and of course all other important events are recorded: Some include material I wouldn't think of mailing. I had to give up a whole volume just before leaving the Solomons since every Jap raid was described. I can get it back after the war, though.

Can't get enough of this South Sea climate. The weather stays sunny and beautiful both here and Hawaii. However, that doesn't mean I would stay here a minute longer than necessary. But it won't hurt to take in the good air with sunbeams while it is plentiful.

The doubt you expressed about my studying Stenotypy by correspondence can be eased some. I can already operate the machine at slow rate and have memorized over 200 abbreviations that are necessary. Of course I have a machine, although I don't think of it as a machine. It's more like a 'pet' and wouldn't part with it for the world. My morale dropped sharply one day on discovering it was out of order. I dismantled part of it and studied the mechanism carefully and found there was a factory defect, then wrote the company. They confirmed my belief and sent instructions to repair it which I did.

Now I can resume my practice.

I should close now so you can read your many other letters for the day.

Very sincerely yours
Cecil Peterson
385th Aviation Squadron
San Francisco, California

[Two pages handwritten]

March 12, 1945

Dear Mr. Peterson:

I am very pleased to know that you have made such strides with your work on the stenotype machine and that you have one and are enjoying mastering its intricacies. I am sure that will make a great difference in your ability to put in these weary months in far away places.

I am glad you like the Marianas but do not let it lessen your liking for the United States.

The President came back from Yalta feeling he had accomplished a great deal that was valuable and he felt that he and Mr. Churchill and Marshall Stalin had worked out a medium for better understanding and cooperation and that now we can look forward to going out to the opening of the conference in San Francisco where I hope good work will be done.[*]

The president is in excellent health[†] and I feel that his report to Congress had, on the whole, a very good effect.

With best wishes to you, I am

Very sincerely yours,

Eleanor Roosevelt

• • •

In her monthly question-and-answer column in the February 1942 Ladies Home Journal, *Mrs. Roosevelt received a question that revealed that the questioner already knew how she would respond:*

"Why not insist on a vindictive peace if stories of German and Jap atrocities are true?

The Bible says "an eye for an eye." Mrs. Roosevelt answered

---

[*] The purpose of the conference was to set in motion the creation of the United Nations.
[†] President Roosevelt died at Warm Springs, Georgia, exactly one month later.

"There are a good many things in the Bible which, if you took them literally, you might find it rather difficult to carry out. Somehow I think it is more important to have a just peace than a vindictive one. We are interested in the future of peoples, and in their ability to learn to live together in peace. We have been brought to a situation where we had to go to war, by the mentality of the Germans and the Japanese which we do not wish to continue in any peoples in the world. The only way I know of to change that mentality is to lay great emphasis on justice."

• • •

Part Four

The Home Front

In a speech on March 15, 1941, President Roosevelt envisioned a world "founded upon four essential human freedoms. The first is freedom of speech and expression—everywhere in the world. The second is freedom of every person to worship God in his own way—everywhere in the world. The third is freedom from want . . . economic understandings which will secure to every nation a healthy peace time life for its inhabitants—everywhere in the world. The fourth is freedom from fear—which means a worldwide reduction of armaments to such a point and in such a thorough fashion that no nation will be in a position to commit an act of physical aggression against any neighbor—anywhere in the world." The president soon found himself leading Americans into a war to secure these freedoms, both at home and abroad.

Eleanor Roosevelt found herself presiding as First Lady over a nation facing wartime privations as well as the loss of sons, husbands, and fathers in battle. Being Eleanor Roosevelt, she managed to find something positive in the situation, seeing it as an opportunity to continue the battle for equal justice: "I could not help feeling that it was the New Deal social objectives that had fostered the spirit that would make it possible for us to fight the war, and I believed it was vastly important to give people the feeling that in fighting the war we were still really fighting for these same objectives." This proved especially important for civilians as they searched for ways to strengthen the war effort.

Americans at home fully demonstrated their desire to contribute, often in unique ways. Mrs. Roosevelt heard from the creators of a new type of bomb, the inventor of an improved airplane wing deicer, a seamstress proffering comfortable clothing to wear on assembly lines in defense industries as a way to increase production, and the owners of large, stately homes, which they offered as convalescent centers for returning invalid soldiers. These were in addition to the more typical letters regarding civil defense issues, "victory" gardens, and war bonds. In order to release men to fight overseas, the government actively encouraged women to work in defense production, hoping to inspire them via a poster of Rosie the Riveter: a woman in a dark blue shirt with her hair tied up in a red-and-white polka dot kerchief, who flexes the muscle revealed by her rolled-up sleeve as she says "We *can* do it!" Such major societal changes carried out in necessary haste created inevitable problems soon reflected in the letters Mrs. Roosevelt received. With the end of the war in sight, new difficulties emerged, among them a severe housing shortage and the problem of how best to integrate millions of servicemen back into the civilian population.

The home-front problem that disturbed Mrs. Roosevelt the most during these years was prejudice and its consequent effect on civil rights. In her "My Day" column of June 18, 1943, she wrote: "I keep getting letters which point up the prejudices in which so many of us indulge, even in war times. They are not always prejudices against a race, sometimes they are religious prejudices. For instance, some people do not wish to be where Catholics or Jews predominate in their environment. Sometimes, it is Protestants who are banned. All this seems out of place in a country with so many racial origins and so many religions. Our soldiers fight and die, side by side, and are comforted by priests and ministers or rabbis, as the case may be, quite regardless of whether the dying boys belong to the particular church represented near him at the moment. It seems to me that this might teach us, as civilians, a lesson. What is really important is not what religion or what race we belong to, but how we live our lives, whether we deal with others with honesty and kindness, or whether we lie and cheat and take advantage of our neighbors. I wish that out of this war might come to us a true evaluation of the worth of human beings and far less interest in the labels of race and religion."

Earlier in the war she had ended an article on civil rights by saying: "It seems to me that the rights of minority groups, whether they are Negro, Jew, Italian, Slav, or German, as long as they are citizens of the Republic of the United States, or are to become citizens, must be observed and enforced. Their non-enforcement menaces not only our minority groups, but the rights of every citizen in the Nation. If we take away such inherent rights from any one group in a Democracy, what is to prevent their being taken away from all of us?" Thus, whether in depression or war, Mrs. Roosevelt maintained her focus on the achievement of basic civil rights and economic well-being for all. After her husband's death on April 12, 1945, she moved out of the White House, back into what she thought would be a quiet life as a private citizen. Instead, given the opportunity to serve as a U.S. delegate to the brand-new United Nations by President Truman, she carried these same goals to the international arena. But that is another story.

—CDK

The Home Front

<hr>

December 3, 1940

My dear Miss Thompson,

Charles A. Frain, a CCC junior whom I had at my old
White Hall camp, doing special work, has, with assistance
from me, invented an idea for a bomb. We have practically
given ourselves a course in thermo-dynamics in an effort
to check our idea, and as nearly as we can figure, the bomb
should go off with a force in excess of 56,000 lbs. to the
square inch. The materials are very inexpensive, and we
believe the bomb would be unusually safe to handle.

But I don't know what to do about it! I know Bill
Byron, who is on the Congressional Defense Committee,
and thought of seeing him. Or possibly it would be better
for us, if it could be arranged, to show our idea to some
qualified member of the Defense Commission. I even
thought of sending the drawings and description to my
University, where they might be interested in experi-
menting with it. Obviously Charles and I have neither the

funds nor equipment for making more than very small, inadequate experiments.

Charles is working for the Bethlehem Steel Company, but as I know the Superintendent, I am sure I could get a day or two off for him, if we can get an appointment to see the proper authorities. I really think it more than probable that we have more than "another hair-brained idea."

Very sincerely yours,

Robert G. Bailey

1327th Company

CCC Camp

Lancaster, Pennsylvania

[One page typed]

Note on top: "Mr. Magee To whom should I refer him?"

December 12, 1940

My dear Mr. Bailey:

After receiving your letter of the third, I inquired and found out that the person you should see about the bomb you and Mr. Frain have invented is the Chief of Ordnance, Major General C. M. Wesson, Munitions Building, here in Washington. I would suggest that you write to him for an appointment and explain what it is you wish to present to him. I am sure that he will see you if it is possible for him to do so.

Very sincerely yours,

Malvina Thompson

Secretary to Mrs. Roosevelt

• • •

[Telegram]

February 20, 1941

Mrs. Eleanor Roosevelt.
The White House
Washington
I am discarding many aluminum pots and pans. It has occurred to me the Red Cross would have a source of income from housewives throughout the United States through their discarded aluminum ware. It seems a terrible waste of this valuable metal to be put in incinerators. What about the discarded tin cans?

Mrs. Otto Harbac
Mamaroneck, New York

• • •

March 26, 1940

Dear Mrs. Roosevelt:—
I am a widow 55 years, well and strong. No money, but there should be some place that I could fit into the National Defense. If I was a man, I'd be in the army right now, so please help me find a place.

Sincerely,
Mrs. C. T. Harding
Duluth, Minnesota

My dear Mrs. Harding:
A committee probably will be appointed soon to prepare a plan for defense work done by women. When a chairman is designated, your letter will be referred for consideration.

Very sincerely yours,
Administrative Officer
Social Correspondence

This same response was used for at least a year during this time period. Eventually women of Mrs. Harding's age who wished to do so found employment in factories supplying war materiel.

. . .

[undated letter]

Dear Mrs. Roosevelt,

As I looked at the rows of bombers last week, standing on the landing field at the Vultee plant near Nashville, awaiting pilots to fly them to the battle front, I thought of the thousands of women all over America, college women in their twenties and thirties, who could be put into service at home, to release the men for war duties.

Many of us who came out of school during the depression, with two or more years of college training, have been unemployed.

Our years of Math, Chemistry and Latin (6 of math, 6 of Latin) should be a solid background for specialized training in a field which is in need of minds of a mechanical turn.

Plenty of us are physically fit (5 feet, 2 in, from 115-120 lbs) with boundless energy and the will to **do**.

Jaqueline Cochrans'[*] idea for training flyers is a good one. I am interested in aeronautics and would like to see a Federal student pilot program for women as well as for men.

Please consider this as the very first application for training in the semi-military phases of aviation.

Sincerely,

Mary Hardin Bernard

Russellville, Kentucky

[Two pages handwritten]

---

[*] Jacqueline Cochran instructed women to fly transport planes and in 1943 was made director of the Women's Air Force Service Pilots.

Enclosed with the letter was a copy of a page from the Courier-Journal *of Louisville, headlined "Just Give Women Fliers a Chance!," and a smaller heading, "American Aviatrices Are Ready and Willing to Share Men's Responsible Flying Duties." The article, by Jacqueline Cochran, includes her picture, captioned "America's foremost woman flier," as well as a photo of Hannah Reitsch, who "has trained hundreds of German war flyers."*

June 6, 1941

My dear Miss Bernard:

In reply to a recent request for information on this subject, we have been advised by the Department of Commerce as follows:

"The Civil Aeronautics Program has been under such severe pressure to provide the maximum of personnel to the air forces that it was deemed necessary to limit the trainees to potential members of these forces. As a result, applications of women for pilot-training were closed March 26.

"This was done with reluctance, of course, and on a temporary basis for the emergency. I am sure you know that this program has trained more women in aviation than any other single force in the history of American flying. It has trained more than 2,400 women. When it was started, there were less than 700 women pilots in the country. I hope and trust that it can resume this splendid service in the not-too-distant future."

Very sincerely yours,
Administrative Officer
Social Correspondence

• • •

January 13, 1942

My dear Mrs. Roosevelt:

We wish to express our deep appreciation for your timely expressions relative to aliens which you made over your national network radio program Sunday.

We are especially thankful for the opinion in which you expressed concern for the morale of those who are now classified enemy aliens, for Japanese aliens residing in this country are prohibited by law from naturalization and the consequent privileges of citizenship and are thus involuntarily aliens.

We are appreciative of the general good will and sympathy which have been shown us who are of Japanese extraction, but whose allegiance to the United States is as undivided as that of any other American. However, we would like to bring to your attention a situation within the local Red Cross chapter which we deem decidedly discouraging to the maintenance of morale: the local chapter of the Red Cross has refused to accept the cooperation extended through our organization by the Japanese American residence here in San Francisco, on the grounds that we might poison the medicines or bandages, treat knitted goods to injure the wearer and deliberately sabotage its work. Would it be possible for you to do something to rectify this deplorable attitude?

We would also like to have a transcript of the radio talk you made Sunday so that we could give it to our members, knowing that its text would prove very encouraging to them and our alien parents.

Thanking you again for your kind thoughts and with best wishes

Very sincerely yours,

Sam Hohri

National Press Agent

Japanese American Citizens League

[One page typed]

The radio broadcast referred to occurred on January 11, 1942, as part of a series sponsored by Pan-American Coffee. This particular program, thirty-five days after the Japanese bombing of Pearl Harbor, focused on the question of morale, especially pertaining to the noncitizens in the U.S. Mrs. Roosevelt said:

"We as citizens, must keep reminding ourselves that at one time our ancestors were newcomers to this country, and also that most of the people to whom the term 'alien' refers, came to the United States a great many years ago to make their homes here, or more recently because they were considered 'enemies' of undemocratic governments and were, therefore, persecuted. Yet in spite of their eagerness to help and to be a part of us, as a united nation defending ourselves against aggression and oppression, we read in newspapers in the 'Help Wanted' advertisements that 'Aliens Need Not Apply.' We hear of employers who are discharging admittedly loyal and efficient workers merely because they are not citizens, or in some cases because they have foreign-sounding names and the employers cannot be sure that they are citizens.

I am concerned with the possible consequences if we do not make every effort to differentiate between the many loyal American non-citizens and the comparatively few who may be truly alien to our way of life. The government has agencies which can be trusted to guard against the people who are disloyal. We must not forget this and we must realize that one cannot tell the difference between a citizen and a non-citizen by just looking at him, by seeing the color of his skin, or by hearing him talk. . . . If we wish a united spirit and united defense so essential to ultimate victory, we must stop thinking in terms of 'alien' or 'alien enemy' and judge and act only on the true tests of loyalty, usefulness, and the love of America."

January 24, 1942

My dear Miss Thompson:

I received your letter of January 19th transmitting the communication from the National Press Agent of the Japanese American Citizens League.

The situation with respect to the use of citizens of Japanese extraction in the volunteer services of the American Red Cross is not one which had previously come to my attention but I am looking into the matter.

Sincerely yours,
Norman H. Davis
Chairman
American Red Cross

January 29, 1942

My dear Mr. Hohri:

Mrs. Roosevelt asks me to tell you that she referred the question to the use of citizens of Japanese extraction in the volunteer services, to the Chairman of the American Red Cross. In his reply to Mrs. Roosevelt, Mr. Davis states that this situation had not previously been brought to his attention and assures Mrs. Roosevelt that he will look into it.

Very sincerely yours,
Malvina Thompson
Secretary to Mrs. Roosevelt

• • •

[Undated]

Mrs. Elenor Roosevelt

Dear Mrs. Roosevelt:

Won't you please read my letter I am not writing to our President's wife but as from one mother to another.

My son Harold was one of the eight men killed in a mine explosion at Peabody Mine 47 better known as Harco, Dec. 28 1941. Harold was a mine examiner to exam the mine for the day men, he went to work at 2 a.m. on Sunday morning the explosion occured apparently at 3:30 am. He was by himself at the time working his territory alone, when found he was lying beside his motor that he used to ride into his working place found dead burned beyond recognition.

Mrs. Roosevelt we find it just almost beyond our strength to give a child up no matter how justifiable the cause but when we know as I know it was caused from greed and carelessness then we feel as if we want to do something about it. I have been a coal miners wife for 31 years my son was 30 years old the father of two boys ages 11 and 3. Mrs. Roosevelt I could write you a book on the things that are breaking my heart but while I truly feel you would turn a sympathetic ear to me I know and realize the responsibilities you have so Mrs. Roosevelt I'll try to make my letter brief. I will try to explain my reason for writing to you in the very first place. Mrs. Roosevelt if I did not have faith in your kindness towards the laboring class, your great interest which you always take, then I could never have written this letter but I know you are fair and just and that is all I am asking is that we be treated that way. The cause of the explosion was from a squeeze in the mine. To explain a squeeze to you Mrs. Roosevelt would be as if you were sitting in a room and the walls began to close in on you, then your first thot would be to get out and stay out as the plastering would be falling all the time also the pieces of wood that supports the ceiling. Well in a squeeze in the mine it is the same with coal falling all the time but the worst part of the squeeze is the gas it forms and on first notice the squeeze should always be tightly sealed at once and abandoned, but in this case and believe me Mrs. Roosevelt I speak truly the condition was allowed to exist for a week with the company trying to get out what coal they could before it all fell in. that is what the seven men who were killed together were trying to do. My son was some where near the explosion but his work was to examine the mine to try and make it safe for the men to work the next day.

Now Mrs. Roosevelt had the company had a safety man there where the seven men were working the safety man would have shut off all the power and then there would have been no explosion as all the men use safety lights to work by but the main reason I am trying to show to you Mrs. Roosevelt is the gas should never have been there and it was greed to make more money for the company that caused it all allowing a condition to exist that had it happened in the day instead of nite how many lives would it have cost as the mine imployes about 500 men, as any practical miner will tell you Mrs. Roosevelt all explosions in the mines are caused by carelessness and what a pity as our undertaker said to me what a pity Mrs. Holden that every precaution is not taken to protect the mens lives in a mine and as Harco has always been known as a very hot mine which means gas, for that reason more precaution should have been taken. At the time of the accident and terrible tragedy so many men were saying it is just pure murder for the men all knew the condition that did exist and while they knew it still they had to go on working trying to earn an honest living, hoping against hope nothing would happen. At the coroner's inquest it was turned over to the grand jury but the States attorney remarked he would not take action till more evidence was produced. Mr. Robert Medill State director of Mines and Minerals who is paid by the tax payers I believe, he is supposed to protect both the operators and miners interests the newspaper quoted Mr. Medill as saying the explosion was just one of those things. Well Mrs. Roosevelt if we have no more protection by the men who are paid to protect us what will we do.

Now Mrs. Roosevelt here is another angle and I believe a very important one, my son always carried a note book he always put the findings down in gas rock falls or just any condition that was supposed to be brought to notice each nite as he examined the mine he put his finding down in his little book then when he went on top there was a large book kept in the office he entered his findings in. Well after the explosion when we got settled enough to ask the undertaker about the book, we found it had remained intact and when we got it we also found the leaves, 3 of them in all, had been removed the last 3 dating from Dec. 5th till the 27th. Then on investigation at the mine office of his morning report we found the same pages had been removed. the manager said he thot Mr. Medill took the pages from the office but who took the ones from Harolds book. They had been torn out before the childs body reached the top of the mine, for the undertaker told me and I sincerely believe he told the truth that no one had touched the book but 2 federal men who did not tear out any pages as he stood over them while they examined it. Now Mrs. Roosevelt there was evidence in the two books to convict, knowing my son as I knew him hearing he and his dad talk together as they did, I know and have every confidence in my sons honesty so did the coal company, they knew what entries my son put in his book. All I ask is a fair and impartial investigation and I know if we have that the guilty will suffer as they should, of course I cant have my boy back but I still have a husband working at the mine. I am sending you a picture of my boy, I want you to see just how fine he looked at the time of his death and imagine what we had left of him after the explosion, the undertaker told me his whole upper body was charred. He was a fine boy Mrs. Roosevelt. I did not see him just through a mothers eyes. Mrs. Roosevelt please forgive me for the bother I've put you to for I know every minute you have is taken up but wont you lend us a helping hand as you have so many others.

So many people advise us not to investigate the accident for fear of my husband losing his job at the mine but how little they understand a parent.

Please answer my letter and give me your honest opinion regardless of my feelings.

Thank you so much.

Yours truly

Mrs. Joe Holden

Harrisburg, Illinois

P.S. Mrs. Roosevelt will you please return the picture.

A news clipping, no date or name of paper, accompanied the letter, with the headline "Put Fan Back on Regular Air Course At Peabody 47." The article stated: "Whether Robert M. Medill, state director of the Department of Mines and Minerals, would make an inspection of Peabody 47 mine before it goes back into operation or whether he would send a commission was not known yesterday. Medill, who has already described the explosion at the mine Dec. 28 as 'just one of those things,' had planned to return yesterday for an inspection. The fan had been put back on the regular air course yesterday to run for 24 hours, ending at 4 a.m. today. George Bagwill, state mine inspector, stated." Written by Mrs. Holden on the top of the article is the question, "Where is the men's protection when these men let you down?"

[Twelve pages handwritten]

February 23, 1942

Dear Mr. Secretary:

Is it possible for the Bureau of Mines, Safety Division, to have a careful investigation made in this case without involving the Holdens?

Very sincerely yours,
Eleanor Roosevelt

March 18, 1942

My dear Mrs. Roosevelt:

An investigation has been made by the Bureau of Mines of the disaster that occurred on December 28, 1941, in the Harco mine, of the Peabody Coal Company, which killed eight men including the son of Mrs. Joe Holden whose letter was enclosed with your letter to me of February 23.

This investigation was undertaken promptly after the Bureau of Mines was notified of the occurrence, in an attempt, if possible, to determine the cause of the explosion. All of the available evidence has been collected, and a report is now being prepared. Upon completion, the report will be made public in accordance with the policy I have established in the Department of making such reports available to the public as soon as possible so that similar disasters might be prevented.

The Harco disaster is another blot on the already dark accident record of the coal mining industry. It was the eighth major disaster, in which five or more lives were lost, that occurred in

1941 and brought the total of fatalities resulting from such catastrophes during the year to 73. The tragedy is that with proper precautions these disasters could have been prevented and therefore the lives lost could have been spared.

Judging from her letter, Mrs. Holden typifies the fortitude and resolution of miners' wives and mothers. She can be assured that the investigation made by the Bureau of Mines is impartial and objective, and that when the report is made public it will reveal all of the pertinent available facts.

Sincerely yours,
Harold L. Ickes
Secretary of the Interior
Washington, D.C.

March 20, 1942

My dear Mrs. Holden:
Mrs. Roosevelt has asked me to send you the enclosed copy of a self-explanatory letter just received from the Secretary of the Interior. As you will see, this letter is in reply to an inquiry made by her after receiving your letter of February 23, 1942.

Mrs. Roosevelt wishes me to convey to you her deepest sympathy in the loss of your son.

Very sincerely yours,
Malvina Thompson
Secretary to Mrs. Roosevelt

Note on the copy: photograph of her son returned with this letter.

March 28, 1942

Dear Mrs. Roosevelt
Please forgive me for taking up more of your time but after receiving the nice letters from Malvina Thompson also from Secretary Harold L. Ickes I just had to try and

express to you my gratitude for the kindness and interest you've shown.

Truthfully Mrs. Roosevelt I expected this from you, for I follow your activities so much and it makes my heart a little less burdened to know my confidence in you is justified.

Mr. Ickes gave me new hope for if as he so nicely stated we have a fair impartial investigation, I know then it will be found to be as I stated to you in my former letter.

Three months today since my son was taken from me and believe me I've lived a life time, some times these things seem to be unavoidable, but this is so different, I have one other child a girl, just as fine as my boy was and to have lost her the blow would have been equally hard, but she still does not take my sons place for each child has its own individual worth to us, you as a mother can understand.

Thank you Mrs. Roosevelt for returning my sons picture, it seems I have so much to thank you for.

My position in life is a very humble one but if my good wishes can mean anything to you and yours, believe me you will always have them.

Very sincerely,
Mrs. Joe Holden
Harrisburg, Illinois

[Two pages handwritten]

• • •

March 3, 1942

Sent to Mr. Collier, Indian Bureau
Monticello, Utah
Mrs. Eleanor Roosevelt
Here we relatives of the two convicts John Chief and Jack Crank I am Mrs. John Chief here include and am in front

and first to speak to Mrs. Roosevelt. I am right calling for help I and the group hereby we exceeding want Mrs. Roosevelt you to suggest attorney for us. Your well know friend that last summer being with you at your residence.

Mrs. John Chief

April 23, 1942

My dear Mrs. Roosevelt:

At various times you have transmitted to us requests from the wife of John Chief, a Navajo charged with murder, that his interests be taken care of by the selection of a good attorney. Under date of April 14, we have had word from the Acting Superintendent of the Navajo Indian Reservation that Mr. Knox Patterson, an excellent attorney at Salt Lake City, will represent John Chief and his co-defendant, Jack Crank, at their trial which has been set for May 18 at Monticello, Utah.

This Office is doing everything possible to see that John Chief and Jack Crank are adequately defended.

Sincerely yours,
John Collier
Commissioner
Office of Indian Affairs
Department of the Interior
Washington, D.C.

April 25, 1942

My dear Mr. Collier:

Mrs. Roosevelt asks me to thank you very much for your letter. She is glad to know that John Chief will be adequately defended at his trial and that the present status of the case is favorable.

Very sincerely yours,
Malvina Thompson
Secretary to Mrs. Roosevelt

• • •

March 23, 1942

Dear Mrs. Roosevelt,

I am forwarding you a copy of the letter dispatched today
to The President by James Y. Sakamoto, general chairman
of the Emergency Defense Council of the Seattle chapter,
Japanese American Citizens League.

As you may be aware, this chapter is one of 66 in the
eight Western States. National headquarters are located in
San Francisco, and total membership is in excess of
20,000, all American citizens.

Because of your well-known interest in the difficulties
of minority groups in the United States, and your efforts
to promote a better spirit of Americanism, I trust that Mr.
Sakamoto's letter will be of interest.

Sincerely,

William Hosokawa

Emergency Defense Council, Seattle Chapter

Japanese American Citizens' League

Seattle, Washington

March 23, 1942

The Honorable Franklin D. Roosevelt
President of the United States of America
The White House, Washington, D.C.
Mr. President:

We, the American Citizens of Japanese parentage in these
United States, have taken seriously your various statements
on the Four Freedoms. Our parents generation too has taken
comfort from those assertions. They have not enjoyed the
rights of citizenship in this country. For that reason they are
at this time particularly open to accusation and suspicion.

We were reassured when war broke out and heard your directions as to the treatment to be accorded aliens of enemy countries. We felt those were commands upon all American citizens to pull together for a common objective. Even when the clamor against us raised by a national organization whose patriotic motives are undoubted seemed about to threaten our very lives, we trusted in your protection.

The picture has changed since then. Evacuation has now become a certainty for all of us, non-citizen and citizen alike. We citizens have been singled out for treatment that has hitherto not been meted out to any American. Though the medicine was bitter, we have attempted to obey without criticism, and to swallow it.

We were prepared to go where we might be sent, to be uprooted permanently from the homes we have known since childhood. Our parents before us had in many instances built up the only homes we knew. They had given us an American education and in some thousands of instances sent us gladly into the service of our country. They, too, were to accompany us. We thought it would simply be a matter of transfer to another locality in which we might carry on, under a cloud indeed, but demonstrating our loyalty none the less, by obeying a humiliating and distasteful command.

We are still so minded. We shall obey willingly. We shall continue to trust you and to give our allegiance to the ideals you enunciate.

In the working out of the details of evacuation, we have noticed an insistence upon the necessity for speed in going to places not designated by anyone. We are willing to go, glad to escape from even the possibility of ever being accused of even being present in the area where sabotage might conceivably take place.

Under the circumstances prevailing, we have been so

completely discredited by the American people at large that it is impossible for us to appear anywhere without giving rise to the hysterically false assumption that we are engaged in some nefarious design against a country that is as much ours as it is that of our fellow-citizens. So marked is this that had we any intention such as we are popularly credited with, the easiest manner in which it might be accomplished would be for us to simply pick up and spread our unwanted presence over the American map and so precipitate, under Army decree, that complete disruption of the war effort.

Our people have not been unconscious of the extent to which our country has been dependent upon them for the production of certain articles of food in areas now filled with Army installations and all lines of war work. Certainly had they any mind to sabotage they could have done so no more completely than by ceasing to produce the food upon which so much of the war effort depended.

Mr. President, we have protested our loyalty in the past. We have not been believed. We are willing to assume the burden of continuing to demonstrate it under all but impossible conditions. We would be deeply grateful if you would point it out to our fellow-citizens that we are not traitors to our country as the above facts, in our opinion amply demonstrate.

Restore our good name to us that our soldiers of Japanese ancestry need no longer hang their heads in shame as their hearts secretly bleed in anxiety over the whereabouts of their parents and loved ones possibly stranded penniless in some desert of the Southwest, or begging their bread in the streets of some strange place.

Give to us some refuge in the heart of the country far removed from even the suspicion or possibility to do harm. We have helped to feed the nation in the past. Let us continue to do so now that it is needed the more. Only let us do so freely and not under that compulsion made notorious in an enemy country. We do not have to be driven to work for a country in which we believe for ideals more precious than our life-blood.

We know there have been dissident elements among us, often unknown to ourselves. We know that some of the customs brought from abroad do lay some members of our parents generation open to suspicion even yet. We, like our fellow-citizens, have complete confidence in the all-seeing eye of the Federal Bureau of Investigation. We have seconded their efforts when told what it was they were searching for and we shall continue so to do.

We hope to find in the hearts of those like ours some understanding of our problems and some surcease from the burdens that oppress us. We have confidence that you yourself may present our case to them as a demonstration here of sincerity toward the promises you have made to the world.

Trusting that you will give us your sympathetic assistance and with the greatest hope for your continued good health, I am, my dear Mr. President,

Faithfully yours,
James Y. Sakamoto
Emergency Defense Council, Seattle Chapter
Japanese American Citizens' League
Seattle, Washington

[Two and a half pages typed]

March 31, 1942

Dear Mr. Hosokawa:

I read your letter and the one from Mr. Sakamoto with much interest.

I know the many difficulties confronting the American born Japanese, and also the loyal Japanese nationals. I am confident that the government will do everything possible to make the evacuation as decent and as comfortable as possible, and it will provide protection against vigilanties and misguided private citizens.

It is still difficult for me to see any reason for a war among people in this 20th Century, when human beings are supposed to have progressed in intelligence and civilization. The ramifications of war are so enormous, many innocent people will suffer and we will all pay the price in one way or another. It chills me to my soul to think of the best of our young men going off to die or to return crippled in mind and body.

Out of this terrific waste of human life must come a realization and a determination on the part of people all over the world that no one really wins a war, and that today's territorial gains provide the fertile field for a future war. No peoples want war. It is the governments who precipitate them, and for future peace the peoples must govern themselves. We must all work for universal understanding.

Very sincerely yours,
Eleanor Roosevelt

• • •

April 3, 1942

Dear Mrs. Roosevelt:

Mrs. Francis Harper, my neighbor in Swarthmore, has kindly permitted me to read your letter to her under date of March 20th in regard to the proposed destruction of Cook Forest State Park with its magnificent stand of virgin white pine, Pennsylvania's most magnificent heritage.

I am indeed glad to learn of your expressed conviction that the Park should be preserved unless the needs
of our war effort cannot otherwise be met satisfactorily.
In reply to this I may say that both of our State Senators, who are thoroughly familiar with the Western part
of the State, are insistent that not much more than half
of our present power equipment is being used. They have
both promised to fight vigorously against this proposed
desecration.

One of our Directors, who is very close to the situation,
has written me as follows: "I have talked with the Pennsylvania engineer in charge and he doesn't like the situation at all. While the letter indicates plainly that no definite
plans have been made, it sets up the Clarion River and the
Cheat River in West Virginia as two sources of needed
power for National defense, and you know they can get
away with murder on that basis."

Naturally we do not wish to impose added burdens
upon you, but if you could steal a moment from your busy
round of activities for a brief word with Mr. Delano and the
others who are so close to the picture, it would indeed be
most helpful and would bring the grateful appreciation of
the citizens of our Commonwealth.

Sincerely yours,
Ellwood B. Chapman
President
Pennsylvania Parks Association
Philadelphia, Pennsylvania

Dear Mr. Chapman:

Mrs. Roosevelt has been kind enough to send me your letter of
April 3, 1942 concerning the proposed Clarion River project
and its effect on the Cook Forest State Park. This proposed
project has received the attention of the National Resources

Planning Board. In fact, to be sure that the State point of view was taken fully into account, several of the members of one of our technical committees and of our Regional Office contacted State officials and inspected the site in person with them. So I can assure you that the relations between the proposed Mill Creek Dam and the stand of virgin white pine in Cook Forest are fully realized and are being given careful consideration.

Available data and statements of interested groups present conflicting testimony on the proportion of Cook Forest virgin timber which would be submerged by the project as proposed. However, there is no doubt that some of the virgin timber would be destroyed if the proposed dam be built. Your especial interest in protecting this stand of timber is being recorded, and you will be glad to know that the preservation of recreational and scenic values in this area, as well as the provision of whatever power facilities are definitely needed in the war effort will continue to be a matter of genuine concern to the Board.

Sincerely yours,
Frederic A. Delano
Chairman
Executive Office of the President
National Resources Planning Board
Washington, D.C.

Frederic Delano was appointed chairman of the National Resources Planning Commission by his nephew, President Roosevelt.

August 28, 1942

Dear Mrs. Roosevelt:

You will be delighted, I know, to learn that we have just received from Senator Joseph M. Guffey a copy of a letter from Mr. Leland Olds, Chairman of the Federal Power Commission, stating that they have abandoned their plans for the Mill Run dam on the Clarion River which would have destroyed such a large proportion of the virgin timber in Cook Forest.

He does not state what their alternative plans may be, but he has given the Senator the assurance that under the new setup the forest will remain untouched.

It is most gratifying to learn that the efforts of our many members and friends have at last borne fruit and we assure you that we are deeply appreciative of your own helpful attitude which may have contributed very materially to the result.

Sincerely yours,
Ellwood B. Chapman
President
Pennsylvania Parks Association
Philadelphia, Pennsylvania

September 1, 1942

My dear Mr. Chapman:

Mrs. Roosevelt asks me to thank you for your letter of August 28. She is glad to know that it was found unnecessary to destroy the virgin timber in Cook Forest and she appreciates your letting her know that the matter has been settled.

Very sincerely yours,
Malvina Thompson
Secretary to Mrs. Roosevelt

Cook Forest State Park, which occupies 7,182 acres in northwestern Pennsylvania, is now a Natural National Landmark. In addition to admiring the scenery of towering white pines and hemlocks, park visitors can hunt, fish, hike, and canoe down the Clarion River.

Mrs. Roosevelt used her "My Day" column of December 12, 1941, to express her views on the environment:

"We are on the train this morning, going up through the mountains of Oregon. Much of this country was settled by New Englanders and the rushing streams which look as though trout and salmon would be plentiful in them, remind one of Maine rivers, though the mountains are so much higher. I wish I could say that wherever I see magnificent trees cut down, I could also see plantations of new trees, but I have not noticed that as yet. One important lesson we still must learn is that we can not use anything which comes from our soil and not return something to the soil for the use of generations to come."

• • •

April 16, 1942

Major General Myron C. Cramer
The Judge Advocate General
District Armory Building
Washington, D.C.
My dear Gen. Cramer:
Today, I called at your personnel office, seeking information concerning the possibilities of and the requirements for obtaining a commission in the Judge Advocate General's Department of the Army, with the intention of offering my services.

Although I did not lose any of my desire to be of service to my country, my morale received no lift when I was told by Capt. Burgess, to whom I talked in Room 209, that the Judge Advocate General's Department does not commission Negroes.

I sought the information on the strength of news

articles and other information that the Army is setting up a new Negro Division to be completely staffed by Negro officer personnel at Fort Huachuca. I surmised that some part of the official staff would be connected with the Judge Advocate General's Department. Several of the recently commissioned officers in the Medical Corps to be stationed at Fort Huachuca are acquaintances of mine.

I am a member of the bar of the District of Columbia, and have practiced here for five years. I have also had seven years of experience in the government, six years of which have been in supervisory or administrative capacities. Included in my duties in these capacities has been the interpretation of legislation, legal matters, and conflicts of policy. I am now doing advanced study in accounting with intention of taking the examination to qualify as a Certified Public Accountant.

I am 35 years of age, married, and have a daughter nine years old. I have a selective service classification of 3A.

Is a commission, such as I seek, possible for one of my qualifications, my race, my loyalty, and my desire to serve?

Respectfully yours,

Harry S. McAlpin

[One page typed]

April 25, 1942

Dear Mr. McAlpin:

I have your letter of April 16 1942, stating that you had called at my personnel office seeking information concerning the possibilities of and the requirements for obtaining a commission in the Judge Advocate General's

Department, with the intention of offering your services, and that you sought the information on the strength of news articles and other information that the Army is activating a new Negro division at Fort Huachuca to be completely staffed by Negro officer personnel. Because of the fact that you state that you were told by Capt. Burgess, to whom you talked, that the Judge Advocate General's Department does not commission Negroes I have delayed answering your letter until I could talk with Captain Burgess.

Captain Burgess informs me that you have evidently misunderstood the statements made to you and that the information he intended to convey was that up to this time this office has not been called upon to furnish a Negro judge advocate for a division to be organized at Fort Huachuca. Captain Burgess further states that he informed you that a great number of well-qualified attorneys throughout the country have written this office expressing their desire to serve with the Judge Advocate General's Department during the war and that in order to process these applications with a view of selecting those best qualified I have established a board of officers in my office for the purpose of classifying and recommending for appointment those applicants whom the board finds are best qualified for the available vacancies, when and if they occur. If you will complete the inclosed forms and return them directly to this office, your application will be carefully considered along with others as the need for new appointments occur.

You ask "Is a commission, such as I seek, possible for one of my qualifications, my race, my loyalty, and my desire to serve?" I think that you will see from the foregoing that the answer is "yes," provided your professional qualifications entitle you to selection on a basis of merit from a very large group of applicants.

Sincerely,
Major General Myron C. Cramer
The Judge Advocate General
Office of the Judge Advocate
Services of Supply
War Department
Washington, D.C.

April 30, 1942

My dear General Cramer:

Thank you for your very pointed and direct reply to my letter of April 16. It would be difficult to explain to you how much it has meant to me, as a loyal and devoted American citizen, to learn that a commission such as I seek is possible for one of my race in the Judge Advocate General's Department. I sincerely regret it if I misunderstood the information Captain Burgess intended to convey to me.

The application forms you enclosed in your letter to me have been completed. I am returning them directly to your office, as you suggested.

I am very hopeful that my qualifications will justify the use of my services in the Judge Advocate General's Department—at Fort Huachuca or elsewhere.

Respectfully yours,
Harry S. McAlpin
May 14, 1942

MEMORANDUM

To: Mrs. Franklin D. Roosevelt

From: Mary McLeod Bethune

Harry S. McAlpin is one of my assistants at the National Youth Administration.

He has applied for a commission in the Judge Advocate

General's Department of the Army. His application was mailed directly to the Judge Advocate General at his request, on April 30, 1942.

The Judge Advocate General's Department is the only branch of the Army in which there are no Negro commissioned officers.

Mr. McAlpin understood from the information given him when he first applied, that the Judge Advocate General's Department did not commission Negroes. He has since written the Judge Advocate General and received a reply stating such a commission as he seeks is possible, provided his qualifications entitle him to selection on a basis of merit from a very large group of other lawyers. (The file of correspondence is attached)

Mr. McAlpin has talked with Major General Cramer on the phone since filing his application, and has been advised that his application has been received, but that no request has yet been made of the Judge Advocate General's Department to provide a staff at the proposed all-Negro Division at Fort Huachuca. If and when such request is received, he was told, he will be given consideration. Mr. McAlpin understands that he meets the qualifications necessary—and I know him to be a person of highest character, possessing an analytical and judicious mind and temperament. I entrust him with the most difficult problems and decisions.

The commissioning of a Negro in this branch of the Army will be a means of lifting the morale of Negroes—as is always the case when hitherto closed doors are opened. The type of service I know Mr. McAlpin would render in such a post would be an additional leavening agent to the morale of Negroes.

It seems needless, and also contrary to stated policy to make his possibilities for such a commission contingent upon the establishment of an all-Negro Division. The thousands of Negroes already in the Army should have a representative in the Army's legal division—the Judge Advocate General's Department.

Would you write a note in Mr. McAlpin's behalf urging the

granting of a commission to him now? It should be addressed to

Major General Myron C. Cramer

The Judge Advocate General

War Department

Washington, D.C.

Whatever else you might do toward obtaining such a commission for this young man, I should appreciate your doing.

May 15, 1942

My dear General Cramer:

Mrs. Roosevelt asks me to write you concerning the commissions to be given by the Judge Advocate General's Department of the Army. She wants me to let you know that if any colored people are being considered for appointments, Mrs. Mary McLeod Bethune, National Youth Administration, has prepared a list of people whom she thinks should be considered.

Very sincerely yours,

Malvina Thompson

Secretary to Mrs. Roosevelt

On February 8, 1944, Harry S. McAlpin, a reporter for the Atlanta Daily World, *attended a White House press conference, thereby becoming the first black White House correspondent. He was told by the head of the White House Press Correspondents Association that if he would refrain from entering the White House, he would be allowed to become a member of their group, upon which he promptly entered the White House. After the press conference, McAlpin strode over to President Roosevelt's desk; Roosevelt made a point of shaking his hand, saying "Harry, I'm glad to have you here."*

• • •

Dear Mrs. Roosevelt,

Do please forgive me for taking any of your valuable time, but I do not know whom I should contact in regard to this matter and thought perhaps you would not mind telling me.

My husband, John Davis, is managing an Ammunition Plant here in Maryland and expects to do so just as long as there is a war—He has inherited his family estate in Massachusetts. It is just eighteen miles from Boston on the Charles River. It is a truly lovely place of 274 acres of valuable farm land. There is a large stone mansion containing about forty large rooms. It has an electric elevator and many bathrooms and fireplaces. I believe it would make an ideal convalescent home.

It has a beautiful swimming pool, gardens, forcing sheds (with heat), caretakers' home, garage, barn, tool sheds, etc. There are many wooded paths with large pine trees on either side.

I am sorry that I can not adequately describe this place but perhaps I have been able to give you some description of it. I read sometime ago where Mrs. Kermit Roosevelt had turned her estate at Oyster Bay over to the Merchant Marine Seamen for the duration and it occurred to me that perhaps this place of ours could be put to some good use for some of our service men for this war or as long as it would be needed. I should be only too glad to send pictures of this place and arrange for anyone to see it. I thank you so much for any advice you can give me.

Sincerely,

Catherine L. Davis

Cool Spring Farm

Annapolis, Maryland

My dear Mrs. Roosevelt:

Your letter of January 13, 1943 forwarding the offer by

Mrs. John Davis of her Massachusetts home for use as a convalescent home, is acknowledged.

The Commandant of the First Naval District has been requested to advise Mrs. John Davis if this property can be of use to any of the Naval activities in that District.

Mrs. Davis' offer and your cooperation are deeply appreciated and it is hoped you will relay our most sincere thanks.

Very sincerely yours,

Frank Knox

Secretary of the Navy

Washington, D.C.

· · ·

February 11, 1943

My dear Mrs. Roosevelt

Wouldn't you like to help make clothes for war workers in industries more comfortable, so that there would be less weary people and fewer accidents in production lines.

Being a teacher of clothing in the High School of this city since 1925, I have acquired some knowledge and experience in this line.

Naturally in a war-minded world one thinks of the things in their profession that would be of service in these trying hours.

Not meaning to boast but I have some inventive trends and have found from past experience it is very hard to get one's ideas safe-guarded.

Besides my day work I teach adults at nite and have some tricks that they in turn have used to make their ready made garments more comfortable.

I do not want my idea exploited for money by people and I myself get no credit. And yet I feel I have an idea to sell (not for dollars) to war workers that would save wear and tear on clothes. Also garments used that would be discarded because the wearer is uncomfortable in them.

We all wear the clothes we feel the best in, even sometimes regardless of the looks.

My idea would be no extra cost to war workers only a little time and work.

Today I tried it on girls welding, girls doing machinists work, cooks in cafeteria and they all agreed the trick made their outfits more comfortable.

Oh yes, I tried it on a man working in coveralls and he said "It sure helps." I've used it for a long time on mens' work shirts.

The idea is not new to me and my family but I feel it is new to hundreds and thousands of workers but how could the idea be given to them for using? I've thot of radio but they need to see as on the screen and I must live and buy war bonds.

I'd love to demonstrate it to you while you are in this area. Only 8 miles from St. Louis and our Steel Industries and Army Deppo.

From one who is enthusiastic to help in some neglected work.

Yours Sincerely,
Grace J. Jordan
Granite City, Illinois

Note penciled in by Mrs. Roosevelt on top of letter: "Acknowledge and suggest she send idea to Dr. L. Stanley * *of Hom Econ who has been working on this."*

February 17, 1943

My dear Miss Jordan:

Mrs. Roosevelt has asked me to acknowledge the receipt of your letter of February 11th.

Mrs. Roosevelt suggests that you send your idea to Dr. Louise Stanley, Bureau of Home Economics, Department of Agriculture, Washington, D.C., as Dr. Stanley has been working on this.

Very sincerely yours,

Secretary to Mrs. Roosevelt

. . .

Letter accompanied by a newspaper article from the *Los Angeles Times,* dated April 29, 1943, headlined "Mrs. Roosevelt Makes Plea for Nisei Youth, They Should Leave Camps, She Says Here."

April 29, 1943

Secretary Please see that Eleanor reads this

Dear Mrs. Roosevelt.

This is my 72nd birthday

The Jap Question.

Every Jap should be sent to Japland and forever—you couldn't breed it out of them in 1000 years.

---

* Louise Stanley earned a Ph.D. in biochemistry from Yale in 1911. She became the highest-ranking woman scientist in the federal government when appointed chief of the U.S. Department of Agriculture's Bureau of Home Economics in 1923. A strong consumer advocate, she developed research and education programs in nutrition during the years of the Great Depression and World War II.

Don't allow **One** in the Americas.

They are an unholy Race—cruel.

Your Husband is a Wonder, yes a World's Wonder and Washington has its dignified [secretary of state] Cordell Hull—the [Undersecretary of State] able Sumner Wells—the independent Senator Willard Tydings

But

If you must free any Japs Turn them loose in your own Back-yard, east of the Mississippi and 200 miles away from the Great Lakes, then if they blow up a Dam they wont drown 50,000 people.

Mrs. Roosevelt you are brilliant and I am for you as long as you are right but I'll have to part with you in regards to the Japs.

Respect

Kimball Patterson

Santa Monica, California

[One page handwritten]

After the Japanese attack on Pearl Harbor, Japanese-Americans, citizens or not, were rounded up and placed in camps. Executive Order No. 9066, signed by President Roosevelt on February 19, 1942, empowered the U.S. Army to designate areas from which "any or all persons may be excluded." The government utilized temporary camps, or "assembly centers," from March through October 1942; these were either large fairgrounds or racetracks. Eventually the War Relocation Authority placed 120,000 Japanese, or Americans of Japanese ancestry, in seven relocation centers throughout the western United States. The Japanese had long faced discrimination; most of them lived in California, feared as competitors for jobs and disliked for their success in growing fruits and vegetables. This dislike led to passage of the Exclusion Act of 1917, which banned all people of the Oriental race from citizenship; however, offspring born in the U.S. were citizens. Latent discrimination gave way to hysteria after Pearl Harbor, leading to the mass internment of Japanese. It is worth noting that no person of Japanese ancestry in the United States was convicted of espionage during the war, while eighteen Caucasians were tried for spying for Japan. Mrs. Roosevelt penned an article in response to letters like the one above:

"I am very conscious of the situation facing many of our citizens who stem from German, Italian and Japanese backgrounds. It is a very difficult situation for them and for the country, because unfortunately, a small minority of German, Italian and Japanese nationals have not been loyal and this, of course, puts the loyal ones on the defensive. We have prided ourselves for years on our ability as a country, to live and work together peacefully regardless of where our forebears came from, or when they came, and we felt our success in this was an example to the world.

I hope that all of our people will think of the people in these three groups as individuals, and not as groups and judge them and treat them as individuals. We believe in the Bill of Rights and we must grant all people the same rights until they violate those rights.... I hope we will stress the need for tolerance, understanding and consideration through every medium of expression that we have. We can not afford to have any number of our citizens in a position where it is hard for them to wholeheartedly accept and endorse democracy as a form of government and way of life."

• • •

[Date-stamped May 27, 1942]

Mrs. Franklin D. Roosevelt
White House
Washington, D.C.
Dear Mrs. President:
I am writing you in behalf of a very unfortunate family. This will be a very long letter, but please read it through.

Mrs. H. had ten children, nine of whom were by her first husband: five girls and four boys. She had the misfortune when very young of becoming infatuated with a man working for her father and married him. He was part Japanese. The nine children were all born within eleven years. Her husband died in 1917.

She moved to another part of the city, changed her name to H., telling her children as they grew up their father was French. Since she was English, no one thought different. She was in hopes any memories the children had of their father would be forgotten, and they were. She remarried a very nice man who has been a Los Angeles City fireman for 18 years. He raised her children. They have a boy seventeen of their own.

Mrs. Roosevelt, I am sure he raised them all to be good, loyal American citizens. These children all married in to good American families and have families of their own. These sons-in-law and daughters-in-law married in to the family, not knowing about this.

But, unfortunately, two of the girls—Mrs. Mabel H. and Mrs. Harold C.—were working in a plant that was taken over for defense. When they had to get their birth certificates, they found out none of the children were registered under the name of H. so they started an investigation which ended in the name being Japanese. The mother confessed to this.

Mrs. Roosevelt, you can not realize the shock to those poor children and the families they had married into. These families were all put in a concentration camp. I am sure if you could only see these families, you would know they do not belong there. They are so out of place there, these little blond babies and young blond American wives. They are trying so hard to keep people from knowing it. It is not only a disgrace to them, but to all the uncles, aunts, cousins, and in-laws. Some of their young girls are just ready for high school.

Mrs. Roosevelt, we don't want to make an issue of this, but I beg of you in God's name and for the sake of humanity to see what you can do. I am not of the family, but I have known them for twenty years and know what nice families they are. They are so afraid this will get in the paper, as this is the only family like that in the camp. The authorities who had to sign them up in camp cried when they saw these dear little children and mothers have to go in there, as they are not Japanese.

It happened so quickly we had no opportunity to contact the proper authorities to whom we might explain their predicament and to plead their case, and knowing them so many years and being familiar with the character of all those affected, I shall never stop trying to help them. It is hard for outsiders to understand the situation and they are trying so hard to keep anyone from knowing about it.

Mrs. Roosevelt, you have done so much good for the poor I am sure you would only have to see them to know it is a mistake. Please in God's name I ask you again, will you help them:

They are in Pomona Camp at Pomona, California. Their names are as follows:

Mr. and Mrs. Harold C.

Mr. and Mrs. Jack S.

Mr. and Mrs. Leonard S. and child

Mr. and Mrs. Edward D. and two children

Mrs. Mable H. and two children

Mr. and Mrs. Arthur H. and two children

Mr. and Mrs. Henry H.

Mr. and Mrs. Fred H. and child

Mr. and Mrs. Frank H. and child

Thanking you for reading this and anticipating your co-operation in the matter, I am

Very respectfully,

Mrs. Ethel Vincent

Los Angeles, California

[Two pages typed]

August 17, 1942

Dear Mrs. Roosevelt:

I wish to thank you on behalf of many of the friends of the H. children who were released from the Pomona Assembly Center, August 15, 1942

As for my self, Mrs. Roosevelt, words cannot express my appreciation for your cooperation in their behalf. I cannot thank you enough for referring my letters to the proper authorities. I am sure the H. children and my self will never forget your kindness.

If you knew the children you would know they are so deserving of our efforts.

I can only thank you again and again for your kindness and interest in the matter.

Very sincerely,

Mrs. Ethel Vincent

Los Angeles, California

• • •

September 30, 1942

Dear Mrs. Roosevelt:

Although I have decided to tell you a few personal matters, I feel I am justified in so doing because these personal matters have a direct bearing on a thing which is of such great importance that it could actually mean Victory or Defeat for the United States and allies.

The enclosed, page 115, May issue, *Popular Science* magazine, will tell you a **little** about the instrument (or in fact one of the instruments) which my husband, John F. Carssow has given years and years of hardship and starving and sacrifice to invent and perfect. Since this article appeared, the instrument was tested in the wind tunnel of Goodrich Rubber Co. by the Army and **proven the best answer to icing**. It has also been tested by Glen L. Martin Co., who state that it is the best de-icer ever invented. The Army says plane models have been frozen to the type fitted for Goodrich Rubber Co.'s **rubber** boot de-icer (with our country's dire need for **rubber**). Plane models have **not** been frozen and rubber boot de-icers do not help do the job of de-icing and are dangerous when the plane gets in strong wind. The number of plane crashes due to ice on the wings, and the loss of lives therefrom, proves that rubber boot de-icers are not adequate.

It is hard for me to write, especially unknown to my husband who definitely would not approve, because it is not my line of work—it is **his**, and we are two, different individuals. It would be easier if my husband could afford to buy a good typewriter. He has priority rating of the highest but just doesn't have the money. I would never have had time to attempt it had I not had very bad trouble with my eyes and had to take a day off from my work. I work swing shift, 6 days a week, for an aircraft company, starting an hour before work and arriving home an hour after. The fluorescent lights used by the company have a constant flicker, even when functioning normally, and when they start flashing on and off, as they do almost every day, in some part of my floor where I work, my eyes play out and they make me terribly sick to my stomach. Yesterday one went bad right above me. It always takes some time before the busy maintenance department can get a man up to take the offending tube out and put in another.

My husband and I have in common that we both went through depression years mostly jobless and discouraged and without money. I now am trying to pay back personal loans to people who **need** the money,—and also get expensive dental work done, which I couldn't have paid for before, etc. I am very much run down and in need of a leave of absence, in order to keep going longer for defense, but, until something **radical** is done to help John's cause and cut through the **eternal** red tape and banish the terrible uncertainty, I can't take any leave of absence until I drop in my tracks. John is going to pieces mentally and, unless I have an answer **immediately** (by which I mean within **days** or hours) after this letter has reached your personal attention, nothing can keep him from going to pieces; and no one will fight, as he has fought, to have these instruments installed in planes for the U.S. and allies. No one would have the bulldog tenacity and moral courage and stamina that he has had.

John's parents fought against his taking an engineer's course at college, as they had always fought his urge to invent things. He took other subjects but since, while going **hungry and shelterless**, studied engineering from libraries. He went without cars and money and music and entertainment. He hasn't even had the bare necessities of life. He is still sacrificing,—still has no money, not even enough to pay off loans, which worries him no end.

You dare to look at things in a new light. You can see that people are wrong in letting the same old rules apply to inventors, 99% of them being trampled in the dust of greed and crooked politics, all their years of sacrifice going for naught, leaving them bitter, their faith in humanity and in God often shattered, and their lives a discouragement to potential inventors who might create things for democracy's sake and to save the very lives of those who, along with your sons, must go to battle and fight for freedom.

John decided to try to get orders from aircraft companies for small parts and, after much suffering and trials, finally landed one,—and then was swamped with orders. I have "procured" (my husband would use the word "swiped") a copy of his letter of application for an RFC loan. This 90% government-guaranteed loan, was turned down by Colonel Azak of the U.S. Army. Colonel Azak pretends to be very much worried over the airplane instrument bottleneck,—yet he gave orders for instruments to a company which turned out bad ones. As a worker in the procurement division of the aircraft co., I know the company is definitely not good.

John had to turn back all those orders for parts (and war production was held up because they can't get parts made fast enough)—because he couldn't get the loan which Frank C. Mortimer, of the WPB, practically assured him he would get.

Any inventor, with a thing worth while, can get financial backing, **if** he wants to turn over half interest to anyone, after all the years of his **life** he has given to it. Can you blame any inventor for refusing to do that? It isn't war-profiteering for him to want enough money, out of all those years of **nothing**, to pay his honest debts,—to clear his credit rating with the banks and to enable him to carry on further research and create new things and improve on those he has created. Isn't a creative mind worth the money to keep it in working order and to keep it creating things for the **safety** of our people? The lives of your sons, out there in battle along with the sons of your beloved American people, may well depend on this ice warning indicator.

There are many other, larger and more **powerful** companies manufacturing de-icers, all of which are inferior to this one, (and that you can **prove** upon investigation), but, because of their **power**, there is more chance that their instrument will be installed on planes than this one.

John will have nothing left out of the payment for those two instruments, after he pays his debts. He will never have much left out of any amount of orders, because he is too good and kindhearted and too much interested in the welfare of all humanity. He doesn't want to profiteer on the war. He wants the war won as quickly as possible, by the U.S. and allies.

If some inventor of such a valuable instrument should break under the terrific strain, under which the United States places an inventor, and lose his mind enough to sell so valuable an instrument to **Hitler** or to **Japan**, all would be over for the U.S. and allies. Hitler doesn't let such talent go unheeded. He sees to it that valuable inventors of **war-winning** factors are financed and encouraged. Why doesn't the United States protect and encourage its inventors? The U.S. inventors are trying to **save**. Hitler's inventors have to have their inventions used to **destroy**. While Hitler is financing and encouraging his inventors of destruction, the U.S. Army, with it's rotten politics, is trampling down inventions for the **savings of lives** and the saving of innocent nation,—the U.S. and allies.

Unless some **explosive** action is taken from headquarters **quick**, cutting thru' all procrastination due to red tape, and issuing a martial law—a command to all aircraft companies to immediately change models to heated wing planes with Ice Warning Indicators, **your sons** may lose their lives in planes with inferior de-icing equipment. John's instrument has been **proven the best**. Why? Why? Why, is it not installed in every U.S. and allied plane? Why is such a huge loss suffered from ice on airplane wings when it could be avoided? In the grim face of war—why? Why the **red tape**, the politics, the greed, when our very nation is at stake?

Mrs. Roosevelt, I **beg** of you! **Investigate**, prove for yourself that this instrument is of **vital** importance, and then please try your best to have **quick** action taken. Every time I see all the **mere babes** in winged aviation suits, either ours or the RAF's, I wonder what kind of a country this is where an instrument designed for their **safety** is denied them.

I am praying tonight that God will cause the secretary, into whose hands this letter falls, to see fit to let you read this letter yourself, and that you will be given the power to act quickly in favor of the safest de-icing device ever known to aviation.

Sincerely yours,
Joyce L. Carssow

P.S. In order to sell an instrument to the Navy, John will have to sign a contract giving the Navy full rights to turn the manufacture of the instrument to any company it chooses. Do you think that is fair treatment of an inventor who has put so much of his life into an invention like that? Unfairness to inventors is not going to further our **Victory**. Unfairness to inventors is discouraging many inventors who could and would give us many more valuable aids to quicker victory. Many an inventor has given up under the injustice they are made to suffer.

[Eight and a half pages handwritten]

The Popular Science *article referred to is entitled "Ice Detector on Plane Wing Warns Pilot to Use De-Icer; Measures Coating Thickness." It begins: "Ice formation on the wings of planes during flight may now be detected and measured by a device set into the leading edge of a wing. Invented by John F. Carssow, of Los Angeles, and tested in operation on a Western Air Lines plane during the winter, it instantly tells a pilot when to turn on the plane's de-icing equipment." Several drawings illustrate how the device works.*

October 14, 1942

MEMORANDUM FOR: Captain John L. McCrea, U.S. Navy

SUBJECT: Ice Detector Invented by John F. Carssow.

1. The Bureau of Aeronautics is extremely interested in the Ice Detector invented by Mr. John F. Carssow. Two of these instruments were purchased and have just recently been received by this bureau. These instruments have been allocated for service tests and consideration will be given to a production order provided service tests are satisfactory.

Ralph E. Davison

Rear Admiral, U.S. Navy

Bureau of Aeronautics

Navy Department

Washington, D.C.

• • •

December 12, 1942

Dear Mrs. Roosevelt:

Recently I read with interest that you said the country women should be organized as land workers as they are in England. I am writing to ask if you will not organize them. They can learn to prune trees, drive tractors, milk, raise vegetables and chickens.

Until eight years ago when my husband died this ranch was our home from which he commuted daily to San Francisco where he was editor of the **Call-Bulletin**. I am a writer, had done no manual labor. Owing to scarcity of labor this year I decided to work the ranch. Much of the summer eight hours a day I gathered apricots, prunes, almonds and walnuts. Soon I found I could carry on with little fatigue. Country women can do far better. I think they would thrill to being Soldiers of the Soil. I hope the Department of Agriculture will see that an organization is begun immediately in order that there be no sag in production. Can you not head the Soldiers of the Soil?

There could be regional directors, one for each section, the Pacific Coast, the NorthWest, the SouthWest, and so on throughout the United States. By consulting with Granges* and farm organizations a Captain in each county could be named. Captains could have a lieutenant in each town to carry out the program. It seems that this is work that each woman in the country can have a small, if not a large share and do her bit to help the war effort.

I first had the pleasure of meeting you at Senator James D. Phelan's luncheon for Vice-President Thomas R. Marshall years ago, and later at the reception at the San Jose Woman's Club on one of your flying trips. Trusting that you will give us your leadership, I am

Sincerely yours,

Cora Older

(Mrs. Fremont Older)

Woodhills Ranch

Cupertino, California

[1 page typed]

---

* An association of farmers organized in 1867 for their mutual welfare.

The article referred to is probably one that appeared in the November 1942 Ladies Home Journal *entitled "Women at War In Great Britain." When Mrs. Roosevelt traveled to England at the suggestion of her husband, she wished especially to learn what she could from the contributions of British women to the war. In her article she stated:*

"You will want to know about the land army because that is Great Britain's answer to the shortage of farm labor. The land army consists entirely of women and they do practically every kind of farm work. There are no men left on the farms except men of fifty-five and over and young boys under eighteen. I visited a farm where the house went back to Elizabethan days and which was surrounded by an old moat. You can imagine that this farm had done certain things in a traditional manner for a great, great, many years. Nevertheless the farmer told me that his land army girls who were all in uniform, were entirely satisfactory. He had a fine herd of cattle and the girls did all the work in connection with it. The girls do every kind of thatching and as you know many farm buildings have thatched roofs. They do threshing and they plow with tractors. Hedging and ditching is done by girls. In fact they learn to do anything that needs to be done."

December 26, 1942

My dear Mrs. Older:

Mrs. Roosevelt asks me to thank you for your letter and to tell you that the organization of a Women's Land Army is under consideration at the present time. The American Women's Voluntary Services has put such a program into effect for unpaid volunteers, and Mrs. Roosevelt hopes that the government will be able to organize something along that line for paid workers. It has worked out very successfully in England and the women there are able to do a great deal of the work on the farms.

Very sincerely yours,
Malvina Thompson
Secretary to Mrs. Roosevelt

• • •

December 29, 1942

Dear Mrs. Roosevelt:

Your December sixteenth "MY DAY" set me to thinking about taking care of all of those babies that were being born to the wives of our men in military service.

We are all very conscious of an "Army Emergency Relief Fund" which has received thousands of dollars especially thru the sport channels of the country.

Many of us have wondered where this money was to be used and still don't know. Why wouldn't this condition mentioned in your article be one that could be remedied thru the use of some of these funds?

If not, and you or your secretary have the time, would appreciate knowing just what this fund is used for.

I am just a salesman with three children so please excuse this typing that gets me by on correspondence with the home office but is hardly good enough for official letter writing.

Sincerely yours,
Walter S. De Haven
Chicago, Illinois

[One page typed]

January 5, 1943

My dear Mr. De Haven:

Mrs. Roosevelt asks me to acknowledge your letter and to tell you she understands the Army Emergency Relief fund is used for maternity care for the wives of Army men, as well as for the care of dependents and the families of men killed in action. It provides a great deal of such help and the Red Cross also assists, but the problem is very great and is almost impossible to solve with funds which are raised by purely voluntary contributions.

Very sincerely yours,
Malvina C. Thompson
Secretary to Mrs. Roosevelt

• • •

April 29, 1943

My dear Mrs. Roosevelt,—

In reference to your recent visit to two relocation camps in Arizona, and the subsequent publicity of your decision that the young internees should be removed from the camps, may I suggest that you give the matter a little more study.

Those of us who have lived in California for many years have had ample opportunity to judge the Japanese, and a great many of us personally know of cases of unsuspected treachery which were revealed after Pearl Harbor.

As an instance. For many years one of the most respected men in town was a Japanese, a highly educated Japanese, who had a flower store in this small village. Everyone knew and liked him and his loyalty to the country was often spoken of. After Pearl Harbor, when he was apprehended by the FBI his place was found to be filled with seditious literature, and it was proved that he had been sending regularly, information to Japan. As we are in the center of an area comprised of Camps, Airfields and Bases, and as you may know, are close to the large airplane factories, this man had plenty of opportunities to attain information. Among the things found in his house, was a citation from the Emperor of Japan, bestowed upon him for valuable assistance.

I am enclosing an editorial from the **San Diego Union**, of April 28th* which explains some of the reasons for the step that was taken to segregate the Japanese, and I repeat that we who live directly on the coast, know of many incidents such as I have told you.

How can you ask people who know, to subscribe to your more or less snap judgement to remove any Japanese from relocation camps? They all sound loyal when you talk to them,—from rather recent experience Washington should know that. Very few of us ordinary citizens would presume to come to your house for a two day's visit, and tell you how to run it.

Very sincerely yours,

Rebecca Rice

(Mrs. Ivan Rice)

Chairman

La Jolla Branch, San Diego Chapter

American Red Cross.

[One and a half pages typed]

May 11, 1943

My dear Mrs. Rice:

I think you must have misunderstood what you read. I did not make any snap judgments. I simply reported on what I saw

---

* The editorial was not in the file.

and was told, and no suggestion was ever made by anyone of having the Japanese return to the West Coast. Both the Federal Bureau of Investigation and the War Relocation Authority believe that carefully checked American-born Japanese might safely be used as needed labor in certain parts of the country. I do not think you want to have to support them indefinitely as we have had to do with the Indians. It is very easy to become institutionalized even when you are an American citizen. I did not suggest that they are not living decently or that any changes should be made in what was being done for them.

Very sincerely yours,

Eleanor Roosevelt

• • •

June 21, 1943

Dear Mrs. Roosevelt:—

I know that I am assuming a great deal in writing a personal letter to the wife of the President but feel you are unwittingly doing the negro race a great wrong with your ill timed and ill advised social reforms. The northern negro takes you seriously and there will be no end of trouble in the north. The southern negro knows you've got a lot to learn but even so it makes him dissatisfied and a poorer worker.

As the inclosed article stated the negro will always pay the price.

I will keep you posted locally.

Respectfully,

C. S. Gordon

Atlanta, Georgia

Enclosed is the beginning part of an article from an unknown newspaper, dated June 22, 1943, headed: "Detroit Quiet Again Under

Army's Guns," with the subheading "President's Action Checks Violence After 23 Are Killed and 700 Are Injured." The portion enclosed reports the following:

"Peace settled upon riot-torn Detroit Tuesday with the guns of the U.S. Army and state troops in grim command of the areas where racial fights spread death, terror and destruction.

Ordered by President Roosevelt in a formal proclamation to desist, and with federal troops carrying out his command, white and Negro antagonists skulked into hiding after having caused the deaths of 23 persons—20 of them Negroes—during a calamitous day and night.

At least 700 persons were injured and approximately 1,300 arrested and held Tuesday. Of the total under arrest police estimated about 85 per cent were Negroes.

On streets 1,100 soldiers marched in patrol to assist the state militia, state police and city police. Early Tuesday authorities said conditions were 'quiet.' "

• • •

June 22, 1943

Dear Mrs. Roosevelt:

I suppose now you are satisfied. Instead of remaining in the White House, and preserving the dignity and honor the people in the United States have always had for its occupants but which through a consistent thread of events since 1932 has been completely destroyed in the minds and hearts of many loyal Americans, *YOU* have been running all over the country sewing seeds of discord and dissension, and such incidents as Detroit, Beaumont, Mobile, etc. are the product of your endeavors.

Thank the Lord, however, the worm is beginning to turn, and real Southerners are just yearning for the opportunity in the fall of 1944 to show their true feelings towards you and the present crowd in Washington, who is causing so much confusion and chaos in the minds of the citizens. We long for the day when the New Deal is completely abolished from even the memory of our citizenry.

Anyone wanting to get at the real root of this racial trouble need only to point to Washington.

Yours truly,

H. Bright Keck

Richmond, Virginia

P.S. I am no radical; I was born in Richmond, Va. in 1897, nearly 46 years ago, and we Southerners understand this negro problem much better than you New Yorkers, and know much better how to handle it.

This letter, and some others sent in at the same time, contained a newspaper editorial apparently cut from a Jackson, Mississippi, newspaper, which said the following:

BLOOD ON HER HANDS

It is blood on your hands, Mrs. Eleanor Roosevelt. More than any other person, you are morally responsible for those race riots in Detroit where two dozen were killed and fully 500 injured in nearly a solid day of street fighting.

You have been personally proclaiming and practising social equality at the White House and wherever you go, Mrs. Roosevelt.

In Detroit, a city noted for the growing impudence and insolence of its negro population, an attempt was made to put your preachments into practice, Mrs. Roosevelt.

What followed is now history. Streets ran red with blood until the President of the United States, who happens to be your husband, declared martial law and sent troops to the scene.

No sort of camouflage or false claiming can hide the ugly facts of what happened in Detroit.

It isn't pleasant to say this concerning the First Lady of the land. It isn't pleasant for millions of people to be living in daily fear of being killed or injured in racial clashes, either.

Claim of the National Association for the Advancement of Colored People was the result of Axis propaganda isn't even decent nonsense. Axis propaganda had nothing whatever to do with it.

It was inevitable that something of this sort should happen. Authorities in scores of our large cities, especially industrial centers, have been for many months in hourly fear of such outbreaks. There is some melancholy gratification in the fact that it happened in one of our northernmost cities, just across from the Canadian border, and not in the Deep South or even the Middle South. Down this way we have tried to use patience, tolerance and forbearance in dealing with all phases of the race problem.

Blood on your hands, Mrs. Roosevelt! And the damned spots won't wash out, either.

Other brief letters or postcards about the Detroit riots said the following:

June 23, 1943

Dear Mrs. R–

That race riot in Detroit is a terrible and horrible thing. Race friction all over our country, due largely, we believe, to your unwise talks and actions. Why don't you stay home and quit talking and writing on every thing under the sun? You and others should forget that 4 and 5th terms and get busy on the WAR and food for the USA.

Jeff Davis
Memphis, Tennessee

June 24, 1943

Dear Madam:

The blood of the dead in Detroit is on your head—and you cannot deny it.

                                        Yours truly,
                                        Frances Jackson
                                        Washington, D.C.

Mrs. E. Roosevelt—

You can now see what you have done to stir up race hatred. Please do not continue. Detroit can blame you and justly.

Mrs. Roosevelt's response was unusually subdued. She ended her June 22, 1943, "My Day" column with this paragraph:

"The domestic scene as you listen to the radio and read the papers today, is anything but encouraging and one would like *not* to think about it, because it gives one a feeling that as a whole we are not really prepared for democracy. We might even fall into the same excesses that some other people whom we look down upon, have fallen into for we do not seem to have learned self-control and obedience to law as yet."

• • •

October 20, 1943

Dear Mrs. Roosevelt:

I am a young girl who recently graduated from high-school. When I heard about the project sponsored by the government for the purpose of training nurses to relieve the current shortage in medical help, I immediately offered my services, thinking I possessed all the qualifications required to fill the position. I was told that they did not take colored applicants as yet. They neglected, however, to tell me just why they did not take colored applicants and since I am an inquisitive individual, I am forced to inquire after a reason. I think that perhaps you can supply that reason if you will.

I am a patriotic American like most Negroes. There isn't a race of people more faithful and loyal to this country than we are. There isn't anyone who is fighting harder than our boys are. I think that they deserve the best. I would appreciate hearing anything you have to say about the matter.

Yours sincerely,
Maudzette Knilown
Milwaukee, Wisconsin

[One page typed]

October 28, 1943

Dr. Thomas Parran
The Surgeon General
Public Health Service
Bethesda, Maryland
Dear Dr. Parran:

Mrs. Roosevelt would appreciate information about any project sponsored by the government for the purpose of training nurses to relieve the current shortage in medical help. She has had several letters from people interested in this project.

Mrs. Roosevelt would also like to know the policy as regards acceptance of Negroes for this work.

Very sincerely yours,
Malvina C. Thompson
Secretary to Mrs. Roosevelt

· · ·

December 13, 1943

Dear Mrs. Roosevelt:–

I read in the newspaper that you were planning a tour
through the over-crowded sections of the Negro district.
I wish that my apartment could be included in this tour.
Let me tell you about it. There are five (5) of us crowded
in (2) rooms kitchen and bath. Three children my husband and myself. This apartment is damp but the bed-
room is driest of the two (2) the children sleep in there.
We share a "Sofa Bed" in the living room. Now here's
where the trouble begins. As I said before, this apartment
is damp my children are kept full of colds. As fast as one
child get rid of a cold the other child contracts this cold
its because there no place for isolation. The room that
they sleep in is very poorly ventilated its small, and the
beds are crowded together and can't be rearranged
without causing a draft. We have tried to apply for a
Defence House and before that a Alley Dwelling House.
In fact I wrote to you, asking for help in obtaining one
of these Alley Dwelling Houses but at that time there was
no vacancy. The Defence Housing Authority said we were
not eligible because we were permanent residence. They
will not even except our application because we were
unfortunate enough to be born here instead of migrating
here.

Mrs. Roosevelt, wouldn't it be smart for the authorities to give us a house to suit our size of the family
because my husband does work at a Defence job. He
works at the Navy Yard. Giving us a larger residence
give the smaller family a chance to take a small residence, it will save the authorities many hours of work
because the private home owners will not have the too

small houses overcrowded thus creating a chance for the communicable diseases spreading unnecessarily. This will enable these children who don't have a chance to survive. The dampness and breaking down the resistance because of frequent colds. Why should these children who are to be future Americans be denied a chance for healthy and normal life due them. Please help them, not for my sake alone but for the sake of the Post-war world that they too are included in.

We Remain,

Sincerely yours,

Another Mother

Mrs. Evelyn Waters

Washington, D.C.

[Two pages handwritten]

December 17, 1943

My dear Mrs. Waters:

Mrs. Roosevelt has asked me to acknowledge the receipt of your letter of December 13th.

Mrs. Roosevelt knows conditions are bad and is trying to arouse public interest.

Very sincerely yours,

Malvina C. Thompson

Secretary to Mrs. Roosevelt

. . .

May 24, 1944

Dear Mrs. Roosevelt.

Our little Negro nursery school (under Lanham Act[*]) has been closed, and in fact I am afraid that not a single Negro nursery school in Palm Beach County is functioning to-day. At the time of your very gracious visit to Azucar we had a very successful colored nursery school in operation—since then it was taken over by the school board—under the Lanham Act—to-day it is **closed**. I feel that the kind people who initiated the Lanham Act could not possibly cover all situations—so that—under the standardized requirements many Negro families could not qualify or meet them—and others were not sufficiently sold on the need to grasp the opportunity.

I feel very strongly on the need—for Negro nursery schools—because I have seen so many colored children, go from nursery school to first grade—and from first grade on and up. The first grade is the "graveyard" for too many Negro children—but not for those who went to nursery school. I just wonder if the Lanham Act is doing what it was expected to do. I pray that it is.

Faithfully yours,

F. E. Bryant

Azucar Recreational Hall

Azucar, Florida

[One page handwritten]

---

[*]The Lanham Act, passed by Congress in February 1941, authorized construction and program assistance for families of those working in defense plants. Assistance included under the program were housing, schools, and other services such as childcare for mothers working in the plants.

Dear Miss Thompson:

This will acknowledge your letter of June 1, 1944, enclosing a letter to Mrs. Roosevelt from Mr. F. E. Bryant, Azucar Recreation Hall, Azucar, Florida, regarding nursery schools assisted by Lanham Act funds.

Lanham Act funds have been allotted to the Board of Education in Palm Beach County for assistance in providing nursery schools for children of working mothers. The responsibility for operation is entirely in the hands of the local school board; however, under the provisions of the Lanham Act, any discrimination on account of race or color is prohibited. It was the intent of this agency to make provisions for the children of working mothers in the County, and the Negro children would be eligible for one or more units if their mothers are working in war connected activities. If, however, the Negro nursery school would be operated on a welfare basis, it would not be eligible for Lanham Act assistance.

I am referring a copy of Mr. Bryant's letter to our Regional Director in Atlanta, with the request for a report on this particular case. As soon as this information is received, I shall relay it to you.

Sincerely yours,
Florence Kerr
Assistant to the Administrator
Director, War Public Services
Federal Works Agency
Washington, D.C.

· · ·

Dear Mrs. Roosevelt:

With the appointment of a new chairman of the American Red Cross, can it not be possible for that organization to reconsider the policy of labeling blood supplied by

Negroes? It is probable that a person not a Negro can not fully understand the inward disturbance the present policy causes Negroes. Discontinuance of this policy might be received with considerable favor by large numbers of white people and in addition bring to the Red Cross full support of the Negroes.

A little consideration may indicate that the time right now is ripe for a change, from several points of view.

Very truly yours,
V. D. Johnston
Howard University
Washington, D.C.

[One page typed]

A typed note, no date: "I will ask but the opposition came not from the Red Cross but from the Army Medical Corps. Send to Mr. O'Connor. E.R."

July 24, 1944

My dear Mr. O'Connor:
I am enclosing a letter from V. D. Johnson, Howard University, Washington, D.C. Mrs. Roosevelt will appreciate it if you will let her know about this.

Very sincerely yours,
Malvina C. Thompson
Secretary to Mrs. Roosevelt.

August 7, 1944

My dear Mrs. Roosevelt:
I received Miss Thompson's letter of July 24, 1944, enclosing a letter to you from Mr. V. D. Johnston, of Howard University,

concerning the policy with respect to the separation of Negro blood in the processing of plasma.

Mr. Johnston's letter is returned herewith, together with a copy of my reply.

As you know, the matter was considered most carefully by the Army, the Navy, and the Red Cross, and I do not see how any other course could have been followed.

Sincerely yours,
Basil O'Connor
American Red Cross
Washington, D.C.

August 7, 1944

My dear Mr. Johnston:

Mrs. Roosevelt has referred to me your letter of July 15, 1944, concerning the policy with respect to the separation of Negro blood in the processing of plasma. Mr. Fieser has also sent me your letter to him.

I have carefully reviewed the situation to which you refer. From the point of view of all the people of the United States—which is the point from which I have to look at things as head of the American Red Cross—I am convinced that the present arrangement is the best possible in all of the circumstances.

You will be pleased, I know, to learn that blood donations are now being received at the rate of approximately one hundred thousand a week, that we are approaching the nine million mark in total blood donations, and that a continuing adequate supply of plasma is being provided for the armed forces.

Sincerely yours,
Basil O'Connor
American Red Cross
Washington, D.C.

• • •

August 16, 1944

My Dear Mrs. Roosevelt,

I do not think I have ever had such a thrill as on the night, after Page School graduation exercises, you so graciously signed autographs and shook hands with everyone, including myself. It was something I had long hoped for, but never really expected to experience. You might possibly remember me, as I am the mother of the boy who gave the salutatory address.

I now have a problem, and knowing how fair, and broadminded you are, I wondered if you might help me.

As you know the Page School admits those who are Pages, and also young workers in Supreme Court, and Capitol Buildings. My boy, Juan, worked in an office at Supreme Court and went to Page School, before work, and after work.

Now my daughter Ruth has a chance for the same job (as Juan has been called in the Navy.) However there is the problem of two more years of high school. If she could only go to the Page School she could manage to do both **work and school** as Juan did. I have found night school would not be satisfactory. I realize the Page School has been an exclusive boys' school. Yet I wish so very much she (Ruth) might have this chance to earn while she is going to school.

She is a quiet girl, very brilliant, and would not, I am sure, cause Mr. Kendall any trouble. I feel there is a first time for everything. I understand they have hired women teachers the last few years, for the first time in the history of the school.

I do **so** hope you may know of some way to help us in this matter.

Sincerely,
Mrs. Muriel Kestner
Washington, D.C.

P.S. We are very proud of this picture. Thought you might like one.

Mrs. Kestner

[Three pages handwritten, accompanied by a photo of Mrs. Roosevelt shaking hands with Juan Kestner.]

The top of the first page has notes in Mrs. Roosevelt's hand, indicating that Mrs. Kestner be thanked for sending the photo, and that a letter should be sent to James Barnes.

[on note paper of The White House, Washington, D.C.]

August 28, 1944

MEMORANDUM
FOR Mrs. Roosevelt
FROM James M. Barnes
We have contacted the Page School and they advised that they did not think it practical that a girl attend their school.

August 30, 1944

My dear Mrs. Kestner:
Mrs. Roosevelt asked the President's Administrative Assistant to find out about the possibility of your daughter attending the Page School and has just received a memorandum which reads as follows:

"We have contacted the Page School and they have advised that they did not think it practical that a girl attend their school."

Mrs. Roosevelt is so sorry.

> Very sincerely yours,
> Malvina C. Thompson
> Secretary to Mrs. Roosevelt.

• • •

December 25, 1944

Dear Mrs. Roosevelt:

Xmas Day, 1944. Here we are, my wife and I, sitting in our comfortable home enjoying the blessings of a free America, listening to the radio programs being sent out to help cheer our fighting men all over the world, making it possible for some of them to talk to their loved ones, here at home. At this moment I am listening to the wonderful Blue Net work program[*] which is no doubt bucking up their Morale on this Xmas Day.

It has just started to snow here in St. Louis and we are having that White Xmas, which so many are today singing about. Yes, we can enjoy it as it drifts down and covers the earth with its beautiful white blanket, but, contrast it over there, our men on the fighting lines lying in the cold bleak weather, some possibly without a hot meal in their stomachs and no protection from the biting winds which numb their bodies. It is for them and our gallant Allies all over the world, that America is thinking. I am sure everything

---

[*]The Federal Communications Commission's 1938-1941 monopoly probe of NBC and CBS radio networks resulted in the creation of a new network, ABC. At the time NBC owned two networks, NBC-Blue and NBC-Red. On October 12, 1943, the FCC created ABC from NBC-Blue network.

possible is being done for their comfort, by this great Nation of ours.

While sitting here enjoying—everything—and reading the paper, at the same time, I came across the enclosed article of the wonderful things you are doing personally, and many others which never get in the news, for I am sure there are many. I am a native of Whitehaven, Cumberland Co. England. Coming to America in 1898 at the age of 10 years. Now, as an American I am interested to know more about this organization, after reading about its great work for these unfortunate children, and think it may be possible that I can contribute in some small way to help at least one British child so unfortunate, if you will send me full information of the organization.

Please accept the Holiday greeting from my wife and self to our Great President, yourself and family, and especially your gallant fighting sons, who are a fine example of what it takes to make America strong.

Respectfully Yours,
Dr. John C. Kitchin
Optometric Eye Specialist
Charles, Missouri

[One page typed]

This letter was accompanied by a newspaper article entitled "First Lady 'Adopts' Another War Victim," describing Mrs. Roosevelt's participation in Foster Parents Plan, whereby each foster parent paid $15 per month for the care of a child.

• • •

March 8, 1945

Dear Mrs. Roosevelt:

I was surprised when I read the enclosed clipping about the negro, Selma Burke, because I understand the Federal Bureau of Investigation investigated her activities in 1940 when she was living as the wife of a German spy, on East Twenty Eighth Street, in New York, in a building where I had my office for a time.

The German, later, fled to Mexico and Selma Burke was active in New Jersey with the Bunds.[*] It is my impression she was sent to prison for a term of years because of her activities against our Government.

Now, in 1945, it does not seem possible this person could be recognised by our President and First Lady in the way they have.

Very Sincerely,

Kathryn Churchill

Flower Consultant

New York, New York

[One page typed]

A small clipping of part of a "My Day" column by Mrs. Roosevelt accompanied the letter, saying, "This morning I went to Miss Selma Burke's studio to look at a head she has done of the President."

March 19, 1945

MEMORANDUM FOR MISS TULLY:

Mrs. Roosevelt says to give you a memo about Selma Burke. She is doing a portrait of the President for the Recorder of

---

* Pro-Nazi German-American Association

Deeds office, which Mrs. Roosevelt saw the other day. She thinks Miss Burke should see the President again. Miss Burke will write you.

March 20, 1945

Dear Mrs. Churchill:

I have your letter of March 8 and I know nothing about Miss Burke. The plaque she is doing was not ordered by us, but is for a government building. I went to look at a plaque done by an artist, and I looked at it for its artistic values only.

Sincerely yours,

Eleanor Roosevelt

March 20, 1945

Mrs. Mary McLeod Bethune
National Council of Negro Women
Washington, D.C.

Dear Mrs. Bethune:

Mrs. Roosevelt has received a letter with the following statement about Selma Burke:

[quotation from Mrs. Churchill's letter].

Can you tell her if this is true?

Sincerely yours,

Malvina C. Thompson

Secretary to Mrs. Roosevelt

March 29, 1945

My dear Mrs. Roosevelt:

I got in touch with the office of Attorney General Biddle regarding the statement which you sent to me concerning Selma Burke. I asked that the records be investigated and his report to me is that there is no record on Selma Burke, and that nowhere does there exist any such statement as was sent to you.

I felt from what I thought of the girl that it was a false accusation. There is much jealousy because of her rapid rise in the field of art. I wish, Mrs. Roosevelt, you would confer with the President to have Selma Burke complete the project which she started with him.

Sincerely,

Mary McLeod Bethune

National Council of Negro Women

Washington, D.C.

March 31, 1945

Dear Mrs. Bethune:

Thank you for your letter about Selma Burke. I will try to get her an appointment with the President when he returns from San Francisco, but since his return from Yalta he has been overloaded with work.

Sincerely,

Eleanor Roosevelt

March 31, 1945

Dear Mrs. Churchill:

I made inquiry about Miss Burke since writing to you and no where is there any record to substantiate the statements you made in your letter to me.

Sincerely yours,

Eleanor Roosevelt

April 4, 1945

Dear Mrs. Roosevelt:

Thank you for your letter of March 31st.

It is my understanding the Federal Bureau of Investigation have investigated Selma Burke's activities and no doubt you can secure the record and information from them.

Sincerely,

Kathryn Churchill

Flower Consultant

April 11, 1945

My dear Mr. Hoover:

Mrs. Roosevelt has received a letter with the following statement about Miss Selma Burke, 88 East 10th Street, New York City:

[quote from original letter]

Mrs. Roosevelt will appreciate it very much if you will let her know whether or not this is true.

Very sincerely yours,

Malvina C. Thompson

Secretary to Mrs. Roosevelt.

PERSONAL AND CONFIDENTIAL

BY SPECIAL MESSENGER

Miss Malvina C. Thompson:

Thank you for your letter of April 11, 1945, in which you request to be advised concerning Selma Burke.

There is no derogatory information in the files of this Bureau concerning Miss Burke and there is no indication that she was ever sent to prison.

Miss Burke was rather intimately associated with one Hans Wolfgang Bohler who was investigated by this Bureau on suspicion of espionage. There was never any indication, however, that

Miss Burke was implicated and investigation of Bohler was discontinued when no evidence of espionage or other subversive activity was developed.

Sincerely yours,

J. Edgar Hoover

Federal Bureau of Investigation

U.S. Department of Justice

Washington, D.C.

On January 30, 1946, the federal government issued the first Roosevelt dime. The designer of the dime, John Sinnock, based his work on a sculpture of Roosevelt done by Selma Burke, who won a national design competition with her profile of the president.

• • •

March 15, 1945

Dear Mrs. Roosevelt:

You will remember me as Grace Turner, the friend of Earl Miller's[*] who had the home up on Lake Champlain where you stopped on your way to Montreal with Earl and Miss Cook. Sometime later you were kind enough to invite me to tea, when I was in Washington on business. Believe I last wrote you when I was working in Jenkintown, Pa. I was remarried two years ago last November to Albert Wood. He was one of our aces in the last war—having started before we were in it—first with the Royal Flying Corps and then with the original Lafayette Esquadrille.

Al is an Engineer with a very fine scholastic background—

---

[*] Mrs. Roosevelt's biographer, Joseph Lash, described Earl Miller as "the handsome ex-state trooper who was one of Eleanor's closest friends." Miller served as bodyguard, chauffeur, and confidante for Mrs. Roosevelt.

having received degrees from Dartmouth and M.I.T. He worked very hard for his education—as he was a poor boy and really got his start because of his foot ball prowess.

We have been very happy and companionable and have had a very quiet life because of heart trouble Al has had—which developed when he was flying in the last war and was made considerably worse the two years he flew in China against the Japs a few years ago. He was grounded after that.

We came here to Hackensack about two years ago and were fortunate to locate a very nice home furnished—owned by a young couple—Capt. Jesser is overseas. We have enjoyed it so much and are seldom out of it—for I have learned when Al was home from work the best thing for his condition was rest.

He has been so good to my dear little mother—73 years old—who is with us—except for a short time during the summer months.

Al has been doing war production work ever since we have been in it—but last July was kept from going to a place on Long Island to represent the firm he was with—Finch Telecommunication Co. of Passaic—on a Radar program—because Naval and Army Intelligence would not pass him. Comdr. Finch, Pres. of the company—who is in Washington now and the acting Pres.—Dr. Bradford—tried their best to find a reason—why Al was not allowed to go and even went to the F.B.I. office in Washington—but there was no reason given.

Al subsequently lost his position with Finch Co.—because of this and when he went to U.S. Employment office here to try and get another job—he was told to go to Army Intelligence office in N.Y.—where a Capt. Russell told him he was barred from any war work from now on—and again—no reason given.

Several influential people have since become interested in Al and have tried their best to get the thing straightened out— but to no avail. A Mr. Abelon—friend of Earl's formerly on the War Production Board—did his best to try and help us—also

Federal Court Judge Fade of Newark and ex U.S. District Attorney—Frederick Pearse—also of Newark. They all agreed that if there was anything really against Al—he would not be walking the streets—a free man.

Finally last fall—Al got a position in N.Y. thru an agency in Newark—but was only there little over a month—when he was let go—no reason given.

The end of Nov. he took one in Englewood—for much less salary than he had ever received and very long hours—but had to get something.

He had been getting along exceptionally well as far as his health was concerned until this happened at Finch—but since then has been going "down hill" rapidly. Doctors have always told him that worry and upsetness was the worst thing for his heart condition and a few weeks ago we found from a blood chemistry that now his kidneys have become involved—and his condition so bad that he had to give up his job or the doctors said he wouldn't be here long—that he must have something with less hours and easier. He has been trying so hard to find something but with the restrictions on war work—he has not been able to find anything and is getting in such a nervous state—I fear that soon he won't be able to work—if he does find something.

I have hesitated so long Mrs. Roosevelt—about writing you for I know how very busy you are and how many requests for help and advice you must receive but—truthfully I am desperate now and I realize my happiness and probably my husband's life depend on straightening out this matter.

All Al wants is to be let alone and to be able to earn an honest living and I also know he is most clever and is needed in war work. He has been considered a mathematical genius and among many other things he has taught navigation.

Can you suggest anything I could do? If at anytime in the near future you are to be in N.Y,. I would so appreciate if I could see you at your apartment and give you more details—or better yet have Al tell you the whole story. We would be as brief as possible for I know how very nearly every minute of your time is taken.

I can't begin to tell you how I would appreciate anything you might do about our trouble—and I also am sorry I have to bother you—but as I explained—I am quite desperate now.

When I was up near Albany last summer—I saw Simone and Earl, Jr. He is such a fine little boy. Simone wrote before Xmas that she is to have another baby. I hope it's a little girl.

With kindest wishes to you—Mrs. Roosevelt.

Very sincerely,
Grace L. Wood
Hackensack, New Jersey

[Seven pages handwritten]

March 27, 1945

My dear Mr. Hoover:

I am enclosing a letter from Mrs. Grace L. Wood, 299 Park Street, Hackensack New Jersey.

Mrs. Roosevelt will appreciate it very much if you would let her know about this case and have the enclosed letter returned with your reply.

Very sincerely yours,
Malvina C. Thompson
Secretary to Mrs. Roosevelt.
March 31, 1945

PERSONAL AND CONFIDENTIAL

Dear Mrs. Roosevelt:

I have carefully reviewed Miss Thompson's letter of March 27,

1945, and its enclosure, the letter written to you by Mrs. Grace L. Wood. I appreciate your interest in referring this matter to me.

I note that Mrs. Wood states that her husband, Albert Wood, was prevented from representing a firm with which he was connected in July, 1944, "because Naval and Army Intelligence did not pass him" and that a Captain Russell of the Army Intelligence Office in New York told him he was barred from any war work without stating any reasons. It was further related that Commander Finch and Dr. Bradford, officials of Mr. Wood's firm, went to the FBI Office in Washington, D.C., for the purpose of ascertaining the reasons for the action taken by Army and Naval Intelligence, but without success.

I can readily understand Mrs. Wood's concern, but, as you know, it is and has been the policy of this Bureau not to interfere in employer and employee relationships and consequently the Federal Bureau of Investigation would not and did not make any recommendation with regard to Mr. Wood's employment. It would appear that Mr. Wood's employment may have been the subject of action by the Army or Naval Intelligence in connection with their security program in war work. I might, therefore, suggest that the reasons for the termination of Mr. Wood's employment may be found in the records of the Office of Army or Naval Intelligence.

I am returning Mrs. Wood's letter as you have requested, together with a brief summary of Mr. Wood's alleged activities as reported to this Bureau.

With kindest personal regards,
Sincerely yours,
J. Edgar Hoover
Federal Bureau of Investigation
U.S. Department of Justice
Washington, D.C.

March 31, 1945

ALBERT WOOD

PERSONAL HISTORY AND BACKGROUND

The above named individual, variously known as Lawrence Goodhue, L. Woods, Al Woods, Bert Hall and as Captain Albert Wood, has been described as a soldier of fortune whose journeys have carried him over a large portion of the globe.

On the night of September 8, 1939, Wood was arrested by an officer of the El Centro Police Department in California on a charge of vagrancy. During an interview at the county jail he provided the following unconfirmed personal history:

Born at Elk River, Minnesota, on May 19, 1885, he left home at the age of thirteen, took to the road and stated that he had been traveling ever since. He embarked on a military career by joining the British Army in 1915, the French Army in 1917 and the United States Army later in 1917. After receiving a discharge from the United States Army in 1919, he claimed to have joined the Polish Forces against the "Reds." He thereafter held all types of odd jobs, was chief gunners mate in the United States Coast Guard in 1926 and in 1932 was in the Aviation Corps of the Chinese Army. He was last steadily employed in 1939 when he acted as a surveyor with the WPA at Minneapolis, Minnesota. However, he was subsequently dismissed from this position.

Among other things, Wood stated that his education had ceased with the eighth year at Lancaster, New Hampshire. However, through constant application he educated himself, and then claimed a thorough knowledge of mathematics, navigation and mechanics. It is interesting to note that on August 16, 1939, when he was arrested by the local authorities in Des Moines, Iowa, in a hobo jungle camp, he claimed to be a graduate of Dartmouth College and a civil engineer by profession. He had in his possession correspondence and plans for a "coincident bomb sight" for which he claimed he was offered the sum of $10,000 by the Military Attache for the Japanese Government in Mexico. It was determined at a later date that the United States Air Force was not interested in his "invention."

At the time of this second arrest he elaborated on his background, claiming that after his activities in Poland he returned to the United States and worked as a research engineer for the Federal Telephone and Telegraph Company, Radio Division, Boston, Massachusetts, where he worked during the years 1921 and 1922. During the same period he claimed he also lectured at Tufts College and wrote articles for the *Boston Post*, and *Herald Examiner*, newspapers in Boston, Massachusetts.

From 1924 to 1932 at irregular intervals his military interests took him to French Morocco in 1923, Nicaragua in 1926, Mexico in 1929, and China in 1932 where for eleven months he joined the forces of General Chiang Chai-shek. Although Wood claimed to be a member of the Lafayette Escadrille, the records of this organization allegedly do not confirm this fact. A further side light of his military career appears in the files of the Veterans Administration Office in Washington in the notation that subsequent to Wood's discharge as a private in the United States Army in March 1919, he reenlisted in December, 1927, and deserted in August of 1928, without thereafter being returned to military control. The above files indicate that he had been diagnosed to be a constitutional psychopath and a victim of neurasthenic anxiety. However, in 1942, when treated for heart disease at Veterans Facilities in Louisiana, no indication of mental disorder was noted.

SECURITY MATTERS

In 1935 he allegedly admitted that he was both in mail and personal communication with Colonel Bito, Japanese Intelligence Officer in New York City, regarding the purchase of information about a radio compass by the Japanese Government. The following year he was reported to possess important military information which he allegedly intended to disclose to unnamed foreign countries. However, this allegation was without confirmation. His information appeared to be in connection with the Panama Canal where he is said to have assisted in the installation of guns through which he became familiar with the locks and details of the Canal.

CITIZENSHIP

Information was received in September of 1941 that Wood may have expatriated himself by taking an oath of allegiance to a foreign government and technically was no longer a citizen of the United States. No additional information is available relating to the status of his citizenship.

CRIMINAL RECORD

From 1931 to 1940, in his wanderings from the West to the East Coast of this country, he was charged on seven different occasions with minor infractions of the law such as vagrancy which would cover conduct ranging from suspicious actions to a desire for a night's lodging.

[On White House memo paper, in Malvina Thompsons' handwriting]

Mrs. R-

Do you think we should send this whole record? She evidently believes in her husband.

[In Mrs. Roosevelt's handwriting]

Well, tell her in general. She can't be left thinking there is no reason.

April 4, 1945

Dear Mrs. Wood:

I asked for a report on your husband's situation and I find that he has worked under several different names and has given information at various times which was not based on fact.

There is nothing I can do and therefore there would be no point in my seeing either you or your husband.

Very sincerely yours,
Eleanor Roosevelt

• • •

April 11, 1945

Dear Mrs. Roosevelt

I am telling you our story because there are thousands of disabled veterans in our predicament.

My husband served in the USAAF from Nov. 3, 1941- Nov. 7, 1944.

Previous to his discharge he spent six months in the hospitals in Texas (May 3-Nov. 7, 1944). Our son was born Nov. 22, 1944 in San Antonio, Texas.

We moved to Denver Colorado on Jan. 15, 1945, on account of my husband's health. He is attending the third year college at the Denver University on Rehabilitation and majors in International Relations.

I am a New York R.N. and we could get along on the $109.25 plus a few nights private duty per month—if—if we **could** only **get a place to live**.

Apartments are scarce but if you have a baby it is impossible to find one. I will not attempt to describe the hardships. I lost sixteen pounds (I weigh eighty four pounds now) and my husband lost eleven pounds since we came here.

There are Federal low income projects and all kinds of other Government projects but when we inquired we were told that they are all reserved for defense workers and we (a disabled veteran–wife R.N. and baby) are no longer essential to the war.

People don't even bother to be polite to us. I'd like to relate an example of Mr. Fabinsky's experiences in apartment hunting in Denver.

We heard of a vacancy on 54 S. Penn St. My husband rushed to the above address but the janitor said that the vacancy was filled. Mr. Fabinsky said "I am a stranger here—a disabled veteran, perhaps you know where or how I can find an apartment in Denver." The janitor replied "I have no time to speak to you" and slammed the door in his face. From March 19–26 (Spring vacation) Mr. Fabinsky visited about one hundred apartment houses and he did not get one civil reply. The reason why you will find in the underlined parts of the newspaper clipping I am enclosing.

What is to become of us who have not profited by this war and cannot compete with the black market, rewards and bribes. Is this what our boys are fighting for, getting crippled and dying? Is this the wonderful "New World" promised to us? Is there nobody to defend the rights to live of the homeless disabled veteran and his family? Is our darling little boy not entitled to a roof over his head?

Yours sincerely,
Rose Fabinsky R.N.
Denver, Colorado

[Three pages handwritten]

The newspaper clipping referred to was not in the file

• • •

April 11, 1945

Dear Mrs. Roosevelt,

I am so aware of your deep interest in so many matters that I would not now be writing you if I didn't think that this matter warranted your interest.

I have been impressed, as you must have been in your travels about this country, by the divergence in the support of the Dumbarton Oaks Proposals, between the religious, social service and liberal groups generally, and the industry and business groups of the country. The Federal Council of Churches, the women's organizations the various Catholic welfare groups, the organizations that have been formed to further the United Nations idea, are doing a fine and active job. On the other hand, the business and industry groups are quiescent and apathetic. We know from surveys that between 38 and 40 United States Senators are either apathetic or against United Nations proposals.

This means, it seems to me, that men and women of good-will everywhere must do their part to try to swing public opinion and, particularly, the public opinion that is inarticulate today, towards a strong and powerful support of United Nations proposals.

One way, of course, in which to do this is to attempt to make the issue and its outcome so inevitable in the minds of all that others will join up.

I know that the State Department is carrying out some activity along these lines, but, of course, it is not and cannot be of the dynamic type that, from my standpoint as a technician, is necessary to swing over those who are passive, on the fence or against the proposition.

I have felt this matter so keenly that I went to work and there will shortly issue from the press, a manual along the lines of "Speak Up for Democracy," which you may recall.

In this manual, I have tried to answer the most important question facing Americans today: "How can I make my opinion felt in shaping a permanent peace based on Dumbarton Oaks Proposals?" I have described methods and tools by which the citizen's opinion can function through the spoken and written word, and be reflected to the media that shape public opinion, as well as to the key individuals in Washington who will determine action itself.

I have also tried in this little manual to provide a bibliography of available literature, and a list of organizations with whom the reader can communicate for further cooperation in securing counsel and material.

I am delighted that Clark M. Eichelberger, Director of the American Association of the United Nations, and Hugh Moore are very keen about the manual and that they and their cooperating organizations will do everything in their power to secure widespread circulation for it among men and women and groups who will use it.

As a result of arrangements made with the publishers and printers, the manual will be supplied at cost—15 cents a copy. I am receiving no profit of any kind from the bulk sales, and the royalties from sales through trade channels at $1.00 a copy, are being given to the Red Cross. This is an indication of my complete disinterestedness in the approach to this problem as far as personal profit is concerned, and I felt I should tell you so.

I am telling you at length about the book and its purpose because I sincerely feel that the situation needs to have some technical dynamics injected into it.

When I worked with General Motors, Ed Stettinius was the liaison between me and the company, and I have taken the liberty of passing on to his office my personal conclusions as to what I believe the situation needs at the present time—that is, a much more vigorous approach on the part of the State Department to the whole problem of engineering the consent of the people for the Dumbarton Oaks Proposals and the United Nations plan to follow them.

I know of your vital interest in this matter and feel that in writing you as I am, I shall keep you in touch with a situation about which you would want to be informed.

Sincerely yours,

Edward L. Bernays

New York, New York

P.S. The name of my manual is "Your Place at the Peace Table"

[Two pages typed]

After her husband's death, on April 12, 1945, Eleanor Roosevelt expected to quietly fade from public life. However, she could not refuse the request of President Harry Truman to serve as a delegate from the United States to the brand-new creation, the United Nations.

· · ·

Conclusion

The people endured. Through the Great Depression they endured physical deprivation hard to imagine in twenty-first century America. They also coped with the deferral or outright collapse of their hopes and dreams. During World War II they lived through privation at home while experiencing continuous anxiety as to the health and well-being of their loved ones overseas. Soldiers, sailors, and flyers, for the first time women as well as men, returned home ill, maimed, or not at all. Throughout this period, Eleanor Roosevelt served as a beacon of light in the darkness, a source of hope. People turned to her for assistance, intercession, solace, and advice. Because they did so, we have their letters, which show us, years later, the monumental efforts they made while trudging onward, day after weary day, year after year.

Throughout American history men such as Abraham Lincoln and Franklin Delano Roosevelt have inspired Americans to rise to the most difficult of occasions. President Roosevelt, especially through his fireside chats, cheered the weary country on, convincing his listeners that everything would, eventually, be all right. Eleanor Roosevelt complemented FDR by means of her travels, showing up anywhere and everywhere to see conditions for herself and report back to her husband. She plunged directly into the world as it was, taking steps both big and small to change it, working always toward that elusive concept most desired by Americans, fairness and equality. She realized that periods of crisis can be opportunities for action and did what she could to aid the ignored and the forgotten.

The letters from this era illustrate the first stirring of change, the tentative small steps taken by women, the poor, and minorities, to demand their fair share. The programs of the New Deal, which reached out to those on the bottom rung of the economic ladder, demonstrated that the government felt even they were worthy of con-sideration and inclusion. Throughout the war years, women took on jobs previously considered fit only for men and did them well. Black men and women, whether serving in the armed forces or helping on the home front, became more active in their demands to be treated fairly. Spurring them all on was Eleanor Roosevelt, the repository of people's hopes and dreams.

Because of her incredibly wide contact with the public, the First Lady felt the pulse of America with its every beat. Because she knew the people so well, she realized their power: "We make our own his-tory," she wrote. "The course of history is directed by the choices we make and our choices grow out of the ideas, the beliefs, the values, the dreams of the people. It is not so much the powerful leaders that determine our destiny as the much more powerful influence of the combined voice of the people themselves."

Notes

Dedication Page

"No woman has ever . . . distressed the comfortable." Said by Clare Boothe Luce, quoted in *Her Star Still Shines*, Franklin D. Roosevelt Presidential Library, 1997, p. 62.

Epigraph

xi.   "I do not ask. . . . as much as another." Eleanor Roosevelt's "My Day" column of November 7, 1944; part of a poem by Bonaro Overstreet, published in her column "American Reasons" on November 5, 1944.

Introduction

xiii. Sunday, December 7, 1941 . . . world changed around her.: Ketchum, Richard M., *The Borrowed Years, 1938-1941*, New York: Random House, 1993, pp. 765-68.

xiv.   "Letters, and letters and letters . . . Then began the avalanche!" "My Mail," p. 1-2, intended for *Vogue* but not published, 1940, Speech and Article File, papers of Eleanor Roosevelt, Franklin D. Roosevelt Presidential Library, Hyde Park, New York.

xiv.   "The invitation which forms the title . . . write to me." *Woman's Home Companion,* August 1933, "Mrs. Roosevelt's Page," p. 4.

xiv.   "a varied collection . . . deal with it." "My Mail," p. 10, *Vogue,* 1940.

xv.   "I have been tempted. . . . my bothering you." See letter, Part III, May 2, 1942, from Mrs. Theodore W. Chanler.

xv.   "I think the fact . . . in what is being done." "Mail of a President's Wife," p. 3, intended for *Cosmopolitan* but not published, 1940, Speech and Article File.

xvi.   "I want . . . after I wrote you." See letter, Part II, January 1942, from Mrs. Geo. Amend.

xvi.   "Knowing that you. . . . Braille Project?" See letter, Part II, October 10, 1939, from Rita D. Oliviera.

xvi.   "Madame, to help . . . what to do." See letter, Part III, July 29, 1941, from Elaine Beck.

xvi.   "American women . . . in high places." See telegram, Part III, July 17, 1940, from Mary Graham and others.

xvii.   "You may never . . . find out more about it?" See letter, Part III, March 26, 1943, from Mrs. George Dalrymple.

xvii.   "With the appointment of. . . . policy causes Negroes." See letter, Part IV, July 1944, from V. D. Johnston.

xvii.   "Very early I became . . . where they could be moderately warm." *The Autobiography of Eleanor Roosevelt* (Boston: G.K. Hall and Co., 1984), p. 12.

xviii. "I first want to tell you . . . even if you were unhappy." See letter, Part II, March 1, 1938, Salamanca, New York.

xix.   "One curious thing is that . . . and finally to the world." *The Autobiography of Eleanor Roosevelt,* p. 413.

xix.   Her constant travel . . . "on the go." Radio Script, "Working in the White House," April 19, 1935, Speech and Article File.

xix.   "Not a brilliant talker, but a brilliant listener." *Eleanor Roosevelt's My Day, Her Acclaimed Columns 1936–1945,* edited by Rochelle Chadakoff, introduction by Martha Gellhorn (New York: Pharos Books, 1989), p. xii.

xx. "I get very critical . . . forget the other things." Interview on the *Kate Smith Radio Show,* December 1937, Speech and Article File.

xxi. "I do think this is . . . I had to protest." Letter from Eleanor Roosevelt to Francis Biddle, attorney general of the United States, dated January 4, 1944.

xxi. "I do not think . . . wisdom of taking action." Letter from Francis Biddle to Eleanor Roosevelt, dated January 13, 1944.

xxi. "My plea to the general public . . . breakdown for any secretary!" Article entitled "Mail," p. 1, undated, Speech and Article File.

xxii. "In several books. . . . it was done without intention." *McCall's,* April 1954, p. 3, Speech and Article File.

xxiii. "The thing which counts. . . . upon the earth." *Her Star Still Shines* by Lynn Bassane and Michelle Metreaud (New York: Franklin D. Roosevelt Library, 1995), p. 24.

xxiii. "The variety of the requests . . . always worried me." *The Autobiography of Eleanor Roosevelt,* p. 171.

xxiii. "Please Mrs. Roosevelt . . . never forget." See letter, Part I, February 26, 1934, Mrs. G. Riddle.

xxiii. From what I have read . . . I am in need." See letter, Part I, February 26, 1934, Mrs. Henry O. Ridgly.

xxiv. "staying aloof is . . . cowardly evasion." *Her Star Still Shines,* p. 59.

xxv. The column in *Woman's Home Companion* lasted until January 1936 when "My Day" began.

xxvi. The individual Mrs. Roosevelt relied on . . . Mrs. Roosevelt's direction." "Keeping Up with Mrs. Roosevelt a Joy, Not a Job," *New York Herald Tribune,* December 18, 1939, p. 20.

xxvii. "There have been days . . . a bit disconcerting." *Eleanor Roosevelt's "My Day,"* pp. 3-4.

xxvii. In a 1939 interview . . . felt her loss greatly. "Malvina Thompson Dies in Hospital, Age 61," *New York Times,* April 13, 1953, p. 27.

xxvii. The *Ladies Home Journal* column lasted from 1941 to 1949.

Part One: The Great Depression

3.   "I see one-third . . . who have too little." President Franklin D. Roosevelt's Second Inaugural Address, January 20, 1937.

3.   "So first of all let me . . . convert retreat into advance." President Roosevelt's First Inaugural Address, March 4, 1933.

3.   "The worst thing that has come . . . life as we live it today." *Her Star Still Shines*, pp. 21-22.

5.   "I have talked to girls . . . which is more fortunate." Radio address, "Social Conditions," 1936, Speech and Article File.

7.   "I will probably never have . . . to be 100 percent American." Radio script, "Letters to Eleanor Roosevelt," April 19, 1935, p. 3. Speech and Article file.

8.   "To give you some idea . . . from school every day." "My Mail," written for *Vogue* in 1940 but never published, Speech and Article File.

11.   "Another task for us to undertake . . . lives of the unfortunate." Speech titled "The Unemployed," given to the Washington Conference on Women's and Professional Projects of the WPA, June 1936, p. 1, Speech and Article File.

22.   "an unofficial organization of some one . . . if it seemed necessary." *Vogue*, 1940, Speech and Article File.

23.   "Other people ask . . . work through them." Radio Script, part of the "Sweetheart Soap Series," July 25, 1940, p. 3, Speech and Article File.

28.   "Some of the most useful . . . our normal lives." *Endeavor* magazine, "Physical Handicaps," October 1945, Speech and Article File.

37.   Later in 1936 . . . anniversary of women's suffrage: Archives of "A Woman a Week," Web Site, re: Adelaide Johnson's career and her sculpture in the capitol, which remains the only national monument to the women's movement.

48.   "The letters which distress . . . know how to reply." Radio Script by Mrs. Roosevelt, part of "Sweetheart Soap Series," July 25, 1940, p. 2.

58.   In 1894 the state of Louisiana . . . they may remain as long as they

wish. Web site of the U.S. Department of Health and Human Services, the National Hansen's Disease Programs, and the Web site of the American Leprosy Missions.

Part Two: The New Deal

75.   "My trips around the country . . . saved many a family from outright disaster." *This I Remember* by Eleanor Roosevelt (New York: Harper and Brothers, 1949), p. 152.

76.   The largest such employment program . . . for young adults. Compiled from William E. Leuchtenburg's *Franklin D. Roosevelt and the New Deal* (New York: Harper and Row, 1963), *The Coming of the New Deal* by Arthur M. Schlesinger, Jr. (Boston: Houghton Mifflin, 1959), and *The New Deal* by Paul K. Conkin (Arlington Heights, Ill.: Harlan Davidson, 1967, reprinted 1992).

77.   The Townsend plan . . . who were desperately seeking help. Paul K. Conkin, *The New Deal,* Chapter Three, "Origins of a Welfare State." (Arlington Heights, Ill.: Harlan Davidson, 1992, third ed.).

78   "One of the basic elements . . . as a human being." *Tommorow Is Now,* (New York: Harper and Row, 1963), pp. 42-43. Speech and Article file.

84.   "I do not feel . . . opposition this year." Found in Speech and Article File.

92.   "the foreclosure on farms . . . urban householders respectively." "Foreclosure of Farms and Homes," sample outline of five-minute talk, 1940, Speech and Article File.

98.   Huey Long, populist Democratic senator . . . over to the Pope. Compiled from references on the New Deal listed above.

128. The Work Projects Administration . . . all WPA programs by June 1943. From books about the New Deal listed above.

131. The American Youth Congress . . . money being diverted to war preparation. *Encyclopedia of the American Left,* (New York: Oxford University Press, 1998), "Student Movements, 1930s" by Robert Cohen.

150. "Now for the personal things . . . help those who help themselves." "The Bright Side of the Depression," undated article or speech, Speech and Article file.

Part Three: The War Years

153. "I have seen war . . . I hate war." From a speech that President Roosevelt gave on August 14, 1936, in Chautauqua, New York, while running for a second term in office.

154. "I imagine every mother . . . had to suffer." *This I Remember,* pp. 292, 311.

156. "I was always a little sorry . . . I sent her a little note." *This I Remember,* p. 306.

164. "She suddenly looked sad . . . I should have done more." Ruth Gruber, *Inside of Time* (New York: Carroll & Graf, 2003), p. 351.

166. Many schemes for the rescue . . . during World War II. *Inside of Time,* pp. 13-14, 158-175.

173. According to the German census . . . took place in September 1943. *The Encyclopedia of Jewish Life Before and During the Holocaust* by Shmuel Spector (New York: New York University Press, 2001), pp. 49-50. From e-mail sent by Laurence Schram, archivist and searcher, Joods Museum van Deportatie en Verzet, April 22, 2004.

174. Israel Schenkel, born December 14, 1886 . . . did not appear in the records. All information found at the United States Holocaust Memorial Museum in Washington, D.C. Material on Drancy found in Serge Klarsfeld's *Memorial to the Jews Deported from France, 1942-1944* (New York: Beate Klarsfeld Foundation, 1983), pp. 182-188. Information on Auschwitz found in Danuta Czech's *Auschwitz Chronicle, 1939-1945* (New York: Henry Holt, 1990), p. 225.

175. Harry Scherman founded . . . and social welfare. From the Scherman Foundation, Inc. Web site.

195. "Where the Negro is concerned . . . other services might do." "The Racial Question," speech by Mrs. Roosevelt for the Joint Commission on Social Reconstruction, October 1945, Speech and Article File.

196. "Over and over again . . . any citizen in our own land." "Race, Religion and Prejudice," *The New Republic,* May 11, 1942, Speech and Article File.

201. Louis Edward Olivera . . . January 31, 1995. Burial records of Willamette National Cemetery, Portland, Oregon.

238. The U.S.S. *Liscombe Bay* . . . an additional 644 men of the navy. The U.S.S. *Liscombe Bay* was named for a bay in Alaska. Information on the ship is found at a Web site on Alaska: juneauempire.com.

265. "Why not insist on . . . great emphasis on justice." *Ladies Home Journal*, February 1942, Speech and Article File.

Part Four: The Home Front

269. "founded upon four essential . . . anywhere in the world." President Roosevelt's address to the annual dinner for the White House Correspondents' Association.

269. "I could not help feeling . . . for these same objectives." *This I Remember*, p. 239.

270. "I keep getting letters . . . labels of race and religion." "My Day," June 18, 1943, papers of Eleanor Roosevelt.

271. "It seems to me that . . . taken away from all of us?" *American Laborite*, "War Brings Curtailment of Rights," July 1, 1941, Speech and Article File.

279. "We as citizens . . . the love of America." Speech and Article File.

296. Cook Forest State Park . . . canoe down the Clarion River. From the Web site of Cook Forest State Park.

297. "We are on the train . . . generations to come." Papers of Eleanor Roosevelt.

302. On February 8, 1944 ". . . glad to have you here." Speech by Dr. Patrick S. Washburn, February 8, 2001, at Utah State University. Dr. Washburn is the author of *A Question of Sedition: The Federal Government's Investigation of the Black Press During World War II* (New York: Oxford University Press, 1986).

306. Louise Stanley earned . . . Great Depression and World War II. A list of her articles and books can be found at the Web site of Cornell University's Mann Library.

307. After the Japanese attack . . . spying for Japan. J. Burton, M. Farrell, F. Lord, and R. Lord, *Confinement and Ethnicity: An Overview of*

World War II Japanese American Relocation Sites (Seattle: University of Washington Press, 2002), Chapters 2 and 3.

308. "I am very conscious . . . way of life." *Common Ground,* "American Germans, Italians and Japanese," Spring 1942, Speech and Article File.

317. The *Popular Science* article . . . how the device works. *Popular Science,* May 1942, vol. 140, No. 5.

327. "The domestic scene . . . to law as yet." Papers of Eleanor Roosevelt.

331. The Lanham Act . . . working in the plants. Cathy D. Knepper, *Greenbelt, Maryland, A Living Legacy of the New Deal* (Baltimore, Md: Johns Hopkins University Press, 2001), p. 68.

337. The Federal Communications Commission . . . from NBC-Blue network. History of the American Broadcasting Company, from the ABC Web site.

343. On January 30, 1946 . . . profile of the president. Information from several Web sites on the history of the coins, such as coinsite.com.

343. Mrs. Roosevelt's biographer . . . confidante for Mrs. Roosevelt. P. Lash Joseph, *A World of Love: Eleanor Roosevelt and Her Friends, 1943-62* (New York: Doubleday, 1984), p. iv.

358. "We make our own . . . voice of the people themselves." *Tomorrow Is Now* (New York: Harper and Row, 1963), p. 4.

List of Abbreviations

The New Deal "Alphabet Agencies" mentioned in the text:

CCC	Civilian Conservation Corps
CWA	Civil Works Administration
FERA	Federal Emergency Relief Administration
FCA	Farm Credit Administration
HOLC	Home Owner's Loan Corporation
NRA	National Recovery Administration
NYA	National Youth Administration
PWA	Public Works Administration
RFC	Reconstruction Finance Corporation
WPA	Work Projects Administration, initially called Works Progress Administration

Wartime abbreviations referred to in the text:

AWOL	Absent Without Official Leave
DD	Dishonorable discharge
PX	Post exchange
RAF	Royal Air Force
WPB	War Production Board
UNRRA	United Nations Relief and Rehabilitation Administration

USAAF   U.S. Army Air Force

USO   United Service Organization

WACs   Women's Army Corps

WASPs   Women Air Force Service Pilots

WAVES   Women Accepted for Voluntary Emergency Service

Index

L

M

N

Postal Telegraph

Mackay Radio — *All America Cables*
Commercial Cables — *Canadian Pacific Telegraphs*

CHARGE ACCOUNT NUMBER		
CASH NO.	TOLLS	
	CHECK	
TIME FILED	(STANDARD TIME)	

Send the following message, subject to the Company's rules, regulations and rates set forth in its tariffs and on file with regulatory authorities   Form 2 L

N100.   LONG. LC507N. 247 NL=MY NEWYORK NY JUN 29 PM 8 36

MRS F D ROOSEVELT=

=HYDE PARK NY=

=MADAME TO HELP SAVE TWO VALUABLE LIVES FOR THIS WORLD PLEASE
CONSIDER THIS CASE STOP ISRAEL SCHENKEL FIFTY SIX AND WIFE
LOTTE BOTH CHEMISTS AUSTRIAN REFUGEES OF HIGHEST INTEGRITY AND
MORALS STOP JEWS OF IMPECCABLE BACKGROUND WITHOUT ANY RELATIVES
IN OCCUPIED EUROPE ASK ME THEIR ONLY DAUGHTER FOR INTERVENTION
IN WASHINGTON WITH FOLLOWING WORDS STOP EVERYBODY HERE IN
MARSEILLES MANAGES THROUGH RELATIVES IN US TO SECURE SENATORIAL
INFLUENCE IN WASHINGTON ONLY WE TWO ARE LEFT TO STARVATION OR
SUICIDE STOP SICK AND STARVING THEY WAITED 3 YEARS FOR VISA
STOP. NOW IT WAS READY AND GRANTED FOR JULY FOURTH BUT NEW
IMMIGRATION LAW PROHIBITED MARSEILLE CONSUL TO WRITE THEM OUT.
MADAME PLEASE IMAGINE STATE OF MIND OF THESE POOR HUMAN BEINGS
STOP THEY FLED FROM HITLERS AUSTRIAN ANNEXATION 1938 TO BELGIUM
AND WAITED FOR US VISA STOP JUST BEFORE ANTWERP CRASHED
ACCEPTED MR SCHERMANS BOOK OF THE MONTH CLUB SPONSOR,
AFFIDAVIT. HITLERS BELGIAN ANNEXATION 1940 SENT THEM FLEEING
TO FRANCE TO CAMP DE GRIS STARVATION AND INCREDIBLE MISERY STOP
NEW AFFIDAVITS NEW WAITING FOR VISA NO PASSAGE MONEY NO
VISAGRANT TILL FINALLY JULY FOURTH STOP MADAME I CAN PROVE
THEIR INTEGRITY I CAN GET NEW SPONSRAFFIDAVITS I CAN TRY TO
BORROW THE PASSAGEMONEY BUT I CANT SPEED UP OR FAVORABLY
INFLUENCE THAT AFFAIR IN WASHINGTON STOP. PLEASE HELP WITH
ADVICE WHOM TO SEE AND WHAT TO DO STOP IT WOULD BE ONE
MORE OF THE INUMMERABLE ANONYMOUS GOOD DEEDS OF A GREAT LADY
STOP RESPECTFULLY=

            =ELAINE BECK.

Even in Hyde Park, New York, home of Franklin and Eleanor Roosevelt,
the world's horrors found the First Lady on a daily basis, through her mail,
and in telegrams such as this wrenching one from the daughter of two
Jewish refugees unable to flee Europe during WW II.

About the Editor

C athy D. Knepper has a B.S. in English Education from the University of Michigan, a B.S. in Social Work from Case Western Reserve University, and a Ph. D. in American Studies from the University of Maryland at College Park. She is an expert on planned communities, past and present, and FDR's New Deal. She works on death penalty issues for Amnesty International in Maryland. The author of *Greenbelt, Maryland: A Living Legacy of the New Deal*, Knepper lives in Kensington, Maryland, with her husband.